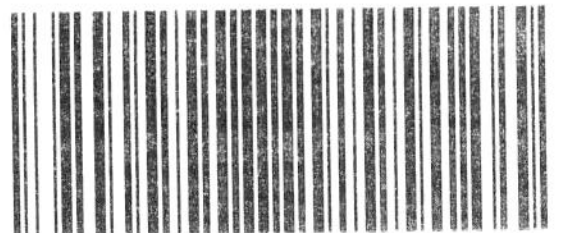
MW00776441

THE HOLLOW CORE OF CONSTITUTIONAL THEORY

The Hollow Core of Constitutional Theory is the first major defense of the central role of the Framers' intentions in constitutional interpretation to appear in years. This book starts with a reminder that, for virtually all of Western legal history, when judges interpreted legal texts, their goal was to identify the lawmaker's will. However, for the past 50 years, constitutional theory has increasingly shifted its focus away from the Framers. Contemporary constitutional theorists, who often disagree with each other about virtually everything else, have come to share the view that the Framers' understandings are unknowable and irrelevant. This book shows why constitutional interpretation needs to return to its historical core inquiry, which is a search for the Framers' intentions. Doing so is practically feasible, theoretically defensible, and equally important not only for discovering the original meaning, but also for deciding how to apply the Constitution today.

Donald L. Drakeman is Distinguished Research Professor in the Program on Constitutional Studies at the University of Notre Dame, and a Fellow of the Centre for Health Leadership and Enterprise at the University of Cambridge. His works have been cited by the Supreme Courts of the United States and the Philippines. His books on the Constitution include *Church, State, and Original Intent*, a Choice Outstanding Academic Title.

The Hollow Core of Constitutional Theory

WHY WE NEED THE FRAMERS

DONALD L. DRAKEMAN
University of Notre Dame

CAMBRIDGE
UNIVERSITY PRESS

University Printing House, Cambridge CB2 8BS, United Kingdom

One Liberty Plaza, 20th Floor, New York, NY 10006, USA

477 Williamstown Road, Port Melbourne, VIC 3207, Australia

314–321, 3rd Floor, Plot 3, Splendor Forum, Jasola District Centre, New Delhi – 110025, India

79 Anson Road, #06–04/06, Singapore 079906

Cambridge University Press is part of the University of Cambridge.

It furthers the University's mission by disseminating knowledge in the pursuit of education, learning, and research at the highest international levels of excellence.

www.cambridge.org
Information on this title: www.cambridge.org/9781108485289
DOI: 10.1017/9781108751001

© Donald L. Drakeman 2020

This publication is in copyright. Subject to statutory exception and to the provisions of relevant collective licensing agreements, no reproduction of any part may take place without the written permission of Cambridge University Press.

First published 2020

A catalogue record for this publication is available from the British Library.

Library of Congress Cataloging-in-Publication Data
NAMES: Drakeman, Donald L. author.
TITLE: The hollow core of constitutional theory : why we need the framers / Donald L. Drakeman, University of Notre Dame, Indiana.
DESCRIPTION: 1. | Cambridge, United Kingdom ; New York, NY : Cambridge University Press, 2020. | Includes bibliographical references and index.
IDENTIFIERS: LCCN 2020018641 | ISBN 9781108485289 (hardback) | ISBN 9781108719391 Paperback | ISBN 9781108751001 (ebook)
SUBJECTS: LCSH: Constitutional law. | Constitutional law – Philosophy. | Constitutional history.
CLASSIFICATION: LCC K3165 .D73 2020 | DDC 342/.001–dc23
LC record available at https://lccn.loc.gov/2020018641

ISBN 978-1-108-48528-9 Hardback
ISBN 978-1-108-71939-1 Paperback

Cambridge University Press has no responsibility for the persistence or accuracy of URLs for external or third-party internet websites referred to in this publication and does not guarantee that any content on such websites is, or will remain, accurate or appropriate.

Contents

Preface

Throughout virtually all Western legal history, when judges have considered the meaning of legal texts, their principal goal has been to identify the will of the lawmaker. There have always been arguments about whether those decisions should be based on the law's meaning as of the date of enactment or as updated in light of current conditions, but the core question for the process of interpretation has been how to apply the lawmaker's decision to the case at hand. Over the past fifty years, however, American constitutional theory has increasingly shifted its focus away from the lawmaker's intentions, not only by arguments for an aspirational, living, or consequentialist Constitution, but even, and perhaps surprisingly, through many contemporary originalists' focus on the search for semantic meaning rather than the Framers' particular policy choices.

This book argues that constitutional theory needs to return to its historical core, which is an understanding of the decision made by the lawmaker in adopting the text. As a practical matter, determining that original choice will require an inquiry into the Framers' understandings despite the fact that most contemporary constitutional theorists – who often disagree with one another about virtually everything else – have been united in the belief that the Framers' understandings are unknowable and, in any event, irrelevant. Returning the Framers to the center of the interpretive process turns out to be an essential basis not only for decisions about the Constitution's original meaning, but also for determining how that meaning can be applied to twenty-first-century circumstances.

Many people have been enormously helpful in shaping the thinking that led to this book, and it is impossible to thank them all adequately. With the standard disclaimer fully in place, I would like to thank Joel Alicea, Helen Baxter, J. Robert Beck, Janice Chik Breidenbach, David Campbell, Marc DeGirolami, Jim Diggins, Matt Franck, Rick Garnett, Christopher Green, Andy Koppelman, Grace Lee, Rich Lizardo, Mark Movsesian, Patrick Nyman, Johnathan O'Neill,

Nektarios Oraiopoulos, Jeff Pojanowski, Kaitlin Pontzer, Philip Sales, Steve Smith, Stephen Tuck, Lynn Uzzell, Steve Whelan, Brad Wilson, John Wilson, and, from Cambridge University Press, three reviewers, and editors Jackie Grant and John Berger. I would especially like to thank Michael Breidenbach, who read, commented on, and vastly improved every version, as well as the participants in discussions of the manuscript at Notre Dame and Princeton, who were extremely helpful in shaping the final version, including Sotirios Barber, Amy Barrett, Rick Garnett, Tom Hardiman, Andy Koppelman, Tyler Moore, Phillip Muñoz, Jeff Pojanowski, Adrian Vermeule, and Keith Whittington, all of whom were convened by Notre Dame's Program on Constitutional Studies; and Roberta Bayer, Matt Franck, Earl Maltz, Mitchell Rocklin, Alf Siewers, Lee Strang, Adam Thomas, and Brad Wilson, who were gathered together by Princeton's James Madison Program in American Ideals and Institutions. Important comments and helpful questions also came from numerous people who attended talks based on earlier versions of book chapters at the Statute Law Society, the Oxford Law Faculty, Notre Dame Law School, Notre Dame's Statutory Interpretation and Constitutional Structure Roundtable Conference, and the University of San Diego.

I am especially grateful for having had the remarkable opportunity to learn about constitutional interpretation from Kent Greenawalt at Columbia and Robby George and Walter Murphy at Princeton; for the students at Princeton and Notre Dame who were wrestling with these issues as I was; for the chance to get to know Richard Ekins and his work as he was setting up the Programme for the Foundations of Law and Constitutional Government at Oxford, which inspired me to dive this deeply into constitutional theory; and for the incredibly valuable and rich conversations I have had over the years with my friend and colleague Phillip Muñoz.

I would also like to express my thanks to the editors of the book and journals who have graciously allowed me to reproduce revised portions of chapters or articles, including: "Which Original Meaning of the Establishment Clause Is the Right One?" in Michael D. Breidenbach and Owen Anderson, eds., *The Cambridge Companion to the First Amendment and Religious Liberty* (Cambridge University Press, 2020); "Charting a New Course in Statutory Interpretation: A Commentary on Richard Ekins' *The Nature of Legislative Intent*," *Cornell Journal of Law and Public Policy* 24, 107 (2014): 107–43; and "What's the Point of Originalism?," *Harvard Journal of Law and Public Policy* 37, 3 (2014): 1124–50. Chapter 6 was first published in *Georgetown Law Journal*. Chapter 9 is derived in part from an article published in *Jurisprudence*, 2018, copyright Taylor & Francis, available online: www.tandfonline.com/doi/10.1080/20403313.2017.1395244.

1

The Framers and Contemporary Constitutional Theory

The Framers are out of fashion. While politicians and the public continue to venerate the American Framers, who built a new nation on the foundation of an enduring Constitution, the academic community has mostly moved on. Harvard's Jill Lepore, speaking for many other leading historians, has recently likened a Framer-focused originalism to astrology, something so completely debunked that it has no place in contemporary academic discussions.[1] Meanwhile, many legal scholars on both the left and the right sides of the political spectrum have deleted the Framers from constitutional debate, even those who are dedicated to discovering the Constitution's original meaning. Still, the public's esteem for the Framers bears potentially powerful political authority, and claiming to speak on their behalf has been a nearly irresistible force. At least in popular debates, Lepore notes, the best strategy is: "When in doubt in American politics, left, right, or center, deploy the Founding Fathers."[2]

The gravitational pull of prominent "Founding Fathers" for constitutional interpreters can clearly be seen in two of the most prominent books of the past decade defending the opposing approaches of originalism and the living Constitution: *Reading Law: The Interpretation of Legal Texts* by Justice Antonin Scalia and Bryan A. Garner, and David Strauss' *The Living Constitution*.[3] They

[1] Jill Lepore, *The Whites of Their Eyes: The Tea Party's Revolution and the Battle over American History* (Princeton, NJ: Princeton University Press, 2011). See also Saul Cornell, "Originalism on Trial: The Use and Abuse of History in *District of Columbia v. Heller*," *Ohio State Law Journal* 69, 4 (2008): 625–40; Martin S. Flaherty, "History 'Lite' in Modern American Constitutionalism," *Columbia Law Review* 95, 3 (April 1995): 523–90; and Jack N. Rakove, "Confessions of an Ambivalent Originalist," *New York University Law Review* 78, 4 (October 2003): 1347.

[2] Lepore, *Whites of Their Eyes*, p. 14.

[3] David A. Strauss, *The Living Constitution* (New York: Oxford University Press, 2010); and Antonin Scalia and Bryan A. Garner, *Reading Law: The Interpretation of Legal Texts* (St. Paul, MN: Thomson/West, 2012).

both invoke the Founders for rhetorical support; then, just as rapidly, the authors switch directions and explain why we need to ignore the Framers in interpreting the Constitution. One favors the original meaning of the text while the other favors the meanings very much rooted in the twenty-first-century judicial process. As a result of these kinds of arguments – and, of course, with notable exceptions[4] – the trajectories of the two principal competing schools of twenty-first-century US constitutional interpretation have been pointing decidedly away from the Framers.[5]

These current views are largely missing what has traditionally been at the core of the process by which judges interpret laws. For centuries before the Constitution was adopted, and until quite recently, judges, lawyers, and scholars shared the view that interpretation meant what Edward Coke said in his *Institutes*: "Every statute ought to be expounded according to the intent of them that made it."[6] To interpret a legally authoritative text was to seek what William Blackstone called the "will of the legislator,"[7] and apply it to the case at hand. The question of whether the law should be understood and applied based *solely* on its meaning as of its enactment, or as circumstances might have changed since that time, has been a second order question. There has also been a long history of debates over whether objective or subjective evidence is the optimal method for determining the will of the lawmaker (especially in light of the complexities of multimember assemblies). But identifying the will of the lawmaker has always been the fundamental basis for interpretation.

With this historical background, it would seem to be a crucial part of the interpretive process to seek the best evidence of the Framers' understandings

4 For notable examples of exceptions, see Larry Alexander and Saikrishna Prakash, "Is that English You're Speaking? Why Intention Free Interpretation Is an Impossibility," *San Diego Law Review* 41, 3 (August–September 2004): 967–95; and Larry Alexander, "Originalism, the Why and the What," *Fordham Law Review* 82, 2 (November 2013): 539–44. See also Steven D. Smith, *Law's Quandary* (Cambridge, MA: Harvard University Press, 2004).

5 As Bassham and Oakley note: "Since at least the 1970s, liberal and conservative constitutional theorists have tended to fall into two sharply divided camps. Conservatives . . . have supported 'originalism.' . . . Liberals . . . have argued for 'living constitutionalism' or 'nonoriginalism'." Gregory Bassham and Ian Oakley, "New Textualism: The Potholes Ahead," *Ratio Juris* 28, 1 (March 2015): 127.

6 Edward Coke, *The Fourth Part of the Institutes of the Laws of England: Concerning the Jurisdiction of Courts* (London, 1817), p. 330, quoted in Richard Ekins and Jeffrey Goldsworthy, "The Reality and Indispensability of Legislative Intentions," *Sydney Law Review* 36, 1 (2014): 40 n8, noting numerous authorities. See also Philip Hamburger, *Law and Judicial Duty* (Cambridge, MA: Harvard University Press, 2008).

7 William Blackstone, *Commentaries on the Laws of England: In Four Books; With an Analysis of the Work*, eds. Edward Christian et al., 19th ed. (New York, 1846), vol. 1, p. 40.

of why a constitutional provision was included, and what it was designed to accomplish. Yet, overreactions by originalists and living constitutionalists alike have downplayed the need for judges to focus their interpretive lens on the Framers. Many originalists, faced with theoretical and practical challenges to the concept of trying to read the Framers' minds, have abandoned a "jurisprudence of original intention" in favor of a search for the original public meaning. Meanwhile, advocates of a living constitution have rejected the idea that the "dead hand" of a group of eighteenth-century elite men should control twenty-first-century constitutional outcomes.

No matter how popular the Framers might continue to be in the popular mind, they have been distinctly unpopular in contemporary constitutional theory. For constitutional theory to return to its historical core, however, it needs to refocus on what I will refer to, from time to time, as the will of the lawmaker, the Framers' intentions, the Framers' end–means decision,[8] or the Framers' understandings – that is, how the Framers, as a group, understood what problem was being solved or opportunity created with the adoption of the provision in question, and what the rationale was for doing it that way. As Blackstone and many other commentators have pointed out, the text is likely to be the best evidence of the lawmaker's intention, but not the only one. Judges will certainly need to understand the meaning(s) of the words the Framers chose, as of the time they chose them, but they also need to explore the debates, disagreements, negotiations, and drafting history, as well as the broader legal and political environment, and so on.

It is important to point out that this is not necessarily an argument in favor of a Framers'-expected-applications approach. Whether the Framers intended to restrict the application of any particular provision to their own preferred outcomes is a question to ask of the documentary record, not an assumption to be made in advance. Nor do I mean for judges necessarily to favor a provision's purpose or rationale over a fair reading of the text. The concept of what Paul Brest called "moderate intentionalism" – that is, applying "a provision consistent with the adopters' intent at a relatively high level of generality, consistent with ... the ... purpose"[9] – is similarly question-begging. Whether the best interpretation of a clause is that it was designed to answer a specific question in a particular way that the Framers expected, or, perhaps, as Ronald Dworkin suggests, that it "enact[s] abstract moral

[8] As discussed in Chapter 2, I am borrowing this phrase, as well as the theoretical basis for employing the Framers' intent, from Richard Ekins, *The Nature of Legislative Intent* (Oxford: Oxford University Press, 2012).

[9] Paul Brest, "The Misconceived Quest for Original Understanding," *Boston University Law Review* 60, 2 (March 1980): 223.

principles" requiring judges to "exercise moral judgment,"[10] cannot be answered in theory. It can only be considered in light of what we can know about the Framers' end–means decisions.

Returning constitutional theory to a core focus on the will of the lawmaker will also provide a foundation for further discussions about how the Constitution should be interpreted over long periods of time. Significant changes in circumstances are inevitable with a Constitution approaching its 250th anniversary, and, for centuries, interpreters have recognized the need for fixed texts to be adapted to unforeseen issues. Those issues have a long enough history to provide a method for defining when and how judges should engage in dynamic interpretations, and I will show how those cases also proceed from an understanding of the Framers and their intentions.

By now, many readers will have thought of a host of objections. Large groups cannot share a common intention. The Framers do not really constitute the constitutional lawmaker. Even if they did, the historical evidence is unreliable and subject to cherry-picking. The text is the law, and it is clear enough without needing to read anyone's mind. The intentions of eighteenth-century Framers cannot possibly be relevant to twenty-first-century legal issues. And so on. Please be patient: the rest of the book is an effort to address those issues.

THE DEAD HAND AND THE LIVING CONSTITUTION

In *The Living Constitution*, David Strauss pronounces originalism to be a "totally inadequate" method for addressing controversial issues, arguing that "[t]he most fundamental problem with originalism is the one that Thomas Jefferson ... identified in the earliest days of the Constitution. 'The earth belongs ... to the living,' Jefferson wrote to James Madison in 1789."[11] Professor Strauss titles this observation "Jefferson's Problem," or "Jefferson's skepticism," and he refers to it many times throughout the book as an early example of what is often called the "dead hand problem." It turns out, however, that the Jeffersonian letter cited in Professor Strauss' argument for

10 Ronald Dworkin, "Comment," in *A Matter of Interpretation: Federal Courts and the Law*, Antonin Scalia (Princeton, NJ: Princeton University Press, 1997), p. 126.

11 Strauss, *Living Constitution*, pp. 4, 24. On Madison's response, especially the idea that "[t]he improvements made by the dead form a debt against the living," see Ilan Wurman, *A Debt Against the Living: An Introduction to Originalism* (Cambridge: Cambridge University Press, 2017), p. 1. For a discussion of how Jefferson has been appropriated by a wide range of political movements, see Andrew Burstein, *Democracy's Muse: How Thomas Jefferson Became an FDR Liberal, a Reagan Republican, and a Tea Party Fanatic, All the While Being Dead* (Charlottesville: University of Virginia Press, 2015).

a living Constitution does not actually point towards an evolving document that each generation should reinterpret for its own purposes.[12] To be sure, Jefferson was worried about the dead hand problem, but his principal interest, at least as expressed in the letter, was to limit the Constitution's duration: "[B]y the law of nature," wrote Jefferson, "one generation is to another as one independent nation to another," and, therefore, "no society can make a perpetual constitution, or even a perpetual law." For Jefferson, then, employing the Comte de Buffon's mortality tables,[13] "Every constitution . . . naturally expires at the end of 19 years."[14] Even the ability to repeal the Constitution is insufficient for Jefferson's purposes because it would not provide adequate protection from the influence of factions and "other impediments" that "prove to every practical man that a law of limited duration is much more manageable than one which needs a repeal."[15]

Jefferson saw the dead hand problem as a central problem of constitutional creation, but his proposed solution was not necessarily a dynamic, ever-changing approach to constitutional interpretation. In fact, had it been obvious that interpreters would continually reshape constitutional meaning in accordance with the changing needs and preferences of each generation, Jefferson would not have had to pen such a lengthy epistle. Instead, because he believed that society should not count on the political process to bring about the necessary generational repeals, Jefferson focused on a self-executing term

[12] Herbert Sloan argues, in commentary on this letter: "Whatever else the principle may have meant to Jefferson, it was decidedly not an invocation of the 'living Constitution.' . . . Jefferson's constitutionalism was decidedly of the strict constructionist variety, and the notion that the text could be interpreted other than through the 'original intent' he rejected out of hand." Herbert Sloan, "The Earth Belongs in Usufruct to the Living," in *Jeffersonian Legacies*, ed. Peter S. Onuf (Charlottesville: University Press of Virginia, 1993), p. 303.

[13] See Merrill D. Peterson, "Mr. Jefferson's 'Sovereignty of the Living Generation,'" *Virginia Quarterly Review* 52, 3 (Summer 1976): 437–47.

[14] Thomas Jefferson, "To James Madison," September 6, 1789, in *The Papers of Thomas Jefferson*, ed. Julian P. Boyd, vol. 15, *27 March 1789 to 30 November 1789* (Princeton, NJ: Princeton University Press, 1958), p. 396. See Ken I. Kersch, "The Talking Cure: How Constitutional Argument Drives Constitutional Development," *Boston University Law Review* 94, 3 (May 2014): 1087; Zachary Elkins, Tom Ginsburg, and James Melton, *The Endurance of National Constitutions* (New York: Cambridge University Press, 2009), p. 2. Compare Chief Justice Marshall in *Cohens v. Virginia*, 19 US 264, 387 (1821): "[A] Constitution is framed for ages to come, and is designed to approach immortality as nearly as human institutions can approach it."

[15] Incidentally, although Jefferson may not have achieved his goal of explicitly limiting the duration of the United States Constitution, he may have been making an impressively sound empirical observation, or, perhaps more likely, an ultimately accurate prediction. Scholars studying international constitutional development have observed that the average lifespan of a constitution is nineteen years. It seems, then, that Jefferson may have been correct if he meant that, on average, "Every constitution . . . expires at the end of 19 years."

limit. In short, if ever-evolving "living" interpretations had been the clear and obvious choice for courts and other interpreters of the Constitution, there would have been no need for Jefferson to propose a nineteen-year limited lifespan.

Whether the Constitution is rewritten or reinterpreted, Strauss' principal concern is: "What possible justification can there be for allowing the dead hand of the past . . . to govern us today?"[16] As he points out, "[T]he world has changed in incalculable ways" since the Constitution was adopted well over two hundred years ago.[17] Rule by the dead hand of the Framers will, as Christopher Eisgruber puts it, "subordinate present-day politics to the will of past super-majorities."[18] Originalists are therefore obliged, says Eisgruber, "to develop a theory that describes the appropriate balance between deference to the past and regard for the present. Not surprisingly, this task turns out to be very difficult, if not impossible, for the simple reason that it is hard to think of any good reason for empowering dead people in the first place."[19] Moreover, he argues that "[o]nce you admit that the dead should have some power over the living, it is exceedingly hard to say how much power is enough."[20]

Among the range of interpretive approaches that today fall generally under the broad "living Constitution" rubric, Strauss' solution to the dead hand problem is a common law approach, which he says, "is what we actually do."[21] The development of constitutional law, he argues, is rarely about the Framers, nor does it necessarily revolve around an interpretation of the specific language of the text; rather, it "is about precedents, and when the precedents leave off, it is about commonsense notions of fairness and good policy."[22]

[16] Strauss, *Living Constitution*, p. 100. The "dead hand" phrase is not unique to American constitutional jurisprudence. See Leslie Zines, "Dead Hands or Living Tree? Stability and Change in Constitutional Law," *Adelaide Law Review* 25, 1 (2004): 3–20. See also William T. Stead, "My First Visit to America: An Open Letter to My Readers," *The Review of Reviews*, March 10, 1894, who wrote: "America is not governed by the sovereign will of the sovereign people expressed at the ballot box; it is governed by the dead hand of those who framed its constitution."

[17] Strauss, p. 1.

[18] Christopher L. Eisgruber, "The Living Hand of the Past: History and Constitutional Justice," *Fordham Law Review* 65, 4 (March 1997): 1613: "I believe . . . the central and most damaging fallacy of modern constitutional theory [is] . . . the 'Dead Hand Fallacy.' The Dead Hand Fallacy holds that the *purpose* of the Constitution is to subordinate present-day politics to the will of past super-majorities . . . . This result is sometimes justified by reference to ideas about popular sovereignty, which I find exceedingly odd, since the people who made the Constitution's most important provisions are all dead."

[19] Eisgruber, "Living Hand," 1614.

[20] Eisgruber, 1614.

[21] Strauss, *Living Constitution*, p. 44.

[22] Strauss, p. 34.

The common law approach is just one of many strands of the collection of arguments made by advocates for a contemporary understanding of the Constitution, not all of whom necessarily agree with one another. While Strauss and others favoring living or evolving, dynamic, or pragmatic interpretive approaches may call on famous Founders for rhetorical support, their primary focus is likely to be elsewhere, such as Strauss' "commonsense notions of fairness and good policy,"[23] popular attitudes about justice,[24] or academic scholarship in moral and political philosophy.[25] If there is a main theme for the diverse collection of constitutional theorists not committed to originalism, it is that there are considerations that should bear on judicial decisions in constitutional cases beyond whatever might have been the eighteenth-century meaning.[26] That is, judges should go about a process of discovering – or perhaps creating – a contemporary constitutional meaning that, in turn, may need continually to evolve to keep up with future times.

Not all of these various approaches to how judges should interpret the Constitution are necessarily compatible with one another, and some theorists argue that there is, in fact, no reason for the courts to employ any one particular method consistently. After listing a range of "established approaches," including "originalism in its various forms, democracy-reinforcement, 'moral readings,' minimalism, or broad deference to political processes," Cass Sunstein proposes that judges should choose, for any particular case, the one that "makes our constitutional system better."[27] Along the same lines, Frank Cross observes: "In practice, the essential alternative to originalism ... is now typically pluralism," which "means that the justices

[23] Strauss, p. 34.

[24] As Justice Brennan wrote in his famous defense of the living Constitution: "When Justices interpret the Constitution, they speak for their community, not for themselves alone. The act of interpretation must be undertaken with full consciousness that it is, in a very real sense, the community's interpretation that is sought." William J. Brennan Jr., "The Constitution of the United States: Contemporary Ratification," *South Texas Law Review* 27, 3 (Fall 1986): 434.

[25] See, especially, Ronald Dworkin's moral reading of the Constitution in Ronald Dworkin, *Freedom's Law: The Moral Reading of the American Constitution* (1996; repr., Oxford: Oxford University Press, 2005); and the works discussed in Scott Hershovitz, ed., *Exploring Law's Empire: The Jurisprudence of Ronald Dworkin* (Oxford: Oxford University Press, 2006).

[26] According to Lawrence Solum: "When 'living constitutionalism' is used by scholars as the name for a constitutional theory, it should be used to refer to nonoriginalist constitutional theories that affirm the view that constitutional practice can and should change in response to changing circumstances and values." Lawrence B. Solum, "Originalism versus Living Constitutionalism: The Conceptual Structure of the Great Debate," *Northwestern University Law Review* 113, 6 (2019): 1246.

[27] Cass R. Sunstein, "There Is Nothing that Interpretation Just Is," *Constitutional Commentary* 30, 2 (2015): 194.

would choose the interpretive method ... depending on the facts of the case before them."[28]

Some theorists are less inclined towards pluralism. James Fleming, for example, distinguishes the "aspirational" and "moral reading" that he, Justice Brennan,[29] and Ronald Dworkin have espoused from what he considers to be the views of contemporary advocates of a living constitution.[30] His concern is that "[l]iving constitutionalists characteristically are more pragmatic, instrumentalist, and forward-looking in their approaches to the Constitution"[31] than those seeking a moral reading. Under the moral reading, or "philosophic approach" to constitutional interpretation developed by Dworkin, Fleming, Sotirios Barber, and numerous others, the Constitution embodies "abstract moral and political principles." Accordingly, the process of interpretation "require[s] judgments of political theory," not the pragmatism of some living constitutionalists or the search "to discover relatively specific original meanings" of many originalists.[32] Whether their interest is in common sense, pragmatism, abstract moral principles, or otherwise, theorists focusing on a contemporary reading of the Constitution are likely to spend little or no time exploring the Framers' intentions.

ORIGINALISM AND THE FRAMERS

It is hardly surprising that proponents of a contemporary Constitution – in spite of methodological disagreements with one another – would agree that judges should diminish or dismiss the importance of the Framers' understandings of the constitutional text and the rationale behind it. Perhaps even more intriguing is the fact that, at least at the moment, much of mainstream originalism does so as well. Instead, numerous leading scholars have rejected any search for the Framers' views (other than as part of the overall semantic context of the time) in favor of a focus on the objective public meaning of the

[28] Frank B. Cross, *The Failed Promise of Originalism* (Stanford, CA: Stanford University Press, 2013), p. 20, citing Stephen M. Griffin, "Rebooting Originalism," *University of Illinois Law Review*, 4 (2008): 1185–223.

[29] See, for example, "The Brennan Center Jorde Symposium: The Living Constitution: A Symposium on the Legacy of Justice William J. Brennan, Jr.," special issue, *California Law Review* 95, 6 (December 2007).

[30] James E. Fleming, *Fidelity to Our Imperfect Constitution: For Moral Readings and Against Originalisms* (New York: Oxford University Press, 2015), p. 27. See also Dworkin, *Freedom's Law*; and Sotirios A. Barber and James E. Fleming, *Constitutional Interpretation: The Basic Questions* (New York: Oxford University Press, 2007).

[31] Fleming, *Fidelity to Our Imperfect Constitution*, pp. 27–8.

[32] Fleming, p. 27.

words in context. Scalia and Garner, for example, base their interpretive approach on how the Framers understood that the Constitution would be interpreted. They argue that the Framers saw the Constitution as an "originalist text," interpreted in light of the usual meanings of the words, because "[t]here were no other sorts of legal texts."[33] Although they embrace the Framers' understanding of interpretation, they do not believe that the Framers' subjective understandings should contribute to the original meaning of specific provisions. As Scalia famously wrote in *A Matter of Interpretation*: "What I look for in the Constitution is . . . the original meaning of the text, not what the original draftsmen intended."[34] As is true for advocates of a living or contemporary constitution, there is a range of specific methods on the originalist spectrum, including proponents of intentionalism. But a considerable number of leading originalist scholars have sought to steer interpreters away from the idea that Framers' subjective understandings are relevant to a determination of the original meaning, and towards the objective public meaning of the constitutional text.

Since the Framers have lost their seats at the interpretive table among many originalist theorists, it may be helpful to see how that happened, since it is a fairly recent phenomenon. President Ronald Reagan's Attorney General, Edwin Meese, called for a much more Framer-friendly jurisprudence of original intention in the 1980s. Emerging as a reaction to what Scalia and Garner describe as the "general acceptance" of "the notion of the living Constitution" during "the time of the Warren Court (1953–1969)," the impetus for a modern originalism movement arrived during the Reagan presidency.[35]

Meese's 1985 speech to the American Bar Association sought to rein in a Supreme Court that had fallen into a "jurisprudence of idiosyncrasy." With the Bicentennial of the Constitution on the horizon, Meese exhorted courts to

33 Scalia and Garner, *Reading Law*, p. 404.

34 Scalia, *A Matter of Interpretation*, p. 38. See also Gary Lawson, "On Reading Recipes . . . and Constitutions," *Georgetown Law Journal* 85, 6 (June 1997): 1834: "The Constitution's meaning is its original public meaning. Other approaches to interpretation are simply wrong."

35 Scalia and Garner, *Reading Law*, p. 405. For the new originalism movement, see Johnathan O'Neill, *Originalism in American Law and Politics: A Constitutional History* (Baltimore, MD: Johns Hopkins University Press, 2005), p. 146; Joel Alicea, "Forty Years of Originalism," *Policy Review*, 173 (June/July 2012): 69–79; and Logan E. Sawyer III, "Principle and Politics in the New History of Originalism," *American Journal of Legal History* 57, 2 (June 2017): 198–222. The originalism movement commencing in the 1980s has had both political and theoretical elements, and in most of this book, I will focus primarily on how theorists argue about interpretive methodologies rather than how originalism has, or has not, been implemented by judges. But since theorists often have strong views about what judges should do, and since the political branches do as well, it is important to set the theoretical issues in their real-world contexts.

return the supreme law of the land to its historical roots. His speech expressly called for a "jurisprudence of original intention": "Those who framed the Constitution chose their words carefully; they debated at great length the most minute points," argued Meese. "The language they chose meant something. It is incumbent upon the Court to determine what that meaning was." Throughout his speech, Meese repeatedly paired the two elements of "text and intention." In describing the proper approach to constitutional interpretation, Meese argued that the "text of the document and the original intention of those who framed it would be the judicial standard in giving effect to the Constitution."[36]

Although Meese had included the Framers in his public appeal for a jurisprudence of original intention, within two years, the Attorney General's own Office of Legal Policy (OLP) began to shift originalism's primary focus away from the Framers and towards the public meaning of the text.[37] Efforts a few years earlier by Robert Bork, Raoul Berger, and others to root constitutional interpretation in a notion of original intent[38] had been met with a barrage of counterarguments,[39] typically from scholars unfriendly either to the concept of originalism in general, or to the particular interpretations that would result from its use. Although these outcome-related legal issues loomed in the background – conservatives were unhappy with progressive decisions, and liberals were anxious to support them – the debates centered on a fascinating mix of factual arguments about the origins of the Constitution, accompanied by theoretical debates over the proper way for courts to interpret that document.

By mid-1980s, Justice Scalia and other originalists began to accept, and even to promote, many of the arguments against using the Framers' intentions that had been raised by opponents of originalism. They instead focused on textualism: a search for the public meaning of the text at the time of enactment.[40]

[36] Edwin Meese III, "Speech of Attorney General Edwin Meese III to the American Bar Association," July 9, 1985, www.justice.gov/sites/default/files/ag/legacy/2011/08/23/07–09-1985.pdf.

[37] US Department of Justice, Office of Legal Policy, *Original Meaning Jurisprudence: A Sourcebook* (Washington, DC: Government Publishing Office, 1988).

[38] See, for example, Robert H. Bork, "Neutral Principles and Some First Amendment Problems," *Indiana Law Journal* 47, 1 (Fall 1971): 1–35; and Raoul Berger, *Government by Judiciary: The Transformation of the Fourteenth Amendment* (Cambridge, MA: Harvard University Press, 1977).

[39] See, for example, Brest, "The Misconceived Quest," 234.

[40] As Joel Alicea notes: "Scalia proposed a theoretical shift: 'Change the label from the Doctrine of Original Intent to the Doctrine of Original Meaning.'" Alicea, "Forty Years of Originalism," 75. See also Department of Justice, *Sourcebook*; and Scalia, *A Matter of Interpretation*.

The jurisprudence of original *intent*, of looking at what the Framers said they were actually trying to accomplish, was thus attacked simultaneously from the right and the left, by progressive advocates of a "living constitution," and by conservative champions of the original public meaning. As a result, the Framers have been missing from much of constitutional theory's mainstream for several decades.

The rationale for the switch from the Framers' intentions to the original public meaning can be seen in the OLP *Sourcebook*, a nearly 200-page analysis of "Original Meaning Jurisprudence" issued in 1987 under Meese's imprimatur but not wholeheartedly embracing his approach. It sought to seize the methodological high ground from the living constitutionalist approach defended by Justice William Brennan by arguing that "original meaning jurisprudence ... predominated in constitutional adjudication for the first 150 years .... Under this approach, a court determines the most plausible meaning of the [text] to the society that ratified it. This original meaning – discerned from the words, structure, and history ... – is then applied to the ... issues before the court."[41] Despite Meese's initial references to the Framers' intentions, the OLP decisively adopted the path of constitutional textualism. The OLP stated its allegiance to textualism plainly: "Our fundamental law is the text ... as ratified, not the subjective intent or purpose of any individual or group."[42]

Since that time, as scholars have generated a sizeable literature dedicated to the methods of original public meaning originalism, the originalism movement, according to Keith Whittington, "is no longer primarily a critique of the Warren Court's rights jurisprudence."[43] The theoretical arguments have been supplemented with historical ones, and originalism's primary focus has continued to shift from the Framers to the text.[44] Over the years, a considerable

[41] Department of Justice, *Sourcebook*, p. 2.

[42] DOJ, 14. The *Sourcebook* cites Judge Thomas Cooley's early-twentieth-century treatise: "Even if we were certain we had attained to the meaning of the convention, it is by no means to be allowed a controlling force .... The constitution does not derive its force from the convention which framed, but from the people who ratified it." Quoted in DOJ, 14.

[43] Keith E. Whittington, "The New Originalism," *Georgetown Journal of Law and Public Policy* 2, 2 (Summer 2004): 607–8.

[44] Whittington, "The New Originalism," 609–10. Whether that shift is an exclusive one remains debatable, and Whittington is more open to seeking insights from the drafting history than some other leading originalist scholars. Compare Whittington's "the history of the drafting process is [not] irrelevant – it may provide important clues as to how the text was understood at the time and the meaningful choices that ... language embodied" with John Manning, who argues that the records of the Constitutional Convention "do not ... provide authoritative evidence of constitutional meaning." Whittington, 610; and John F. Manning, "The Role of the Philadelphia Convention in Constitutional Adjudication," *George Washington Law Review* 80, 6 (November 2012): 1753.

number of other constitutional theorists have further explicated and applied the public meaning approach, and much of contemporary originalism, often called "New Originalism," is therefore not "another way of referring to the subjective intent of the Framers and ratifiers," which has become "Old Originalism."[45]

For New Originalists, Founding Era dictionaries can be a more valuable source of constitutional meaning than the Framer's debates, although, in a wonderful example of unintended irony, modern dictionaries describe "originalism" not as a devotion to the objective meaning of the constitutional language, but as the "interpretation of the constitution which aims to follow closely the original intentions of those who drafted it."[46] That definition describes the Framer-focused "old" originalism of Attorney General Meese and Judge Bork half a century ago, not the original public meaning of many originalists today. In other words, the main current of today's originalist theory, which is based in part on the fundamental notion that the meaning of words should not evolve, has chosen a name that is itself the result of semantic evolution.

It is a sign of the strength of originalism's popularity in the early-twenty-first century that it is virtually impossible to list all of the leading descriptions of contemporary originalism. With the growth of scholarly interest in originalism since the early days of Attorney General Meese's call for a "jurisprudence of original intent," Steven Smith finds a "dazzling list of conceptual claims, shadings and distinctions" as "the subject has become scholasticized."[47] Mitchell Berman, perhaps somewhat tendentiously, identifies "72 distinct theses" in the "originalist logical space."[48] Noting the addition of the work of more progressive scholars such as Jack Balkin's "Living Originalism" into the originalist fold, Smith suggests that, "in gaining Balkin and like-minded thinkers, originalism loses ... well, its soul."[49]

45 Department of Justice, *Sourcebook*, p. 14. For this distinction, see especially Whittington, "The New Originalism," 599–613.

46 *Oxford Dictionaries Online*, s.v. "originalism," accessed January 15, 2020, https://en.oxforddictionaries.com/definition/originalism.

47 Steven D. Smith, "That Old-Time Originalism," in *The Challenge of Originalism: Theories of Constitutional Interpretation*, eds. Grant Huscroft and Bradley W. Miller (Cambridge: Cambridge University Press, 2011), pp. 226–7.

48 Mitchell N. Berman, "Originalism Is Bunk," *New York University Law Review* 84, 1 (April 2009): 14. See also Lawrence Solum, who has pointed out, "originalism means different things to different people," and he calls it a "family of related theories." Lawrence B. Solum, "We Are All Originalists Now," in *Constitutional Originalism: A Debate*, by Lawrence B. Solum and Robert W. Bennett (Ithaca, NY: Cornell University Press, 2011), p. 2. See also Sawyer, "Principle and Politics."

49 Smith, "That Old-Time Originalism," 230. See Jack M. Balkin, *Living Originalism* (Cambridge, MA: Harvard University Press, 2011).

Despite the diversity of views, a number of constitutional theorists have identified what they see as the central themes of public meaning originalism. Most prominent among them is Lawrence Solum, who has identified:

> [F]our core ideas that define one version of what is sometimes called the "*new originalism.*" First ... originalism claims that the meaning of each provision of the Constitution becomes *fixed* when that provision is framed and ratified .... The second idea that forms part of the core of contemporary originalism is that sound interpretation of the Constitution requires the recovery of its original public meaning .... A third notion at the core of contemporary originalism is the claim the *original public meaning* has the *force of law.*

The fourth, which he acknowledges is the most controversial, is: "Constitutional practice includes two distinct activities: (1) constitutional interpretation, which discerns the linguistic meaning of the text, and (2) constitutional construction, which determines the legal effect of the text."[50] While some prominent originalists have continued to argue for the importance of identifying the subjective understanding of the Framers,[51] the primary approach to contemporary originalism over the past few decades encompasses what appears to be a simple and straightforward method: the words must be interpreted based on their objective public meaning, in context, at the time the Constitution (or the relevant constitutional amendment) was ratified and became the law of the land.[52]

Once interpreters have identified the original public meaning, that meaning remains unchanged based on what Solum calls the "fixation thesis," that is, the principle "that the meaning of each provision ... becomes *fixed* when that

[50] Solum, "We Are All Originalists Now," 2–4. See also Aileen Kavanagh, "Original Intention, Enacted Text, and Constitutional Interpretation," *American Journal of Jurisprudence* 47 (2002): 255–98.

[51] McGinnis and Rappaport identify as "prominent intentionalists ... Larry Alexander, Raoul Berger, Sai Prakash, and Keith Whittington." John O. McGinnis and Michael B. Rappaport, "Original Methods Originalism: A New Theory of Interpretation and the Case Against Construction," *Northwestern University Law Review* 103, 2 (2009): 758–9.

[52] Especially useful places to find examples of descriptions of contemporary originalism include: Vasan Kesavan and Michael Stokes Paulsen, "The Interpretive Force of the Constitution's Secret Drafting History," *Georgetown Law Journal* 91, 6 (August 2003): 1134–48; Lawrence B. Solum, "What Is Originalism? The Evolution of Contemporary Originalist Theory," in Huscroft and Miller, *Challenge of Originalism*; Whittington, "The New Originalism"; Steven G. Calabresi, ed., *Originalism: A Quarter-Century of Debate* (Washington, DC: Regnery, 2007); Wurman, *A Debt Against the Living*; and Dennis J. Goldford, *The American Constitution and the Debate over Originalism* (New York: Cambridge University Press, 2005). For a history of constitutional originalism, see, generally, O'Neill, *Originalism in American Law and Politics*.

provision is framed and ratified."[53] In the words of nineteenth-century constitutional commentator Thomas Cooley, echoing one of the major strands of interpretive thought throughout the ages: "The meaning of the Constitution is fixed when it is adopted, and it is not different at any subsequent time when a court has occasion to pass upon it."[54] Since the search for the public meaning is the core originalist inquiry, according to this view, the Framers' subjective understandings are not relevant. If there is any reason to look to the Framers themselves, it is to see how prominent people in the Founding Era used the kind of language found in the Constitution. As John Manning has argued, while "it is impossible to imagine trying to reconstruct ... the intentions of a lawmaking process that consists of the Philadelphia Convention and thirteen ratifying conventions," the records of the Convention could be employed by the Framers as linguistic exemplars, demonstrating how particular words may have been used at the time of ratification, but "only to confirm propositions that can be derived from other sources."[55]

A PARTIAL RETURN TO THE FRAMERS?

Despite the various objections to a Framer-focused search for the original meaning, there has been a recent move by some originalist theorists towards including the Framers in the process of determining the meaning of the text, but not nearly to the degree for which I will argue. Lawrence Solum, for example, had previously written that constitutional meaning is fixed by "the linguistic practices of the public and not by the intentions of the Framers."[56] More recently, however, he has turned to the practical question of how an interpreter should discern that public meaning. Citing Randy Barnett's observation that the "public meaning ... could be gleaned from a number of sources, including the records of the convention,"[57] Solum points out that some of these materials "may provide evidence of the public context" for the "constitutional communication."[58] He remains uninterested in the subjective

[53] Solum, "We Are All Originalists Now," 2.

[54] Thomas M. Cooley, A *Treatise on the Constitutional Limitations which Rest upon the Legislative Power of the States of the American Union* (Boston, 1868), p. 55. Solum points out that this language was quoted by Justice George Sutherland in his dissenting opinion in *West Coast Hotel v. Parrish*, 300 US 379, 404 (1937).

[55] Manning, "Role of the Philadelphia Convention," 1792.

[56] Solum, "We Are All Originalists Now," 4.

[57] Randy E. Barnett, "An Originalism for Nonoriginalists," *Loyola Law Review* 45, 4 (Winter 1999): 627–8.

[58] Lawrence B. Solum, "Originalist Methodology," *University of Chicago Law Review* 84, 1 (2017): 291.

understandings of the Framers, however. He cautions that "it is important to distinguish between the use of the record of framing, ratification, and implementation as evidence of communicative content ... from the use ... as evidence of the legal content of constitutional doctrine."[59] Public meaning originalism, he argues, "rejects the use ... for the purpose of establishing the legal content of early constitutional doctrine that is supposed to be binding on the present."[60]

Solum develops a three-pronged approach – the "method of triangulation" – to "recover the original public meaning."[61] The three components are (1) corpus linguistics, that is, searches of digital databases of word usages in the relevant period; (2) immersion, that is, studying the "linguistic and conceptual world of the authors and readers"[62] of the relevant provision; and (3) the constitutional record, including "the drafting process, ... debates during the drafting and ratification process, and the early history of implementation of the constitutional provision."[63] Including the drafting history does not, for Solum, signal a shift to an interest in the subjective meaning often referred to as the Framers' intentions. The drafting history instead plays a "limited role ... like any other text from the period" in that it "can provide evidence of conventional semantic meaning."[64]

Solum's injunction that interpreters should go beyond dictionaries and commentaries, and immerse themselves in the language, history, law, and politics of the relevant era is an important contribution to contemporary originalism. As I will argue in the following chapters, Solum points to the right places to look for the original meaning, although I will diverge from his approach in two important ways. First, I will show that corpus linguistics-based analyses can, at best, provide data that will be helpful for the immersion process but cannot (or can only rarely) point directly to an answer to the question of original public meaning. It is more likely to show that there are multiple viable candidates for the semantic meaning. Second, the constitutional record can provide meaningful and even definitive evidence of the original meaning in at least two ways. It can identify a specific understanding of provisions that otherwise appear vague or ambiguous either from a nineteenth-century or a twenty-first-century perspective, and it can provide

[59] Lawrence B. Solum, "Triangulating Public Meaning: Corpus Linguistics, Immersion, and the Constitutional Record," *Brigham Young University Law Review*, 6 (2017): 1663.
[60] Solum, "Triangulating Public Meaning," 1663–4.
[61] Solum, 1667.
[62] Solum, 1624.
[63] Solum, 1624.
[64] Solum, 1656.

evidence of the Framers' rationale for adopting the provision, which will be necessary when interpreters need to apply the provision, especially (but not exclusively) to new and different circumstances.

Even more recently, Lee Strang has also reasserted the importance of the Framers in his "natural law account" of the Constitution.[65] His "Constitutional Communication Model" approach to originalism seeks to unite various schools of originalist thought, and he points out that "to enable effective constitutional communication to happen, all the parties" – the Framers, the ratifiers, government officials, and the public – "utilized original meaning."[66] That is, to "change the law . . . and secure the common good," the Framers needed to use "public meaning," rather than "privately intended . . . meaning"[67] so that they would be understood. Along the same lines, the Framers and ratifiers operated in the same communications milieu that included "conventional methods of interpretation."[68] Accordingly, although he starts by arguing that the "focal case of legal interpretation is understanding the lawmaker's intentional act," that element of intention necessarily includes "the communication of the legal reasons in a legal text to guide the conduct of the law's subjects,"[69] which itself must rely on public, not private, meaning. Strang also embraces the conventional interpretive methods of the time under his understanding of the constitutional context. As a result, there should be no divergence among original intent, original methods, and original public meaning interpretations because, as Strang puts it: "[T]he Framers resorted to the Constitution's public meaning, funneled through terms of art and the conventional interpretive rules, to convey their intended meaning to the Ratifiers and the American people."[70]

Solum and Strang open the door for a return of the Framers to constitutional history, but then they close it much of the way. Their focus remains on the objective public meaning. For Solum, the records of the Framers' debates can only provide evidence of how people employed language at the time. For Strang, the Framers knew that they could only achieve their goal of setting policies to advance the common good if they used publicly available meanings. Hence both are attracted by the potential power of computer-aided

[65] Lee J. Strang, *Originalism's Promise: A Natural Law Account of the American Constitution* (Cambridge: Cambridge University Press, 2019).

[66] Strang, *Originalism's Promise*, p. 44.

[67] Strang, 45, noting: "The Ratifiers, government officers, and Americans . . . knew that they did not have access to the Framers' private intentions, and *they knew the Framers knew they knew this*" (original emphasis).

[68] Strang, 45.

[69] Strang, 48, citing Ekins, *The Nature of Legislative Intent*, pp. 180–284.

[70] Strang, 56.

searches of corpus linguistics databases to provide critical insights into the objective meaning of the text.[71] Yet, identifying just one public meaning in large databases of material published in the Founding Era turns out to be much harder in practice than it is in theory.

The concept of using corpus linguistics to ascertain the public meaning of a text is simple: by counting all of the identifiable uses of constitutional terms in materials printed in America, scholars and judges using corpus linguistics databases can provide a reliable, reproducible, scientific determination of the objective public meaning. In practice, however, corpus linguistics demonstrates a foundational weakness of much of contemporary originalism – the assumption that interpreters can reliably identify a single objective (or conventional) meaning of enough highly contested terms to make the search for objective meaning a practically viable method of constitutional interpretation that is capable of resolving difficult cases. As numerous scholars have pointed out, we do not need an interpretive theory to tell us what it means when the Constitution says that the president must "have attained to the Age of thirty-five years." Where judges need guidance from constitutional theory is in dealing with the provisions that have dominated many constitutional debates over the past century or more, some of which are discussed in detail in later chapters, including: what does "an establishment of religion" mean, and is the excise tax clause broad enough to encompass the Social Security Act and the Affordable Care Act? Those chapters will show in detail why many originalists' enthusiasm for corpus linguistics – and, in fact, their dedication to the concept that a single, clear, objective public meaning can be determined without reference to the Framers' subjective understandings – is seriously misplaced.

However, Strang has made a critical point that bears emphasizing: the Framers knew that their goals could be achieved only if they used language that would make sense to the ratifiers, public officials, and to the public itself. Any secret or private understanding would remain just that – secret and private – and would not contribute to anyone else's perception of constitutional meaning. This important observation removes one of the theoretical objections to a Framer-focused search for the original meaning – namely, that it could lead to justices selecting an original constitutional meaning based on private, undisclosed understandings, perhaps found in an otherwise hidden scrap of notepaper squirreled away in a Framer's attic. The fact that some justices have done just that – as in Justice Souter's use in *Lee v. Weisman* of an elderly James Madison's unpublished musings about church–state issues – is an example of both the importance of the Framers and the need for a sound

[71] For Strang's contribution to corpus linguistics theory and practice, see Chapter 7.

method for employing their views.[72] For the Constitution to achieve the communicative goals noted by Strang, the Framers' meaning needed to be intelligible to the public. Yet identifying any intelligible meaning is not enough. What interpreters need to look for is evidence of which meaning, of the range of possible meanings – broad or narrow, for example – that the Framers had in mind in their effort to "secure the common good."[73]

Randy Barnett and Evan Bernick have proposed that faithfully construing the Constitution requires an understanding of both the "letter" and the "spirit."[74] That spirit is found in "the functions, purposes, goals, or aims implicit in its individual clauses and structural design."[75] They suggest that their method will also "unify original public meaning originalists with originalists who remain intentionalists,"[76] as long as the definition of "intention" matches their conception of the spirit, "as distinct from any subjective expectations concerning how particular provisions would be applied."[77] That is certainly a helpful distinction, and they are clearly right that "[e]ach constitutional provision and structural design element was crafted for a reason or multiple reasons."[78] Their emphasis on the design process and their recognition of the crucial importance of the reasoning process that led to the text of a provision are important advances in originalist theory, even as they distance themselves from what they call the "proto-originalism" involved in seeking the "intentions of the Framers."[79]

THE THESIS

The recent turn towards the Framers sets the stage for the thesis of this book: following Coke, Blackstone, and countless American judges and scholars,

72 *Lee v. Weisman*, 505 US 577, 617 (1992). The notes are called the Detached Memoranda. The document was discovered among the papers of one of Madison's biographers in 1946, "its yellowed pages folded and tied with a shoestring." It was written in the nineteenth century and showed that Madison had second thoughts about legislative chaplains and other topics. See Elizabeth Fleet, "Madison's 'Detached Memoranda,'" *The William and Mary Quarterly* 3, 4 (October 1946): 534–60. Irrespective of whether we agree with the opinions advanced in Madison's nineteenth-century private notes, we should share the view that they provide no reasonable evidence of what the members of the First Federal Congress thought they were doing when they adopted the Establishment Clause at least thirty years earlier.

73 Strang, *Originalism's Promise*, p. 45.

74 Randy E. Barnett and Evan D. Bernick, "The Letter and the Spirit: A Unified Theory of Originalism," *The Georgetown Law Journal* 107, no. 1 (October 2018): 5.

75 Barnett and Bernick, 3.

76 Barnett and Bernick, 5.

77 Barnett and Bernick, 5.

78 Barnett and Bernick, 46.

79 Barnett and Bernick, 46.

I will argue that the central goal of interpretation is discerning the will of the lawmaker. In the positivistic terms described by William Baude, that is "our law" of interpretation,[80] in spite of recent arguments by Sunstein and other scholars that "There is Nothing that Interpretation Just Is."[81] Seeking the will of the lawmaker involves not only knowing the objective meaning of the words, but also, to the extent possible, the subjective understanding of the Framers. I will, therefore, continue down the pathway established by Richard Ekins, who has argued that the Constitution "is an intentional lawmaking act rather than a text floating free in the world, and that the point of ... interpretation is primarily to understand the meaning that those who made [it] intended to convey."[82] Doing so involves a search for the policy judgment – the end–means decision – made by the Framers when they debated and drafted the Constitution. That search will require an investigation into how the Framers understood the provision they approved as well as the rationale that supported it.

Strang is right that the Framers needed to use publicly comprehensible meanings, but I will show that, for important constitutional terms, the range of public meanings in the relevant context is too diverse to allow judges to identify the right one without inquiring directly into the Framers' intentions. This approach would revise Justice Scalia's well-known statement of contemporary originalism: "What I look for in the Constitution is ... the original meaning of the text, not what the original draftsmen intended."[83] Interpreters need to look for the Framers' end–means decision in light of what may be a range of possible objective meanings of the text. That will require going beyond Solum's injunction to allow the drafting history only to play a "limited [semantic] role ... like any other text from the period,"[84] and instead use that drafting history as a potentially important guide to the provision's meaning and rationale. This search for the lawmaker's will was part of the Framers' understanding of the concept of interpretation, and thus should also be seen as an essential element of the "original methods" approach described by John McGinnis and Michael Rappaport.[85]

80 William Baude, "Is Originalism Our Law?" *Columbia Law Review* 115, 8 (December 2015): 2349–408.

81 See Sunstein, "There Is Nothing."

82 Richard Ekins, "Objects of Interpretation," *Constitutional Commentary* 32, 1 (2017): 1.

83 Scalia, *A Matter of Interpretation*, p. 38.

84 Solum, "Triangulating Public Meaning," 1656.

85 McGinnis and Rappaport, "Original Methods Originalism," 752. They note, for example, that "there is evidence both for intentionalism and textualism." McGinnis and Rappaport, 791, citing Philip Hamburger, *Law and Judicial Duty* (Cambridge, MA: Harvard University Press, 2008), p. 54.

The approach described in this book does not limit interpretation to the Framers' expected applications to eighteenth-century America, however. Judges, lawyers, and political leaders at the time of the Constitution understood the need to apply fixed texts to the new circumstances that come from the passage of time, as well as the importance of the lawmaker's rationale for doing so in a manner that is consistent with the Framers' intentions. Although such an approach to original methods "updating" allows for a degree of constitutional adaptability to changing circumstances, it is clearly distinguished from the approach advocated by Judge Richard Posner, who says: "I see absolutely no value to a judge of spending decades, years, months, weeks, day, hours, minutes, or seconds studying the Constitution, the history of its enactment, its amendments, and its implementation."[86] Judge Posner's point is simply that modern society's current concerns are "not what those 18th century guys were worrying about."[87] Similarly, scholars such as William Eskridge and Philip Frickey argue that judges interpreting statutes "should engage in 'practical reasoning' – a form of pragmatic, dynamic, multifactor analysis that does not depend upon unearthing some decision actually made by the legislature," an approach to the Constitution encouraged by various advocates of pragmatism, consequentialism, and other forms of policy analysis.[88] To the contrary, following a long-established tradition of legal interpretation identified by Coke, Blackstone, and others, judges seeking to interpret the Constitution in light of modern circumstances need to start by "discover[ing] relatively specific original meanings,"[89] in spite of Fleming's argument to the contrary.

My goal is to describe the well-precedented and theoretically sound approach to the interpretation of legal texts that has been "our law" for a very long time, and to apply it specifically to the Constitution. It is important to note, however, that this book does not attempt to set out a complete account of judicial decision making. Its focus is on the concept of interpretation. How interpretation relates to precedent, canons of construction, judicial review, the separation of powers, and other related topics will remain important subjects for further study.

86 Richard A. Posner, "Law School Professors Need More Practical Experience: Entry 9; The Academy Is out of Its Depth," *The Breakfast Table* (blog), *Slate*, June 24, 2016, https://slate.com/news-and-politics/2016/06/law-school-professors-need-more-practical-experience.html. He continues: "Eighteenth-century guys, however smart, could not foresee the culture, technology, etc., of the 21st century."

87 Posner, "Law School Professors."

88 John F. Manning, "Inside Congress' Mind," *Columbia Law Review* 115, 7 (November 2015): 1920, citing William N. Eskridge Jr. and Philip P. Frickey, "Statutory Interpretation as Practical Reasoning," *Stanford Law Review* 42, 2 (January 1990): 347–8.

89 Fleming, *Fidelity to Our Imperfect Constitution*, p. 27.

THE ARGUMENTS FOR THIS THESIS – CHAPTER BY CHAPTER

James Wilson, a law professor, Framer, ratifier, and Supreme Court justice, pointed out that: "The first and governing maxim in the interpretation of a statute is … to discover the meaning of those … who made it."[90] Nonetheless, much of contemporary interpretive theory has identified a series of both theoretical and practical obstacles to doing so in both statutory and constitutional interpretation. The book will demonstrate why those potential impediments have unnecessarily (and often inaccurately) relegated the Framers' subjective understandings to the interpretive sidelines.

Chapter 2 builds on Richard Ekins' influential work in defining and describing "The Nature of Legislative Intent."[91] This chapter deals with the question of whether the Framers or the ratifiers represent the actual lawmaker, analyzes what it means for the Framers to have an intention, and addresses the most frequently cited drawback of seeking the subjective understanding of the Framers, which is the "summing problem."[92] Whereas there is only one text, there are dozens of Framers and many more ratifiers with many different goals and mindsets. This issue is probably as old as the concept of laws being adopted by legislative bodies rather than by individual kings or emperors. Well before the US Constitution, interpreters noted that there are likely to be as "many myndes" as there are "statute makers."[93] The crux of this complaint is that, even if we wanted to determine the intention of the Framers, the barriers would simply be too high. This is a powerful criticism, but it is important to put it into a broader interpretive context.

I will address the issue of group intent and the "many myndes" objection in Chapter 2 in greater detail, but even beyond those Framer-related arguments, a central theme of the remainder of the book is that there will almost always be a summing problem in the search for the meaning of many important constitutional provisions. Whether constitutional interpreters rest their cases on the ratifiers' or the public's understandings (in either case, representing many more "myndes" than just the limited collection of Framers), a key challenge will be determining how to go about identifying the nature of the meaning that will govern the outcome. In a geographically diverse country of immigrants,

90 James Wilson, "Of the Study of the Law in the United States," in *The Works of James Wilson*, ed. Robert Green McCloskey (Cambridge, MA: Harvard University Press, 1967), vol. 1, p. 75.

91 Ekins, *The Nature of Legislative Intent*.

92 See, for example, Brest, "The Misconceived Quest," 204; and Max Radin, "Statutory Interpretation," *Harvard Law Review* 43, 6 (April 1930): 863–85. That concern is a serious challenge to seeking the Framers' understandings that has been raised by originalism's friends and foes alike. See also Manning, "Role of the Philadelphia Convention," 1756–68.

93 Quoted in Hamburger, *Law and Judicial Duty*, p. 52.

key constitutional terms could have multiple, sometimes inconsistent meanings. Interpreters in virtually all schools of thought will therefore encounter the same summing problem that has been attached primarily to the Framers.

Chapter 3 will then offer an essential backdrop for many of the remaining arguments. It surveys the jurisprudential landscape at the time of the Constitution, which reflected a very long experience in Western history in which legal scholars addressed just these kinds of interpretive questions. When Scalia and Garner, McGinnis and Rappaport, and others have made the original-methods-as-textualism argument, they have often based their conclusions on the historical assertions that even the Framers did not believe that their own understandings were relevant to constitutional interpretation, and that dynamic interpretations did not appear for another century or more.[94] They cite prominent Framers' statements in support of those arguments, but a broader analysis of the historical record shows that there is also strong evidence of a focus on the Framers' subjective understandings, and that the Founding Era was replete with examples of updated interpretations of old texts, including the Magna Carta.

The original methods discussion in Chapter 3 describes a very long pedigree for the concept that judges need an interpretative method that will enable them to apply unchanging texts to changing circumstances. Chapter 4 discusses how to do so without departing from the nature of the decisions made by the Framers in adopting the text. This method for dealing with a text written long ago has its roots in the jurisprudence of Coke and Blackstone, and will show where updating interpretations end and noninterpretive judicial decisions begin. The key question is whether the updating analysis is based on the end–means decision made by the Framers. As discussed in Chapter 4, updating interpretations are cases where the justices are essentially applying the Framers' policy choice to new circumstances, rather than changing the policy to one that they believe to be better.

Chapter 5 analyzes two continually contested constitutional provisions – the tax clauses and the Establishment Clause – to show the degree to which the search for a constitutional term's single public meaning can potentially suffer from an even larger summing problem than a search for the subjective understandings of the Framers. The eighteenth-century Supreme Court declared that there were two equally persuasive arguments for the semantic

[94] See, for instance, John O. McGinnis and Michael B. Rappaport, "Unifying Original Intent and Original Public Meaning," *Northwestern University Law Review* 113, 6 (2019): 1371–418; see also H. Jefferson Powell, "The Original Understanding of Original Intent," *Harvard Law Review* 98, 5 (March 1985): 885–948; and various others.

meanings of an "excise" tax. Meanwhile, Supreme Court justices and constitutional scholars have identified at least four potential meanings of the First Amendment's clause: "Congress shall make no law respecting an establishment of religion."

A number of scholars have recently identified a different answer to the semantic summing problem than the one that I will propose. They point to the new tool of computer-aided searches in corpus linguistics databases. Chapter 6 takes a detailed look at how the corpus is constructed and evaluated, and shows that the use of "Big Data" to answer constitutional questions is unlikely to live up to its promise of providing "reliable and reproducible" scientifically defined meanings. Corpus linguistics is a powerful tool for studying language use, but the materials collected in the corpus will not necessarily represent conventional American usage, and, even if they did, there is a distinct lack of adequate data analysis tools necessary to turn the research results into clear constitutional answers. Ultimately, this chapter asks: "Is Corpus Linguistics Better Than Flipping a Coin?" The answer to that is "no."

Chapter 7 demonstrates how seeking the Framers' understandings can resolve the difficult cases involving multiple potential meanings, and it returns to the tax clauses and the Establishment Clause as examples. The point of seeking the Framers' intentions in determining the original meaning in this manner is to select from the pool of semantically viable candidates rather than to propose a meaning at odds with a reasonable objective reading of the text. While evidence from the Framers will not always be able to point clearly to the original intentions, there is no way for interpreters to know without exploring the relevant sources in as much depth as possible.

Chapter 8 addresses factors that might inhibit constitutional interpreters from focusing on the Framers in spite of the arguments of the previous chapters. As the justices consider the Court's "sociological legitimacy," as Richard Fallon has defined it, or what Lawrence Lessig calls their own "fidelity to role," they may be concerned about how their decisions are perceived by scholars, by their peers in other countries, and by the public.[95] A number of scholars of comparative law have suggested that any commitment to originalism in general, and to the Framers in particular, is out of step with what judges do in other modern democracies. Additionally, some journalists and scholars have argued that originalism is primarily a "cover" for

[95] Richard H. Fallon Jr., *Law and Legitimacy in the Supreme Court* (Cambridge, MA: Harvard University Press, 2018), pp. 21–4; and Lawrence Lessig, *Fidelity and Constraint: How the Supreme Court Has Read the American Constitution* (New York: Oxford University Press, 2019), pp. 17–18.

conservative politics. This chapter will show that the evidence does not adequately support either assertion, and that there is an impressively bipartisan public interest in the Framers' intentions. These results are consistent with how the justices have written their opinions in the Court's ongoing effort to describe their decisions in ways that will maintain the Court's sociological legitimacy.

Chapter 9 returns to the Court's role as an interpretive body and points to a further critical reason for paying attention to the Framers. Judicial decisions that go beyond the policies embodied within the text of the Constitution place the Supreme Court in an independent policy-setting role for which, according to modern decision theory, it is ill prepared. An interpretation of the Constitution necessarily proceeds from, as Blackstone put it, "exploring [the lawmaker's] intentions at the time when the law was made." Whether the Court, under its equity powers, federal common law or otherwise, has the power to decide cases on any other basis is a separate matter. I will argue that the Supreme Court should be aware that its noninterpretive decisions are less likely to lead to good outcome than the justices might expect, and that if the Court were to make such a decision, it should be transparent in describing its rationale, and not try to make the decision sound as if it involved constitutional interpretation.

The Conclusion, Chapter 10, is a reminder that there is much to be learned in the long history of interpretation. In particular, the debates over the proper balance between static and dynamic interpretations, and sticking strictly to the text versus flexible constructions, are likely to continue for the next millennium, as they have in the last one.

THE FRAMERS, CONSTITUTIONAL INTERPRETATION, AND JUDICIAL POWER

Throughout Western legal history – at least until quite recently – one constant refrain has accompanied virtually every debate over interpretive methods: whatever approach legal theorists or judges have advocated from time to time, they have claimed that they are seeking the will of the lawmaker.[96] There have been disagreements of equally long standing over the benefits and drawbacks of seeking the lawmakers' actual or presumed intent but, until fairly

[96] "For at least six centuries," Ekins and Goldsworthy write, "courts have maintained that the primary object" of interpretation is "to give effect to the intention of the [lawmaker]." Richard Ekins and Jeffrey Goldsworthy, "The Reality and Indispensability of Legislative Intentions," *Sydney Law Review* 36, 1 (2014): 39, quoting *Attorney-General v. Carlton Bank* [1899] 2 QB 158, 164.

recently, it has been difficult to find the lawmaker excluded from many of those considerations, not only by scholars preferring updated applications of that intent, but even by those who are committed to seeking the original meaning.

The goal of this book is to demonstrate why a search for the will of the lawmaker – that is, the Framers' intentions, or the end–means decisions they were making and the reasons for those choices – is an essential element of the interpretive process. Exploring the proposals, drafts, debates, and discussions that took place in the Constitutional Convention or the First Federal Congress can provide documentary evidence of those intentions. Bringing the Framers back into a more central role in the constitutional conversation will be valuable not only because of the impressively deep tradition of doing so throughout Western legal history, but also because the modern Supreme Court has raised the interpretive stakes to an arguably unprecedented level. Throughout most of the vast expanse of Western legal history, judges' and commentators' arguments about interpretive methods have related to statutes. In America, a judicial interpretation of a statute can be overridden by a legislative act amending the statute. Similarly, the common law jurisprudence in the United Kingdom in effect at the time of the Constitution, and still today, says that if Parliament is unhappy with a judicial interpretation, even an interpretation of the Magna Carta, it can be corrected or overridden by a normal act of the legislature.[97] That is not the case for the US Constitution.

Justice Kennedy wrote in *Boerne v. Flores* (1997): "The power to interpret the Constitution . . . remains in the Judiciary."[98] If Congress could change the meaning by statute, Justice Kennedy continued, citing *Marbury v. Madison* (1803), "no longer would the Constitution be 'superior paramount law, unchangeable by ordinary means'."[99] As a result, the political branches can only change the Court's interpretation via the difficult process of amending the Constitution. Justice Kennedy's statement thus demonstrates the degree to which the Court's current approach to judicial review elevates the importance of getting interpretive theory and practice right, even compared to the many centuries prior to the Constitution.

97 See David Neuberger, "The UK Constitutional Settlement and the Role of the UK Supreme Court" (lecture, Legal Wales Conference, Bangor, Wales, October 10, 2014), www.supremecourt.uk/docs/speech-141010.pdf.

98 *City of Boerne v. Flores*, 521 US 507, 524 (1997).

99 *Boerne*, 521 US at 529, quoting *Marbury v. Madison*, 5 US 137, 177 (1803).

2

The Framers' Intentions

Who, What, and Where

"Every statute ought to be expounded according to the intent of them that made it," wrote Lord Coke in his influential *Institutes*, summarizing what had become, by that time, a very long and well-established jurisprudential tradition.[1] Blackstone echoed the same theme: the "fairest and most rational method to interpret the will of the legislator is by exploring his intentions at the time when the law was made."[2] Supreme Court Justice, law professor, and constitutional Framer James Wilson concurred with that approach in his law lectures at the University of Pennsylvania. In a rare instance of a Framer discussing interpretive theory in the abstract rather than as an advocate debating a particular issue, he said: "The first and governing maxim in the interpretation of a statute is . . . to discover the meaning of those . . . who made it."[3]

William Rawle, in one of the earliest commentaries on the Constitution, pronounced in the 1820s that the "true rule" of construing the Constitution is "to deduce the meaning from its known intention and its entire text."[4] A few years later, Justice Joseph Story's *Commentaries* cited the "first and fundamental rule" of interpreting legal instruments, which is "to construe them according to the sense of the terms, and the intention of the parties."[5] At the

1 Edward Coke, *The Fourth Part of the Institutes of the Laws of England: Concerning the Jurisdiction of Courts* (London, 1817), p. 330, quoted in Richard Ekins and Jeffrey Goldsworthy, "The Reality and Indispensability of Legislative Intentions," *Sydney Law Review* 36, 1 (2014): 40 n8, noting numerous authorities. See also Philip Hamburger, *Law and Judicial Duty* (Cambridge, MA: Harvard University Press, 2008).

2 William Blackstone, *Commentaries on the Laws of England: In Four Books; With an Analysis of the Work*, eds. Edward Christian et al., 19th ed. (New York, 1846), vol. 1, p. 40.

3 James Wilson, "Of the Study of the Law in the United States," in *The Works of James Wilson*, ed. Robert Green McCloskey (Cambridge, MA: Harvard University Press, 1967), vol. 1, p. 75.

4 William Rawle, *A View of the Constitution of the United States of America* (Philadelphia, 1829), pp. 31–2.

5 Joseph Story, *Commentaries on the Constitution of the United States: With a Preliminary Review of the Constitutional History* [. . .] (Boston, 1833), vol. 1, p. 383.

end of the nineteenth century, one of James Wilson's successors at the University of Pennsylvania Law School, Dean George Sharswood, stated the position even more strongly in his notes to an American edition of Blackstone's *Commentaries*: "It may be laid down that the intention of the makers of a statute is to govern, even though the construction grounded upon such intention may appear to be contrary to the literal import of the words."[6] Professor John Manning, also writing at the turn of the century, declared: "The method of interpretation employed in the Roman Law is the will of the prince or law maker, and in all free countries the will of the legislative body."[7] After tracing many centuries of statutory interpretation in Anglophone countries, Richard Ekins and Jeffrey Goldsworthy have written: "The proposition that the will or intention of [the lawmaking body] is the object of interpretation has been affirmed in leading cases and textbooks on statutory interpretation in England, Australia, Canada and the United States for ages (literally)."[8]

In summary, identifying the will of the lawmaker has long been the central interpretive inquiry in American jurisprudence, an approach this nation inherited from a very lengthy set of legal predecessors. A great deal of commentary throughout Western legal history has been devoted to the questions of *what* constitutes the will of the lawmaker, and *where* interpreters should find evidence of that will, but there has been impressive agreement on the question of *whether* interpreters should do so. This chapter will address both *what* and *where*, but, first, there is a question that is peculiar to the American constitutional setting: *who* is the lawmaker?

WHO IS THE CONSTITUTIONAL LAWMAKER?

When we speak of the Framers, we generally mean the delegates to the Constitutional Convention, in the case of the unamended version, or the First Federal Congress, in the case of the Bill of Rights (and subsequent Congresses that framed other amendments). Although both judges and scholars were essentially united across many centuries in the understanding that the object of interpretation was to identify the intention of the lawmaker, there

6 George Sharswood, ed., *Commentaries on the Laws of England: In Four Books*, by William Blackstone (Philadelphia, 1893), vol. 1, p. 60 n19.

7 John Manning, *Commentaries on the First Book of Blackstone* (Chapel Hill, NC, 1899), p. 12. Harvard Law Dean John Manning has had a long and distinguished record of scholarship on interpretive methods, but not quite this long. This commentary on Blackstone was written by the John Manning who was a professor of law at the University of North Carolina in the nineteenth century.

8 Ekins and Goldsworthy, "Reality and Indispensability," 40.

has rarely been a question of who constituted the lawmaker. But, by its terms, the Constitution did not become law until it was ratified; accordingly, the people whose action transformed that language into law were the ratifiers. This two-step process requires us to determine whether the lawmaker, for constitutional purposes, is the group that made the legal language or the one that, via ratification, officially made it into law.

The determination of who constitutes the lawmaker in the constitutional setting is important so that interpreters know where to look for evidence of the lawmaker's will. There are only helpful records for some of the state ratifying conventions, for example.[9] Since there is little evidence concerning the subjective understandings of the large number of ratifiers, it is easy to see why interpreters would generally have little choice but to look at the objective public meaning of the language as the best evidence of the ratifiers' understanding of the Constitution. "In ratifying the document," as Keith Whittington notes, "the people appropriated it, giving its text the meaning that was publicly understood."[10] Meanwhile, we have records from the Constitutional Convention and the First Congress,[11] but to figure out what role they should play in interpretation, we need to consider whether the *Framers* should actually count as lawmakers. The answer to that question is yes.

Article VII of the Constitution would appear to settle this question to the contrary: "The ratification of the conventions of nine states, shall be sufficient for the establishment of this Constitution between the states so ratifying the same."[12] But the story of constitutional formation is considerably murkier than the plain language of Article VII. As has been discussed since the ratification debates,[13] the Congress' charge to the Constitutional Convention in Philadelphia stated that "the sole and express purpose" was to revise the

9 See Gregory E. Maggs, "A Concise Guide to the Records of the State Ratifying Conventions as a Source of the Original Meaning of the U.S. Constitution," *University of Illinois Law Review* 2 (2009): 457–96.

10 Keith E. Whittington, *Constitutional Interpretation: Textual Meaning, Original Intent, and Judicial Review* (Lawrence: University Press of Kansas, 1999), p. 60. See also Thomas B. Colby, "The Sacrifice of the New Originalism," *Georgetown Law Journal* 99, 3 (March 2011): 722–4; and Vasan Kesavan and Michael Stokes Paulsen, "The Interpretive Force of the Constitution's Secret Drafting History," *Georgetown Law Journal* 91, 6 (August 2003): 1137.

11 For a guide, see William Baude and Jud Campbell, "Early American Constitutional History: A Source Guide" (unpublished manuscript, October 31, 2018), 11–12, https://perma.cc/326P-Q9V7.

12 US Const. Art. VII.

13 See, for example, *The Federalist Papers*, no. 40 (James Madison), in *The Avalon Project: Documents in Law, History and Diplomacy*, http://avalon.law.yale.edu/18th_century/fed40.asp.

Articles of Confederation.[14] The Articles, which provided for a "perpetual union," could only be amended if "such alteration be agreed to in a congress of the United States, and be afterwards confirmed by the legislatures of every state."[15] Nevertheless, the Convention proposed an entirely new Constitution, which, by its terms, would be effective on ratification by conventions (not legislatures) of only nine states.

Whether the Constitution was lawfully enacted has generated considerable debate.[16] As historian Joseph Ellis has written: "Critics of the Constitutional Convention have called attention to several of its more unseemly features," including the facts that "the convention was extralegal, since its explicit mandate was to revise the Articles of Confederation, not replace them ... [and] the machinery for ratification did not require the unanimous consent dictated by the Articles themselves."[17] In spite of those issues, even those who are not committed legal positivists will recognize that the Constitution has been treated as the supreme law of the land long enough to make its lawfulness a moot point.

As Richard Fallon points out: "[W]hen enough people embraced the Constitution as the operative framework of government, there was no need for further questioning."[18] That is, its "sociological legitimacy gave it legal legitimacy."[19] For our purposes, however, the essential point is that *the ratification process had whatever authority it possessed only because the Framers said so*. The power of nine ratifying state conventions to "establish" the Constitution was devised by the Framers who then announced it in the constitutional text, in spite of the fact that it was not consistent with the explicit requirements for modifying the Articles of Confederation. In other

14 *Federalist*, no. 40.

15 Articles of Confederation, Art. XIII.

16 See, for example, Bruce A. Ackerman, "The Storrs Lectures: Discovering the Constitution," *Yale Law Journal* 93, 6 (1984): 1058–9; Sanford Levinson, *Constitutional Faith* (Princeton, NJ: Princeton University Press, 1988), pp. 130–31; David C. Hendrickson, *Peace Pact: The Lost World of the American Founding* (Lawrence: University Press of Kansas, 2003), pp. 153–4; Pauline Maier, *Ratification: The People Debate the Constitution, 1787–1788* (New York: Simon & Schuster, 2011), p. 62; Akhil Reed Amar, *America's Constitution: A Biography* (New York: Random House, 2005), p. 517; Akhil Reed Amar, "Philadelphia Revisited: Amending the Constitution Outside Article V," *University of Chicago Law Review* 55, 4 (1988): 1043–104; Francisco Forrest Martin, *The Constitution as Treaty: The International Legal Constructionalist Approach to the U.S. Constitution* (New York: Cambridge University Press, 2007), p. 5 n11.

17 Joseph J. Ellis, *Founding Brothers: The Revolutionary Generation* (New York: Knopf, 2000), p. 8.

18 Richard H. Fallon Jr., *Law and Legitimacy in the Supreme Court* (Cambridge, MA: Harvard University Press, 2018), p. 86.

19 Fallon, *Law and Legitimacy*, p. 86.

words, the process of ratification was one of the many things the Framers framed.

When pressed by the Antifederalists on the basic issue of whether the Framers had gone well beyond their mandate, the Federalists responded that the Framers had not overstepped their legal boundaries because Article VII said that it was the ratifiers who made it into law. The Federalists' argument was a clever one, and, ultimately, it was successful, but it necessarily contained a Wizard of Oz-ian element of "pay no attention to [the Framers] behind the curtain." If they lacked authority to write an entirely new constitution, they certainly lacked authority to say that it would become law as a result of a process they invented and called ratification, especially since that process did not fulfill the requirements for amending the Articles of Confederation. Along the same lines, when the Congress "resolved unanimously" to send the Constitution to the state conventions "in conformity to the resolves of The [Philadelphia] Convention," Washington hoped that people would get the misimpression that Congress had unanimously approved the Constitution itself, saying, "Not every one has opportunities to peep behind the curtain ... ; as the multitude often judge from externals, the appearance of unanimity ... will be of great importance."[20]

The Framers thus successfully bootstrapped their way into a new constitutional order by designing a ratification process that would be "sufficient" to "establish" the Constitution, in the words of Article VII. As Charles Lofgren points out, the notion of ratification was new, one of the "new sett [sic] of ideas" that Connecticut's Oliver Ellsworth said "seemed to have crept in since the articles of Confederation were established."[21] The Framers' creative effort in successfully inventing the ratification concept should remind us that they were engaged in the process of inventing other solutions to the difficult issues associated with national governance, and we should pay close attention to the other choices they made as well.

One of the arguments of this chapter is that interpreters need to study the debates and negotiations involved in that problem-solving process (to the extent possible in light of the available records) to understand what prior interpreters have, for a millennium or more, called the *ratio* behind the Constitution's various provisions. As Ian Maclean writes in his review of interpretation in the centuries leading up to the time of Blackstone's

[20] Washington to Madison, October 10, 1787, quoted in Pauline Maier, *Ratification: The People Debate the Constitution, 1787–1788* (New York: Simon & Schuster, 2010), p. 58.

[21] Quoted in Charles A. Lofgren, "The Original Understanding of Original Intent?," *Constitutional Commentary* 5, 1 (Winter 1988): 82–3.

Commentaries, *ratio* typically included one or more of three things: "first, the cause of the law (i.e., the mischief which the law is designed to remedy); second, the purpose of the law ... ; third, the rationality of the law."[22] Maclean is describing the tradition that Blackstone was summarizing when he wrote: "There are three points to be considered ... ; the old law, the mischief, and the remedy .... [I]t is the business of the judges so to construe the act as to suppress the mischief and advance the remedy."[23] Furthermore, Maclean points out that *ratio* was closely related to, and perhaps inseparable from, the allied concept of the *mens legislatoris*, or the intent of the lawmaker.[24]

The text will provide strong evidence of the lawmaker's will, as Blackstone and many other commentators have pointed out.[25] But the text, in isolation, may not as clearly point to the *ratio* as the text in combination with a search for the *mens legislatoris*, the intent of the lawmaker. The further we are removed from the environment in which the text was created – and the past 200 plus years have seen many, many changes in American life and law – the harder it is for interpreters to comprehend the lawmaker's will solely by examining the text. That search for the original rationale and remedy requires a broader effort to comprehend the specific context and negotiations that led to that particular constitutional solution. Since the Framers not only debated and drafted the text, but also created the ratification rule by which that text would become law, it is their *ratio* we should seek *in the first instance*. They were the ones who considered what the Constitution should address, and how it should do so. Their debates, disagreements, and negotiated settlements created the text that was ratified without alteration. That being said, in providing for the ratification process, the Framers positioned the ratifiers in such a way that they would be perceived by the public as the lawmaker, and, therefore, the Framers could not reasonably have believed that the ratifying conventions would vote in favor of a completely unknown package of unvoiced intentions and secret meanings.[26] Accordingly, we need to look for evidence of the Framers' understandings of the mischief, remedy, and *ratio* that the ratifiers were likely to have known in light of a text whose words would be understood by the ratifiers.

22 Ian Maclean, *Interpretation and Meaning in the Renaissance: The Case of Law* (Cambridge: Cambridge University Press, 1992), pp. 152–3.

23 Blackstone, *Commentaries*, vol. 1, p. 60.

24 Maclean, *Interpretation and Meaning*, pp. 142–58.

25 See, for example, the discussion of Blackstone in Chapter 3.

26 See Lee J. Strang, *Originalism's Promise: A Natural Law Account of the American Constitution* (Cambridge: Cambridge University Press, 2019), pp. 45–8.

These classic interpretive theories may sound as if they will inevitably lead to the kind of flexible, purposive interpretations that are anathema to textualists and others who are nervous about offering judges the opportunity to construe the purpose or *ratio* so broadly that they pay little or no attention to the limitations otherwise signaled in the text. Those same issues were appreciated by the jurisprudential theorists who provided the Founding Era – and us – with the methodological foundations of interpretation. "Extensive" interpretations were highly controversial then, as they continue to be today. Legal scholar Alessandro Turamini wrote in 1542, for example, that "one can scarcely ever assume that the legislator intended something other than what he said,"[27] but, at the same time, the *ratio* remains essential because, in the words of Justinian's *Digest*, "to know the law is not to know the words of the law, but its force and power."[28] Nevertheless, purposive interpretations can inappropriately focus interpreters so completely on eradicating the mischief by any means possible that they do not pay sufficient attention to the remedy, which may have been limited to particular means. Constitutional interpreters need to be aware that the text was written well over 200 years ago, and that our initial twenty-first-century impression of the meaning of the language may not be an accurate reflection of either the eighteenth-century meaning, or its intended purpose and effect. Evidence of how the Framers understood what they were doing and why they were doing it can be essential to identifying the actual meaning as adopted by the Framers and approved by the ratifiers. The next section will consider in more detail exactly what it means for the Framers, as a group, to have an intention.

WHAT IS THE CONSTITUTIONAL LAWMAKER'S INTENTION?

The fact that there is a frequently cited and deeply rooted judicial commitment to interpreting legal texts in light of the lawmakers' intention would lead a casual observer to assume that such intentions actually exist. That seemingly commonsensical approach has nevertheless been questioned for centuries. Surveying much of the same jurisprudential landscape that inspired Ekins and Goldsworthy to focus on intention, Philip Hamburger has pointed out that "lawyers began in the fifteenth century and especially the sixteenth to wrestle with problems such as the hidden character of a lawmaker's mind and the divergent minds of multiple legislators," which has made it hard, and perhaps

[27] Quoted and translated in Maclean, *Interpretation and Meaning*, p. 151.
[28] Quoted and translated in Maclean, p. 144.

even impossible, to discern a single legislative intention.[29] Then, as now, there are "apt to be as 'many wittes' as 'heades' and as 'many myndes' as 'statute makers'."[30] The problem of "many myndes" creates both conceptual and practical issues. It is difficult to imagine that the hundreds of politicians who make up modern legislatures – or even the dozens participating in the drafting of the Constitution – were of one mind with respect to every clause. In light of these concerns, it is not hard to see why scholars, and textualists in particular, have been made nervous by statements from Supreme Court opinions suggesting that the primary source of meaning is not necessarily found in the text at all but in the background to its adoption.

As a result of the various concerns about identifying a genuine intention of the lawmaker, the hallmark of modern scholarship on interpretation has become what John Manning has called "intent skepticism."[31] Many "[t]heories as diverse as legal realism, pragmatism, and Dworkinism," not to mention the Manichaean opposites of textualism and purposivism, "all build out from the idea that interpreters cannot reasonably expect to identify what 'Congress' actually decided about the litigated issue in hard cases."[32] That is, many scholars agree that it is impossible to identify a clear, single intention of a large legislative body made up of men and women with a widely varying array of interests, intents, and motivations, especially regarding the kinds of provisions that end up in litigation over difficult issues of textual interpretation. Justice Scalia has argued that seeking the legislature's actual intent is nothing more than a "wild-goose chase."[33]

If a large lawmaking body cannot realistically have a single intention, as the scholarly consensus seems to have decided, then there is no point in looking for it.[34] Thus, for Justice Scalia, records of debates, committee reports, and similar sources are not "reliable indication[s] of what a majority of both Houses of Congress intended when they voted for the statute .... The *only*

29 Hamburger, *Law and Judicial Duty*, p. 52.

30 Hamburger, p. 52, citing *A Discourse upon the Exposicion and Understandinge of Statutes: With Sir Thomas Egerton's Additions*, ed. Samuel E. Thorne (San Marino, CA: Huntington Library, 1942), pp. 151–2.

31 John F. Manning, "Inside Congress' Mind," *Columbia Law Review* 115, 7 (November 2015): 1912. This is especially true in statutory interpretation, although all the same issues affect constitutional interpretation.

32 Manning, "Inside Congress' Mind," 1912.

33 Antonin Scalia, "Judicial Deference to Administrative Interpretations of Law," *Duke Law Journal*, 3 (June 1989): 517.

34 As in all areas of interpretation, there are dissenters from this consensus, and, as discussed below, I believe that the dissenters have the better argument. For summary of the recent literature, see Victoria Nourse, "What Is Legislative Intent? Evidence of Context," chap. 5 in *Misreading Law, Misreading Democracy* (Cambridge, MA: Harvard University Press, 2016).

reliable indication of *that* intent – the only thing we know for sure can be attributed to *all* of them – is the words ... that they voted to make law."[35] Except for occasional searches for background context, commentators following Justice Scalia's view have foresworn any references to the legislative history in interpreting either statutes or the Constitution, even where doing so would bolster their arguments about the meaning of a text. As Ralph Rossum has pointed out with respect to Justice Scalia, "Scalia's refusal to consult ... the debates over the drafting of the Constitution and the Bill of Rights occasionally keeps him from making as strong an argument as he otherwise could make."[36]

Moreover, the search for any sort of intention, especially in the legislative history, is jurisprudentially risky, as it provides "willful judges" the opportunity to implement their own "policy preferences, rather than neutral principles of law."[37] Citing federal Judge Harold Leventhal's memorable analogy, Justice Scalia has pointed out that "the trick is to look over the heads of the crowd," as at a cocktail party, and "pick out your friends," thus finding ways to justify a judge's preconceived conclusion about what the Constitution should mean by invoking any helpful statement by a Framer, even if it is taken well out of context.[38]

A clear example of this friend-at-a-cocktail party version of original intent can be found in Justice Wiley Rutledge's opinion in the *Everson* parochial school busing case. That opinion gave the appearance that James Madison's writings about church–state controversies in Virginia provided the decisive rationale leading to a strict separationist conclusion, but the historical analysis was just a cover story. Rutledge's actual concerns were reflected in the derisive comments about Catholic aggression that he expressed in a confidential memorandum to his judicial colleagues. When it came time to write his opinion, however, Rutledge shifted to history, saying "[A]ll the great

[35] *Crosby v. Nat'l Foreign Trade Council*, 530 US 363, 390–91 (2000) (Scalia, J., concurring) (original emphasis). Justice Scalia's nonjudicial writings urge readers not to search his judicial opinions for inconsistencies in his application of the interpretive principles he has espoused elsewhere. While Professor Rostrum has highlighted one case in which the justice was devoted to his principles, Andrei Marmor has pointed out that "many of his opinions refer to historical evidence that can only be taken as evidence about the Framers' further intentions, motives, or purposes, and the like." Andrei Marmor, "Meaning and Belief in Constitutional Interpretation," *Fordham Law Review* 82, 2 (November 2013): 579 n2.

[36] Ralph A. Rossum, *Understanding Clarence Thomas: The Jurisprudence of Constitutional Restoration* (Lawrence: University Press of Kansas, 2014), p. 16, citing, in particular, the meaning of the Second Amendment's right to bear arms.

[37] Antonin Scalia, A *Matter of Interpretation: Federal Courts and the Law* (Princeton, NJ: Princeton University Press, 1997), p. 35.

[38] Scalia, A *Matter of Interpretation*, p. 36.

instruments of the Virginia struggle for religious liberty ... became warp and woof of our constitutional tradition ... by the common unifying force of Madison's life, thought and sponsorship."[39] Rutledge even attached a copy of Madison's "Memorial and Remonstrance" to his opinion because "it behooves us in the dimming distance of time not to lose sight of what [he] *and his coworkers had in mind*" when they adopted the First Amendment.[40]

It was important for Rutledge, as he later put it in a letter to a friend, "to avoid pointing what I had to say in the direction of any specific sect," so he buried his concerns about religious aggression beneath an avalanche of Madisonian footnotes, saying that he "felt pretty strongly" about the case, and that he found the "Virginia history ... admirable for the ... purpose" of keeping the tone "moderate."[41] Despite its origins as convenient camouflage for his concerns about Catholic aggression, Justice Rutledge's one-sided, law office history has been very effective since *Everson* in linking the Framers with a strict separation of church and state.

It is not surprising that Justice Scalia and many other originalists sought to exclude that kind of material by saying that the process of interpretation should focus exclusively on the words of the Constitution, rather than the attitudes of any or even all of the drafters. In fact, the OLP Sourcebook called out Rutledge's opinion as an example of a bad interpretive method: "Rutledge ... improperly treated Madison's 'Memorial and Remonstrance ... ' as the equivalent of a constitutional amendment."[42] So as to be more effective in restraining judges from this kind of goal-oriented "law office history," Edwin Meese's earlier call for a jurisprudence of original intention was replaced by a search for the objective semantic meaning of the text, where sources such as dictionaries and commentaries could provide ostensibly objective metes and bounds limiting judges' creative ability to cite friendly history in support of their preferred interpretations. Since Meese had singled out cases involving religion as an area whether the Court had overstepped its interpretive bounds,[43] one of the attractions of jettisoning the concept of looking for the Framers' intent would be to free church–state jurisprudence from Madison's "Memorial" and Jefferson's "Wall of Separation." In doing so, however, they eliminated an important

39 *Everson v. Bd. of Educ.*, 330 US 1, 39 (1947) (Rutledge, J., dissenting).

40 *Everson*, 330 US at 37–38 (emphasis added).

41 Wiley Rutledge to Ernest Kirschten, February 20, 1947, Wiley Rutledge Papers, Box 143, quoted in Donald L. Drakeman, *Church, State and Original Intent* (New York: Cambridge University Press, 2010), p. 131.

42 US Department of Justice, Office of Legal Policy, *Original Meaning Jurisprudence: A Sourcebook* (Washington, DC: Government Publishing Office, 1988), p. 19 n38.

43 Edwin Meese III, "The Supreme Court of the United States: Bulwark of a Limited Constitution," *South Texas Law Review* 27, 3 (Fall 1986): 461–4.

source of constitutional meaning. To see why, we need to back up to consider the meaning of meaning.

MEANING

In interpreting any communication, is the speaker's intended meaning the core of the search for meaning? There have been energetic debates surrounding this issue for a very long time. As Maclean observes, "the distinction between speaker's meaning and hearer's meaning is ... a feature of ancient rhetoric."[44] Scholars in multiple fields – law, philosophy, linguistics, and probably others – have all worked to define meaning. The most successful of the definitions have primarily been descriptive, with prescriptive maxims designed to enhance the likelihood of successful communication, such as Paul Grice's "co-operative principle" and Donald Davidson's "principle of charity."[45] Defining a single method for determining meaning in the context of authoritative legal texts has been more challenging, in spite of many centuries of attempts.[46] For Kent Greenawalt, these arguments remain inconclusive: "[N]either the philosophy of language nor linguistics provides convincing bases to prefer one approach to statutory and constitutional interpretation over all its competitors; they can highlight reasons to question certain techniques but do not provide ... grounds to reject an approach that otherwise seems attractive."[47]

44 Maclean, *Interpretation and Meaning*, p. 101.

45 These insights are from Maclean, pp. 121, 140, citing Donald Davidson, "Radical Interpretation," *Dialectica* 27, 3/4 (1973): 313–28; and H. P. Grice, "Logic and Conversation," in *Syntax and Semantics*, eds. Peter Cole and Jerry L. Morgan, vol. 3, *Speech Acts* (New York: Academic Press, 1975).

46 For recent examples, as well as analyses of the challenges, see Paul Grice, *Studies in the Way of Words* (Cambridge, MA: Harvard University Press, 1989); H. P. Grice, "Utterer's Meaning, Sentence-Meaning, and Word-Meaning," *Foundations of Language* 4, 3 (August 1968): 225–42; and H. P. Grice, "Utterer's Meaning and Intentions," *Philosophical Review* 78, 2 (April 1969): 147–77. For a discussion of the limits of applying Grice's insights to legal texts, see Andrei Marmor, "The Pragmatics of Legal Language," *Ratio Juris* 21, 4 (December 2008): 423–52; and Andrei Marmor, *Social Conventions: From Language to Law* (Princeton, NJ: Princeton University Press, 2009). For an approach employing the source/reference distinction from Gottlob Frege and others, see Christopher R. Green, "'This Constitution': Constitutional Indexicals as a Basis for Textualist Semi-Originalism," *Notre Dame Law Review* 84, 4 (2009): 1607–74. For several different views of how Hans Georg Gadamer's insights into language may be relevant to legal interpretation, see the essays by Frank S. Ravitch, Lawrence B. Solum, and Francis J. Mootz III in Brian G. Slocum, ed., *The Nature of Legal Interpretation: What Jurists Can Learn about Legal Interpretation from Linguistics and Philosophy* (Chicago: University of Chicago Press, 2017).

47 Kent Greenawalt, "Philosophy of Language, Linguistics, and Possible Lessons about Originalism," in Slocum, *Nature of Legal Interpretation*, p. 48. See also Fallon, *Law and*

It would be valuable, nevertheless, briefly to review the leading theoretical options, which are intentionalism, in which meaning is found in what the speaker intended to convey, and a focus on conventional meaning (or at least the meaning derived from the conventions of a particular community, such as legal professionals). There are good arguments for and against both of these theoretical options. Generally, for intentionalists, the meaning of a text is what the author meant. As Stanley Fish writes: "My answer to the question 'What is the meaning of a text?' is simple and categorical: A text means what its author or authors intend."[48] This statement is, for Fish, not a theory of interpretation, but simply the "definition" of meaning.[49] Fellow intentionalist Larry Alexander calls himself a "simple-minded originalist" because he believes that "the proper way to interpret the Constitution ... is to seek its authors' intended meanings – the same thing we do when we read a letter from Mom, a shopping list from our spouse," and so on.[50]

Many of the intentionalist arguments and their supporting hypothetical scenarios deal with cases involving Mom, our spouse, or another single speaker or author. The intentionalist position becomes considerably more complicated when there are multiple authors. Discerning what the authors of legal texts had in mind and distilling those thoughts into a single, comprehensible intention is considerably more challenging than interpreting what a single speaker had in mind. For intentionalism skeptics, the solution is to focus on the most reasonable semantic meaning at that time. John Manning, quoting Joseph Raz, thus argues:

> Even if we cannot know the actual intent of the legislature, we can at least charge each legislator with the intention "to say what one would be normally understood as saying, given the circumstances in which one said it." Ascribing that sort of objectified intent to legislators offers an intelligible

Legitimacy, pp. 57–65. He writes: "Philosophers of language have no authority to legislate how you and I properly use nontechnical concepts." Fallon, pp. 64–65.

48 Stanley Fish, "The Intentionalist Thesis Once More," in *The Challenge of Originalism: Theories of Constitutional Interpretation*, eds. Grant Huscroft and Bradley W. Miller (Cambridge: Cambridge University Press, 2011), p. 100. See also Steven D. Smith, *Law's Quandary* (Cambridge, MA: Harvard University Press, 2004), pp. 101–25.

49 Fish, "Intentionalist Thesis," 100.

50 Larry Alexander, "Simple-Minded Originalism," in Huscroft and Miller, *Challenge of Originalism*, p. 87. As Steven D. Smith writes: "[P]art of the appeal of originalism, I suspect, has always been its inclusively commonsensical quality .... It made interpretation seem much like the sort of communication we all engage in routinely .... Just do basically the same thing you do when you talk with a colleague, or shop from a grocery list, or make dinner from an old recipe for fried chicken." Steven D. Smith, "That Old-Time Originalism," in Huscroft and Miller, *Challenge of Originalism*, pp. 229–30.

way to hold legislators accountable for the laws they have passed, whether or not they have *any* actual intent, singly or collectively, respecting its details.[51]

The Raz and Manning argument raises two questions. First, it is not clear who constitutes the "we" in that sentence who have the authority "to charge" the lawmakers with such an assumed intention. If it refers to "We the People" of the Preamble, then the Constitution offers little guidance on how lawmakers must use language (or how courts should interpret it).[52] "We" could also refer to twenty-first-century judges, who, practically speaking, have a more direct ability to charge lawmakers with the responsibility for using language in a certain way. Doing so – that is, saying that lawmakers may only use words in ways specified by judges – has been a controversial claim throughout much of legal history.[53] At least from the time of the Emperor Justinian, lawmakers have periodically issued edicts that have taken the opposite view: judges (and even scholars[54]) are charged to interpret words in ways specified by the lawmaker, not the other way around. Additionally, neither Raz nor Manning specifies the actor behind the passive connection involved in determining "what one would be normally understood as saying." Figuring out what that normal meaning is can lead to the semantic version of the summing problem normally associated with the "many myndes" of a lawmaking body – that is, various people may use words somewhat differently. As Justice Story wrote, words "expand or contract . . . from the more loose or exact uses, to which men

[51] John F. Manning, "Textualism and the Role of *The Federalist* in Constitutional Adjudication," *George Washington Law Review* 66, 5/6 (June–August 1998): 1341 (original emphasis), quoting Joseph Raz, "Intention in Interpretation," in *The Autonomy of Law: Essays on Legal Positivism*, ed. Robert P. George (New York: Oxford University Press, 1996), p. 268.

[52] A number of new originalist scholars have made a version of the following argument from Michael Stokes Paulsen, which focuses on the portion of the Supremacy Clause that describes the words "this Constitution" as pointing to the semantic meaning of the words at the time: "The straightforward internal textual argument for original-meaning textualism is that the Constitution is a written document; that it specifies 'this Constitution' as the thing that is to be considered supreme law; [and] that the default rule for textual interpretation was, at the time of the Constitution's adoption, the natural and original linguistic meaning of the words of the text." Michael Stokes Paulsen, "How to Interpret the Constitution (and How Not To)," *Yale Law Journal* 115, 8 (June 2006): 2056. As discussed in the earlier chapters, it is hard to sustain the argument that the objective public meaning was necessarily the "default rule" at the time of ratification.

[53] See Chapter 3 and, in the context of statutory interpretation, Nourse, *Misreading Law*; Abbe R. Gluck and Lisa Schultz Bressman, "Statutory Interpretation from the Inside: An Empirical Study of Congressional Drafting, Delegation, and the Canons, Part I," *Stanford Law Review* 65, 5 (May 2013): 901–1025; and Lisa Schultz Bressman and Abbe R. Gluck, "Statutory Interpretation from the Inside: An Empirical Study of Congressional Drafting, Delegation, and the Canons, Part II," *Stanford Law Review* 66, 4 (April 2014): 725–63.

[54] See the examples in Chapters 3 and 5.

of different talents, acquirements, and tastes, from choice or necessity apply them."[55] (These factual issues involving multiple conventional meanings of constitutional terms are explored in detail in Chapters 5 and 6.)

Intentionalists argue not only that language conventions can lead to vagueness, ambiguity, and other indeterminacies, but also that normal, or objective, semantic meaning may be insufficient to understand what the lawmakers were doing. Richard Ekins, for example, rejects the thesis that language can be fully explained in terms of linguistic conventions, arguing that "the use of language is an act, which means that it is undertaken for reasons. [Therefore,] [w]hat defines the communicative act is ... the speaker's intention to convey something ... to his audience."[56] A successful communication occurs when that audience "understand[s] the speaker's intention including its highly particular meaning-content, which the speaker intends the audience to identify."[57] Because the "semantic content of a sentence underdetermines what a speaker may mean," it can be "much thinner than ordinarily assumed."[58] So the "literal meaning of the sentence is sometimes a candidate for what the speaker may intend to mean, although often it will be too sparse and uninformative to be a proposition the speaker has good reason to convey."[59]

In response to these kinds of arguments, Manning and other textualists point to the use of the relevant lawmaking context to narrow the range of possible meanings. In turn, Ekins argues that, although context is also an important element in the search for meaning, context and semantics cannot "together constitute sentence meaning" because the "much more detailed, highly specific set of conventions" that would allow context to settle meaning does not exist.[60] Rather, context is more likely to serve as one of several tools

[55] Story, *Commentaries*, vol. 1, p. 437.

[56] Richard Ekins, *The Nature of Legislative Intent* (Oxford: Oxford University Press, 2012), p. 194. In this section, Ekins takes on a number of proponents of the view that statutes have as their meaning the conventional or ordinary meaning of the words employed. See, for example, Joseph Raz, *Between Authority and Interpretation: On the Theory of Law and Practical Reason* (New York: Oxford University Press, 2009), pp. 284–5; Frederick Schauer, *Playing by the Rules: A Philosophical Examination of Rule-Based Decision-Making in Law and in Life* (New York: Oxford University Press, 1991), pp. 55–8; and Jeremy Waldron, *Law and Disagreement* (Oxford: Oxford University Press, 1999), pp. 82–3. These arguments are complex, and they bear serious attention. In the end, Ekins concludes that these scholars fail to determine "whether conventions in fact explain (exhaustively or even sufficiently) how persons use language." Ekins, *Nature of Legislative Intent*, p. 193.

[57] Ekins, p. 194.

[58] Ekins, pp. 196, 198.

[59] Ekins, p. 202.

[60] Ekins, p. 209.

"to capture the best judgment of what the speaker is likely to have intended."[61] But, in the end, "[a] successful instance of communication occurs when the hearer identifies the intended meaning by recognizing the speaker's intention to this effect."[62] If the hearer does not get the intended message, "there is no third category of meaning, [what various scholars tend to call] utterance meaning. There is just what the speaker meant and what the hearer wrongly but reasonably understood him to mean."[63]

If the meaning of a legal text (and Ekins is writing specifically about statutes, but his insights can encompass our constitutional considerations, as well) were to be limited to the semantic meaning, interpreters would be stymied by cases when the language is ambiguous or otherwise poorly drafted: "Failures in precise, direct expression are likely to occur when legislators form and enact complex statutory texts .... Interpreters strive to grasp the meaning that the legislature intended to convey because they realize that what the legislature means does not reduce to what it says."[64] Moreover, the "text should be clear and clarity is not in general best achieved by exacting, exhaustive precision."[65]

Objective public meaning originalists nevertheless argue that meaning is a function not of intention but of the use of conventional communication practices and semantic meanings, which, together with a reasonable understanding of the relevant context, should be able to allow judges fully to determine the meaning. If that were actually true, however, we would not see so many letters from authors claiming to have been misunderstood in reviews of scholarly books in the *New York Review of Books*, *Times Literary Supplement*, or *Claremont Review of Books*, not to mention the countless works appearing in a Google Scholar search for the phrase "misinterpreted my" by scholars complaining that their peers had not properly understood what they meant (including scholars writing about semantic meaning in legal interpretation).[66] In each of these cases, the complaints are made by some of the world's most intelligent,

[61] Ekins, p. 209.

[62] Ekins, p. 210.

[63] Ekins, p. 210. Although modern thinkers frequently are cited, philosophers have been arguing about meaning for millennia. Grice has done so in a way that appeals to a number of New Originalist scholars, but see Saul Cornell, "The People's Constitution vs. The Lawyer's Constitution: Popular Constitutionalism and the Original Debate over Originalism," *Yale Journal of Law and the Humanities* 23, 2 (Summer 2011): 297 n9: "Philosopher Paul Grice's work has been cited by some new originalists .... It is important to recognize the divisions among philosophers of language regarding Grice."

[64] Ekins, *Nature of Legislative Intent*, p. 215.

[65] Ekins, p. 215.

[66] See, among many others, David O. Brink, "Semantics and Legal Interpretation (Further Thoughts)," *Canadian Journal of Law and Jurisprudence* 2, 2 (July 1989): 186: "Patterson ... misinterprets my interpretive claims."

well-educated, and well-trained users of the English language, arguing that some equally capable communicator has failed to understand their intended point. In our own writing, we (or at least those who complain about being misinterpreted) clearly believe, with Ekins, that a communication successfully occurs only when the audience "understand[s] the speaker's intention including its highly particular meaning-content."[67]

For the purpose of this book, it is unnecessary to address all of the most difficult theoretical conflicts between speakers' meaning and conventional meaning, especially where the two are arguably in conflict. On this point, Lee Strang is clearly right when he observes that the Framers knew that they needed to use words in a way that ratifiers and public officials would understand.[68] Instead, my focus is on the use of evidence of the speaker's meaning to determine which of multiple conventional meanings is the right one. Later chapters will show that there are likely to be more cases of multiple meanings than might be expected. This brings us to the question of whether there is an identifiable group intention of the Framers.

INTENTION

In discussing the Framers' subjective understandings, it is important to avoid simplistic notions of "intent." Many of the most trenchant critiques of looking for original intent are based on the observation that it is (virtually or perhaps actually) impossible to aggregate the intentions of dozens or hundreds of lawmakers.[69] Richard Ekins' powerful defense of intentionalism starts by clearing away the old notion of legislative intention as "an aggregation of the intentions of the many individual legislators," a formulation that has previously been critiqued by a host of skeptics, from Max Radin's pithy comments of a century ago (which, as we have seen, echo the voices of judges and scholars over many centuries) to more recent works by Ronald Dworkin and Jeremy Waldron.[70] If such an intention were to be, in Dworkin's words, "what someone has in mind and means to communicate by a vote," then it seems

[67] Ekins, *Nature of Legislative Intent*, p. 194.

[68] Strang, *Originalism's Promise*, p. 45.

[69] See Paul Brest, "The Misconceived Quest for Original Understanding," *Boston University Law Review* 60, 2 (March 1980): 214–15. See also Max Radin, "Statutory Interpretation," *Harvard Law Review* 43, 6 (April 1930): 870: "The chances that of several hundred men each will have exactly the same determinate situations in mind as possible reductions of a given determinable, are infinitesimally small." See also John F. Manning, "Textualism as a Nondelegation Doctrine," *Columbia Law Review* 97, 3 (April 1997): 684.

[70] Ekins, *Nature of Legislative Intent*, p. 9. See Radin, "Statutory Interpretation"; Ronald Dworkin, *Law's Empire* (Cambridge, MA: Harvard University Press, 1986), pp. 313–54; and Waldron, *Law*

that "we must take as primary the mental states of particular people because institutions do not have minds."[71] This formulation obliges the interpreter to "worry about how to consolidate individual intentions into a collective, fictitious group intention."[72] Both Ekins and Dworkin suggest that we refocus the issue, however. They point out that the legislator (in Dworkin's case, the ordinary legislator who does not control the drafting) "is like a signatory to a group letter," a formulation that shifts "the focus of attention away from the mental states of each person considered independently."[73] Then Ekins and Dworkin take that shared conclusion in very different directions. Ekins argues that "Dworkin is driven to conclude that the document is the author," a position which Ekins considers to be "absurd (an author is a person who writes a document to convey something)," whereas, for Ekins, the "joint intention on which [a] group acts is the plan of action that coordinates and structures the joint action of the members of the group."[74] For either scholar, however, the point is that the individuals comprising the lawmaking body take an action *as a group*.

For Ekins, who follows a "classical understanding of social action found in Aquinas," and restated and updated more recently by John Finnis and others, a "group is an association of two or more persons who unite in the coordinated pursuit of a common purpose." "Group action," then, "is action by the members of the group on a group intention. That group intention ... [is] the means to the shared end that defines the group."[75] To "understand the nature of [those] group intentions ... is to understand how they coordinate individual acts into a group action and how they relate to the reasoning of

and Disagreement, pp. 125–6. See also William N. Eskridge Jr., "The New Textualism," *UCLA Law Review* 37, 4 (April 1990): 642: "To talk about the collective intent of a legislature is fiction compounded, not just by the greater number of people whose intent must be discovered, but also by the muteness of most of these people and the special conventions of the legislative process, such as the requirements that a bill must be passed in the same form by both chambers (bicameralism) and that it must then be presented to the President (presentment)."

[71] Dworkin, *Law's Empire*, pp. 335–6.

[72] Dworkin, p. 336. Here I am relying on Ekins's interpretive description of Dworkin's approach.

[73] Ekins, *Nature of Legislative Intent*, p. 25.

[74] Ekins, p. 47.

[75] Ekins, *Nature of Legislative Intent*, pp. 52, 64, citing John Finnis, *Aquinas: Moral, Political, and Legal Theory* (New York: Oxford University Press, 1998), pp. 23–37; and John Finnis, Joseph Boyle, and Germain Grisez, *Nuclear Deterrence, Morality and Realism* (New York: Oxford University Press, 1987), pp. 120–23, 288–91, 344–7. Ekins also relies on Bratman's approach to interlocking intentions. See Ekins, *Nature of Legislative Intent*, pp. 59, 63–4, citing Michael E. Bratman, *Faces of Intention: Selected Essays on Intention and Agency* (Cambridge: Cambridge University Press, 1999), p. 107.

individual members."[76] This notion of group agency is based on "the joint intention to form and maintain a group that responds coherently to reasons."[77] That is, the members of the body not only take action as a group, but they take *reasoned* action.

For all of us who have seen the often unruly and complicated process that goes into lawmaking, it is important to note that Ekins here is describing the "central case" (or what some social scientists would call the "ideal-type") of the "well-formed legislature," which is "an institution capable of reasoned choice."[78] Whether actual lawmaking bodies can live up to the descriptions "well-formed" and "capable of reasoned choice" remains an open and complex issue, and there are certainly numerous examples of when they have not. Yet his focus on the group takes us in a potentially fruitful direction: the idea that a lawmaking body is – or at least can be – a group of people who are reasoning and debating together in the context of a question of whether and how a law should be enacted or changed in order to serve the common good.

Speaking still of the ideal case, Ekins sees the exercise of "legitimate [legislative] authority" as "respond[ing] to reasons with reasoned action" and thus "[r]ational lawmaking is action to change the law in specific ways for (what the legislature takes to be) good reasons."[79] In doing so, the legislature has not only one intention, it actually has two of them, a standing intention and a series of particular intentions. These intentions contribute to the "defining end of the assembly," which is "to be in a fit state to legislate on particular occasions for the common good."[80] The standing intention is essentially to be capable of making reasoned choices based on the concept

[76] Ekins, *Nature of Legislative Intent*, p. 53.

[77] Ekins, p. 73.

[78] Ekins, pp. 77, 118. In discussing the "well-formed" legislature, Ekins has adopted the "central case" jurisprudential method. See John Finnis, *Natural Law and Natural Rights*, 2nd ed. (New York: Oxford University Press, 2011), pp. 9–10, which Ekins describes as: "Adopt[ing] the perspective of the practically reasonable person to identify the ends, or objects, of fully reasonable human action and thence to understand more or less confused or in other ways rationally defective purposes, actions, and institutions. The central case of the legislature . . . is the form that the legislature has . . . when it is chosen and maintained by practically reasonable persons." Ekins, *Nature of Legislative Intent*, p. 118. See also Finnis, *Natural Law*, p. 11: "One's descriptive explanation of the central cases should be as conceptually rich and complex as is required to answer all appropriate questions about [them]. And then one's account of the other instances can trace the network of similarities and differences, the analogies and disanalogies . . . between them and the central cases." In developing the central case approach, Finnis cites both Max Weber's "ideal-type" and Aristotle's "focal meaning." Finnis, p. 20. For an application of Ekins's approach to the US Constitution, especially in the context of the central or focal case, see Strang, *Originalism's Promise*.

[79] Ekins, *Nature of Legislative Intent*, pp. 112–13.

[80] Ekins, p. 219.

that "each lawmaking act ... [is] reasoned and coherent."[81] Then, when it does act, the legislature's particular intention is the "intention on which it acts ... which is both that for which it acts – changes in the law that are means to valuable ends – and the plan it adopts to introduce those changes – a complex set of meanings that expresses a complex set of propositions."[82]

For Ekins, the goal for interpreters is thus to identify "the legal changes that the legislature has [enacted] by understanding the intended meaning of the ... text."[83] To do so is to "understand what was intended by inference, which in turn requires reflection on why the [legislature] acted."[84] In that effort, it is important, in Ekins' formulation, to acknowledge the essential role of reasons to the meaning of the law. That is, the text itself, or the semantic meaning of the words, cannot capture the legal effect of the statute. Rather, the legal effect of the statute is the set of legally true propositions that the statute stands for."[85] The text does not exist in isolation but "is a contribution to an existing legal order, in which there are prevailing assumptions, antecedent rules, and general qualifying principles."[86] It stands "together with other such acts [to] constitute[] a scheme of social coordination towards the common good."[87] The "content of the law ... is [thus] the set of normative propositions" that is "made known" by the text.[88]

This Ekinsian conclusion – that the text only signals the content of the law, which takes the form of "normative propositions" that reflect reasoned choices – has a very distinguished history. The law, according to Cicero, "is nothing more than right reason."[89] It is an important reminder that those searching for the objective public meaning can be tempted to overlook or too quickly dismiss the fact that the text resulted from a reasoning process in which its Framers deliberated about how to address a particular issue (the mischief) and ultimately made what Ekins calls an "end–means" choice (the remedy).

81 Ekins, p. 223.
82 Ekins, p. 220. The point is that the legislature's intention is not that of the majority that votes in favor of a particular piece of legislation. Rather, the standing intention – that the majority's act is the act of the entire group – leads to a particular intention that is the reasoned choice represented by the act. The majority thus does not enact a statute by itself; only the legislature as a whole enacts a statute, and through the process of drafting and debate the legislation's meaning becomes available to all the legislators, whether they vote in the majority or not. See Ekins, p. 236.
83 Ekins, p. 236.
84 Ekins, p. 236.
85 Ekins, p. 126.
86 Ekins, p. 126.
87 Ekins, p. 126.
88 Ekins, p. 127.
89 Quoted and translated in Maclean, *Interpretation and Meaning*, p. 154.

As he concludes: "[T]he focus of the interpretive inquiry is rightly on what it is plausible to infer [the legislature] intended in enacting the relevant statutory text – that is, what meaning – content it intended to convey . . . . The legislature acts for reasons and uses language rationally, which means that interpreters have good reason to reflect on the legislature's likely chain of reasoning in order to determine the meaning that the legislature likely acted to convey," with the text essentially being "the conclusion of the reasoning."[90]

In summary, solely focusing on the four corners of the text – even the text in its relevant context – may also cause interpreters to lose sight of the possibility that the Framers' decision to adopt that provision involved a rational thought process over how to address a particular issue. It is important to keep in mind, however, that Ekins has described the central case scenario, where we can assume that, as Cicero put it, "law is the highest degree of reason set in nature."[91] In the context of the real life events associated with the framing of the Constitution, it is not clear that every provision was the conclusion of a consistent and thoughtful process leading to a conclusion best characterized as "right reason." The Constitution was the result of a combination of reasoned arguments and the negotiated compromises needed to address difficult sectional rivalries. The three-fifths clause and other slavery-related provisions, for example, are not examples of "right reason," but they are the result of a coherent process of problem solving involving essential participants employing take-it-or-leave-it arguments. They were hard-fought, negotiated compromises without which the Constitution may not have come to pass. In the real world constitutional context, Ekins' first intention still stands – to be in a proper state to act together as a group – and the second, to change the law in a particular way (means) to achieve specific ends, stands as well, but we cannot necessarily assume that interpreters can determine what the Framers' meant by inferring the "chain of reasoning"[92] that led to the "legally true propositions that the [text] stands for."[93] Instead, we need to look for the best evidence that tells us what the Framers actually understood the provision to mean – what were its ends and means – irrespective of whether any particular Framer wanted it to be adopted in that particular fashion, or whether there is a single, consistent chain of reasoning leading to the law's proposition. In the case of the Constitutional Convention and the congresses that adopted the texts of the Bill of Rights and other amendments, these bodies did, in fact,

90 Ekins, *Nature of Legislative Intent*, pp. 249–50.
91 Quoted and translated in Maclean, *Interpretation and Meaning*, p. 154.
92 Ekins, *Nature of Legislative Intent*, p. 249.
93 Ekins, p. 126.

deliberate over ends and means, and that evidence of their thinking and negotiation contributes vital information for our understanding of the original meaning of the constitutional text.[94]

WHERE DO INTERPRETERS FIND THE FRAMERS' UNDERSTANDINGS?

Even Ekins does not think that the lawmaker's intention can be found in the records of speeches and debates. He argues that it is "unsound to assume that what the legislature truly intends is best gleaned from the legislative history rather than from the text uttered in context."[95] He would only reluctantly seek evidence of that intention from the debates since "legislative history is capable of making a difference only when what is intended is not otherwise clearly promulgated, which is a failure of legislative action."[96] That overstates the case, however. He admits that "what the legislature means does not [always] reduce to what it says."[97] He counts on the fact that the law is a reasoned response to a specific need to change the law to achieve the common good to allow interpreters to infer – essentially reverse engineer – the reasoning process, and hence the meaning intended by the lawmaker.[98] But outside the central case that he addresses in which lawmakers can be assumed to choose well-reasoned means to address rational public policy ends, the legislative history can be a valuable source for those seeking to identify that intention, especially when interpreters need to try to understand a reasoning and bargaining process that took place two centuries ago.

[94] See Nourse, *Misreading Law*, p. 159: "Jurisprudential experts have debated the question of 'legislative intent' for long enough. That is the wrong question. The question to ask is how Congress makes decisions, and what evidence should count to determine its decisions." A similar call to focus more intently on what the lawmakers were trying to accomplish has been made by Danny Frost's effort to "rehabilitate and elaborate the so-called 'mischief rule' of English law." Daniel Frost, "Getting into Mischief: On What It Means to Appeal to the U.S. Constitution," *International Journal for the Semiotics of Law* 28, 2 (2015): 267.

[95] Ekins, *Nature of Legislative Intent*, p. 270.

[96] Ekins, p. 271. For a considerably more friendly view towards the legislative record, see Nourse, *Misreading Law*, p. 157: "The reality is that bills change over and over again; the final text should be the starting place for any analysis of legislative evidence. From there, the debate on the conference report and the conference report's joint explanation is the best evidence of what happened in the final bill .... If there is no debate on the conference report, or no conference report, then the floor debate and amendments leading to the text should be consulted." She then continues to discuss approaches to employing evidence from the Senate.

[97] Ekins, *Nature of Legislative Intent*, p. 215.

[98] Ekins, pp. 112–13, 126.

THE BENEFITS AND RISKS OF LOOKING FOR MEANING IN THE DRAFTING RECORD

A variety of records describe the discussions at the Constitutional Convention, the ratification debates, and the comments in the First Congress about the proposed Bill of Rights, including contemporaneous notes, reports, and letters written by various participants, newspaper accounts, and so on. The fact that Madison's notes of the Convention were not available to the ratifiers (and that the accuracy of some of his notes has been called into question) has become something of a red herring in arguments about the Convention.[99] Leading scholars assume that the ratifiers lacked insights into what the Philadelphia Framers were thinking. With the exception of Rhode Island, which did not send delegates to Philadelphia, all of the state ratifying conventions included at least one member who had been a delegate to the Constitutional Convention.[100] Like all documentary sources from the period, Madison's notes offer interpreters a potentially useful window through which to view the proceedings that led to the text, and may well reflect what the other

[99] Madison's detailed notes of the convention were not available for several decades. See *The Papers of James Madison: Purchased by Order of Congress; Being His Correspondence And Reports of Debates* [...], ed. Henry D. Gilpin, vol. 2 (New York, 1841). But information about the Convention debates *was* available through published essays by other delegates. See Luther Martin, "The Genuine Information, Delivered to the Legislature of the State of Maryland, Relative to the Proceedings of the General Convention, Lately Held at Philadelphia," in *The Complete Anti-Federalist*, ed. Herbert J. Storing, vol. 2, *Objections of Non-Signers of the Constitution and Major Series of Essays at the Outset* (Chicago: University of Chicago Press, 1981), pp. 27–82. Regarding Martin's pamphlet, see Kesavan and Paulsen, "Interpretive Force," 1152 n143: "Luther Martin's Letter revealed no small portion of the hitherto secret proceedings of the Philadelphia Convention – including the drafting history (in some detail) of various clauses." There has been a lively debate over the reliability of Madison's notes for a long time. For the most recent arguments, see Mary Sarah Bilder, *Madison's Hand: Revising the Constitutional Convention* (Cambridge, MA: Harvard University Press, 2015); and the response by Lynn Uzzell, *Redeeming Madison's Notes* (unpublished manuscript). For the ratification debates, see Merrill Jensen, ed., *The Documentary History of the Ratification of the Constitution*, vol. 1, *Constitutional Documents and Records, 1776–1787* (Madison: State Historical Society of Wisconsin, 1976). For the First Congress, see, for example, Joseph Gales, ed., *The Debates and Proceedings in the Congress of the United States, with an Appendix* [...], vol. 2, *Comprising (with Volume I) the Period from March 3, 1789 to March 3, 1791, Inclusive* (Washington, DC, 1834). These sources are not always ideal. For a discussion of their limitations, see generally Marion Tinling, "Thomas Lloyd's Reports of the First Federal Congress," *William and Mary Quarterly* 18, 4 (October 1961): 519–45; and James H. Hutson, "The Creation of the Constitution: The Integrity of the Documentary Record," *Texas Law Review* 65, 1 (November 1986): 1–39.

[100] See Gregory E. Maggs, "A Concise Guide to the Records of the State Ratifying Conventions as a Source of the Original Meaning of the U.S. Constitution," *University of Illinois Law Review*, 2 (2009): 457–96.

Convention delegates were reporting when they attended their own state conventions. Whether Madison's notes appear to be accurate as to any particular issue will require further investigation, but the need to confirm the veracity of any historical "witness" to meaning, from Madison to the authors of dictionaries to the Federalist-Antifederalist debates, is simply an essential part of recovering the original meaning in its original context.

The best records of the Framers' understandings are those that tell us about the issues, disagreements, debates, negotiations, and decisions – that is, documents describing the Convention or the First Congress in the case of the Bill of Rights (or other congresses responsible for proposing constitutional amendments). These records can be supplemented by contemporaneous documents containing information about those proceedings, such as *The Federalist* and Antifederalist Luther Martin's widely reprinted *General Information*. The most valuable ones will more closely resemble reportage than editorials, with *The Federalist* and the *General Information*, for example, falling into the latter category, although the topics debated publicly by the Federalists (in *the Federalist* and elsewhere) and the Antifederalists (for example, in the *General Information*), as well as any records from the ratifiers, can help us understand the principal concerns and controversies on multiple sides of the arguments. Moreover, while statements from individual Framers about how a provision should be interpreted, or how it would apply to specific issues (that is, what is sometimes called the Framers' "expected applications"), may be useful information, we need to bear in mind that those statements were often made in the context of controversial cases, and the various Framers often disagreed about specific applications. Looking for what the Framers, acting together *as a group*, understood regarding the meaning of the text is the goal of interpretation.

This concept of using the records of lawmakers' debates for the purposes of interpretation is a common one. Judges acknowledge that they do it regularly, frequently looking for evidence of that intention in the documents recording the proceedings by which the provision was debated and ultimately became law. As former Appellate Judge Kenneth Starr has written: "One of the workaday tools which federal judges are called upon to employ regularly in their daily labors is the body of materials called 'legislative history.' Like a trusty old teapot, legislative history is readily available whenever the need for it arises."[101] Fellow Appellate Judge Robert Katzmann agrees, arguing that legislative history, including the proposals, committee reports, floor debates, and similar

[101] Kenneth W. Starr, "Observations about the Use of Legislative History," *Duke Law Journal*, 3 (June 1987): 371.

materials, can be helpful not only to judges, but is often expected to be part of the interpretive process by the lawmakers themselves. One influential member of Congress has said that "[d]isregarding legislative history 'is an assault on the integrity of the legislative process'."[102] Similarly, according to Katzmann, ranking members of the Senate's judiciary committee from both major parties "have consistently supported judicial resort to legislative history."[103] Victoria Nourse cites numerous other examples in her powerful case for incorporating both legislative history and a realistic appreciation for legislative context in the interpretation of statutes.[104]

Some scholars have cited preconstitutional English legal history to say that the Framers would not have expected courts to refer to the proceedings of the Convention or the First Congress in an effort to ascertain the Framers' intentions. Hans Baade, for example, argued that intent is "ascertained primarily from within the four corners of" the enactment, along with "matters presumed to be within the [lawmaker's] knowledge," but that "[e]vidence of legislative history is generally inadmissible."[105] This rule against reference to records of parliamentary proceedings, often called "the exclusionary rule," is not found until 1769,[106] well after most lawyers and judges in the Founding Era finished their legal education. Since then, it has sometimes been honored in the breach, and has been substantially relaxed over time. Otherwise, from the earliest days of Parliament, English courts would seek help in determining the "mente legislatorum," including by directly asking the "statute makers"

[102] Robert A. Katzmann, *Judging Statutes* (New York: Oxford University Press, 2014), p. 36, quoting "then-Congressman Robert W. Kastenmeier (D-WI), the longtime chair of the House Judiciary Subcommittee on Courts[, Intellectual Property, and the Administration of Justice]."

[103] Katzmann, *Judging Statutes*, p. 36, citing, in particular, "Senators Orrin Hatch (R-UT) and Charles E. Grassley (R-IA) as Republican chairs or ranking members of the Judiciary Committee, and Senator Patrick Leahy (D-VT), as Democratic chair or ranking member."

[104] Nourse, *Misreading Law*. See also Kent Greenawalt, *Statutory and Common Law Interpretation* (Oxford: Oxford University Press, 2013), p. 84: "Among state legislatures that have adopted rules of interpretation, every one has authorized judicial use of legislative history." He further predicts, "Were the federal courts consistently to refuse to look at legislative history, it is doubtful whether Congress would remain passive or would, instead, enact guides to interpretation that would include that history." Greenawalt, *Statutory and Common Law Interpretation*, p. 84.

[105] Hans W. Baade, "'Original Intent' in Historical Perspective: Some Critical Glosses," *Texas Law Review* 69, 5 (April 1991): 1007.

[106] James J. Brudney, "Below the Surface: Comparing Legislative History Usage by the House of Lords and the Supreme Court," *Washington University Law Review* 85, 1 (2007): 7, citing *Millar v. Taylor* (1769) 98 ER 201, 217 (KB) (Willes, J.).

and hearing "their lyvinge voice."[107] As Raoul Berger notes, quoting historian Samuel Thorne: "Actual intent ... is controlling from Hengham's day [thirteenth century] to that of Lord Nottingham (1678)."[108]

In practice, constitutional interpretation has focused on the Framers' intent both early and fairly often. In the US Supreme Court's first case considering the constitutionality of a federal excise tax statute in 1796, Justice William Paterson showed no hesitation in basing his opinion on "the intention of the Framers of the Constitution," for which he needed no documentary evidence, as he had been a delegate to the Convention.[109] More than two centuries later, in yet another controversy over the constitutionality of a statute involving provisions of Article I about taxes (and many other things), all of the justices' opinions referenced the intentions of the Framers of the Constitution or the legislators responsible for the statute.[110]

Among other things, the records make it clear that there were numerous opinions among the Framers about many, if not all, of the still-controversial constitutional provisions. From the range of points of view expressed, we can see that when the Framers arrived at the Constitutional Convention or the First Congress (in the case of the Bill of Rights), they hoped for a number of different, and often conflicting, constitutional outcomes.[111] At the beginning of the process, then, we can find a sizeable collection of individual Framer's specific intentions – if, by "intentions," we refer to the common notion of intention as what an individual will try to accomplish. Some of those viewpoints originated in a Framer's personal beliefs about how governments should be structured, while others resulted from instructions from their home states. In the end, however, the final form of the Constitution was the result of a series of compromises made by the delegates who negotiated its provisions and framed its language. The search for evidence of those constitutional compromises is the place to begin the quest for an identifiable original meaning in the intentions of the Framers acting as a lawmaking body, as defined earlier.

[107] See Brudney, "Below the Surface," 7; and *Pepper (Inspector of Taxes) v. Hart*, [1993] AC 593.

[108] Thorne, *Discourse*, p. 60 n126, quoted in Raoul Berger, "'Original Intention' in Historical Perspective," *George Washington Law Review* 54, 2/3 (1985–86): 302–3. Compare H. Jefferson Powell, "The Original Understanding of Original Intent," *Harvard Law Review* 98, 5 (March 1985): 885–948; and Lofgren, "Original Understanding of Original Intent?"

[109] *Hylton v. United States*, 3 US 171, 176 (1796).

[110] *Nat'l Fed'n of Indep. Bus. v. Sebelius*, 567 US 519 (2012).

[111] See, generally, Woody Holton, *Unruly Americans and the Origins of the Constitution* (New York: Hill & Wang, 2007); Richard Labunski, *James Madison and the Struggle for the Bill of Rights* (New York: Oxford University Press, 2006); Maier, *Ratification*; and David O. Stewart, *The Summer of 1787: The Men Who Invented the Constitution* (New York: Simon & Schuster, 2007).

By focusing on the debates and compromises involved in resolving specific constitutional issues, we will potentially be able to see what end–means choices were in competition, and even how any conflicts were ultimately resolved. As Keith Whittington has pointed out:

> The process of negotiation and compromise that marked the framing process indicates that the authors of the Constitution were making efforts to unite behind a single text . . . . This is not to contend that all were satisfied with those changes but that such negotiated amendments create a presumption that all understood the language being used.[112]

Or, I would argue, even if they did not necessarily all understand the precise meaning of the terms in the same way, at least they may have shared a view of what the language was being used *for*. That is, whether or not they shared a common understanding of the meaning of each word employed (and sometimes they did not), they nevertheless are likely to have had a shared idea of what the provision was designed to accomplish, that is, the end–means choice that was made to apply a specific remedy to a particular mischief. Whether that choice represents a narrow answer to a specific question, or a broad principle is, as Whittington observes, "not an a priori theoretical question but a contextualized historical one."[113]

A focus on the nature of the final constitutional deal is exactly how the early Supreme Court interpreted the taxation clauses in Article I in the first substantive case involving the constitutionality of a federal law, *Hylton v. United States*, as discussed in Chapter 7.[114] When the analysis of dictionaries, commentaries, and similar sources led to two entirely plausible but contradictory results, Justice Paterson focused on what was "'obviously the intention' of his fellow constitutional Framers."[115] Pointing out that "[t]he Constitution has been considered as an accommodating system; it was the effect of mutual sacrifices and concessions; it was the work of compromise," Justice Paterson went along with the final deal struck by the Convention, even though he was unhappy with it.[116]

When there is a dispute over the meaning of a heavily debated provision, litigants on both sides of a case will undoubtedly seek to highlight those

[112] Whittington, *Constitutional Interpretation*, p. 97.

[113] Whittington, p. 187. He further argues that "just as Dworkin was misguided in subsuming specific conceptions under a broad concept, originalists would be equally misguided in simply dismissing the possibility that the founders intended to constitutionalize broader concepts." Whittington, p. 187.

[114] *Hylton*, 3 US.

[115] Joel Alicea and Donald L. Drakeman, "The Limits of New Originalism," *University of Pennsylvania Journal of Constitutional Law* 15, 4 (April 2013): 1183.

[116] *Hylton*, 3 US at 177–8.

Framers whose *initial* positions align with their own interests, much as they are likely to point to the dictionaries and commentaries that support their preferred semantic interpretations. The goal for the Court, however, is to identify the *final* constitutional compromise, that is, the Framers' end–means choice.[117] In the contemporary debates over statutory interpretation in an academic environment of intent skepticism, this focus on negotiation and compromise has primarily been claimed by the textualists. In rejecting broadly purposive interpretations, textualists, according to John Manning, "believe that focusing on semantic cues – the way a reasonable person would read the text – enables legislators to use their words to draw effective lines of legislative compromise that specify both the means and the ends of legislation."[118]

Manning's "premium on facilitating legislative compromise" may differentiate textualists from purposivists, but it is not clear why the evidence of legislative compromise needs to be drawn solely from research into the semantic meaning without the benefit of guidance that might be available in the record of the negotiations. If knowledge of the lawmaker's end–means choice as expressed in the text is the goal of interpretation, then evidence relating to the negotiations during the debates has the potential to contribute to that knowledge, especially when the language is susceptible to multiple readings. That is, the theoretical challenge to summing the individual intentions of a lawmaking body is no longer a relevant point because many individual preferences have been replaced by specific compromises, for which we may have additional documentary evidence beyond the text itself. If textualists are comfortable consulting external documentary evidence such as dictionaries or commentaries to determine the meaning of the text, it is not clear why documentary evidence of what the lawmakers themselves thought the text was meant to accomplish should be discarded, except perhaps out of fear of the friend-at-a-cocktail party problem. But concerns about this kind of evidentiary cherry-picking do not demonstrate that the documents showing the development of the final compromise are inherently unreliable; they merely draw our attention to the possibility that many kinds of sources can be employed to serve partisan ends by ingenious interpreters.

[117] As Nourse argues, "The final text should be the starting place for any analysis of legislative evidence." Nourse, *Misreading Law*, p. 157.

[118] Manning, "Inside Congress' Mind," 1913, citing Frank Easterbrook to the effect that "strict adherence to text enables the legislature to select the means as well as ends of legislation." Manning, 1913 n12. See Frank H. Easterbrook, "Statutes' Domains," *University of Chicago Law Review* 50, 2 (Spring 1983): 533–52.

The various materials describing how the Framers disagreed on important issues when they entered the debates, and the lack of good records of the views of numerous others, can make it difficult to identify what the Framers as a group were trying to accomplish after they completed their debates and negotiations. Whether doing so is possible in light of the evidentiary issues will be determined on a provision-by-provision basis, and, in some cases, the inquiry into a single identifiable understanding of the Framers will be defeated. That is not a criticism of searching for the Framers' understandings per se, but a practical issue.[119] As Keith Whittington has argued, "Analytically, the concept of collective intent creates no difficulties .... The real difficulty of collective intent is in its empirical discovery, not in its conceptual viability."[120] There may well be cases where it is possible to find persuasive evidence of such an intended meaning.

The critical methodological point that helps avoid the summing problem is, therefore, to focus on the end–means choice, that is, the fully negotiated conclusion rather than the initial preferences of the individual Framers. At the same time, this what's-the-final-deal approach will minimize the cocktail-party concern that a judge, following Justice Rutledge's example, will conduct Founding Fathers research with the sole goal of reaching a preferred outcome, ultimately concluding that the Framer with the most desirable views is somehow representative of all the others.[121] No matter how fascinating individual Framers' views may be as a matter of political philosophy, in the factual inquiry into the Framers acting as a group, it is necessary to focus solely on the Framers' *constitutional* understandings.[122] To achieve this particular understanding, we should not focus on what they have written on the topic in general or in the context of their state constitutions, where different

[119] See Alicea and Drakeman, "Limits of New Originalism," 1213 n319, arguing that, for at least some provisions, it may be impossible to identify a single objective public meaning using the techniques of the New Originalists.

[120] Whittington, *Constitutional Interpretation*, p. 96.

[121] See, for example, Antonin Scalia and Bryan A. Garner, *Reading Law: The Interpretation of Legal Texts* (St. Paul, MN: Thomson/West, 2012).

[122] It is possible, of course, that the Framers, in adopting the constitutional text, could have meant to incorporate in that language something that Madison or Hamilton or other well-known individuals may have written about on similar topics in other settings. Whether that is the case can be determined by examining the record for evidence that the Framers agreed to do so. Similarly, extraconstitutional writings could provide evidence of, and insights into, broader philosophical commitments shared by the Founding generation. For an example, see Vincent Phillip Muñoz's argument regarding the Founders' natural rights philosophy of religious liberty in Vincent Phillip Muñoz, "Two Concepts of Religious Liberty: The Natural Rights and Moral Autonomy Approaches to the Free Exercise of Religion," *American Political Science Review* 110, 2 (May 2016): 369–81.

end–means choices may have been made, but what they said about this particular constitutional provision. If there is no evidence of such a shared understanding of the end–means choice, the conclusion is that the Court is unable to determine the original subjective meaning from an analysis of the records of the Framers' debate. The answer is simply, "We don't know." At that point, the text itself will be the only – and still the best – evidence of the lawmaker's intention.

CONCLUSION

This chapter has sought to answer the "Who, What, and Where" questions regarding the Framers' intentions. In particular, it has argued that the primary lawmaker whose will needs to be identified by interpreters is the Framers, and only secondarily, the ratifiers. With the help of work by Richard Ekins and others, it has shown that there actually can be an intention of the constitutional lawmakers that is recoverable by interpreters. Then it has shown that the records of the constitutional debates and drafting can potentially provide essential information for interpreters seeking to determine what policy choice was made by the adoption of the constitutional language – that is, the ends and means represented by the text. The next chapter will move to an analysis of how the search for the Framers' end–means choice was the central element of their "original methods" of interpretation.

3

Original Methods and the Limits of Interpretation

About 60 percent of the constitutional Framers were trained as lawyers in pre-Revolutionary colonial law, and they read a great deal of Blackstone's *Commentaries* and Coke's *Institutes*.[1] As Ellen Holmes Pearson writes: "A significant percentage of delegates to the Continental Congress and the Constitutional Convention had been trained in the law."[2] They would inevitably bring their familiarity with the *Commentaries* and the *Institutes*, and with English law in general, to the process of both drafting the Constitution, and thinking about how courts would interpret it. Reviewing this inherited tradition can, therefore, help us better understand the interpretive context for the drafting and ratification of the Constitution.

John McGinnis and Michael Rappaport have argued that, since the "Constitution is a formal, legal document," the interpretive rules "applicable to a document of this type"[3] come from "the statutory interpretive rules that existed in England during the eighteenth century," that is, the "common law method."[4] Noting that "[n]othing guarantees that the original methods were originalist in this sense," they concede that if those interpretive rules were "nonoriginalist, the proper interpretation of the Constitution would not be originalist."[5] Nevertheless, McGinnis and Rappaport report that they have been unable to identify "strong evidence that the rules were dynamic or

[1] See, for example, Peter Charles Hoffer, *Law and People in Colonial America* (Baltimore, MD: Johns Hopkins University Press, 1998).

[2] Ellen Holmes Pearson, "1775–1815," in *A Companion to American Legal History*, eds. Sally E. Hadden and Alfred L. Brophy (Malden, MA: Wiley-Blackwell, 2013), p. 46.

[3] John O. McGinnis and Michael B. Rappaport, "Original Methods Originalism: A New Theory of Interpretation and the Case against Construction," *Northwestern University Law Review* 103, 2 (2009): 758.

[4] John O. McGinnis and Michael B. Rappaport, "Unifying Original Intent and Original Public Meaning," *Northwestern University Law Review* 113, 6 (2019): 1395.

[5] McGinnis and Rappaport, "Original Methods Originalism," 786.

otherwise nonoriginalist."[6] They therefore conclude that the "original methods were broadly originalist in the modern sense of the term."[7] In a more recent article, they have sharpened their point as to the degree to which those "broadly originalist" methods found support among knowledgeable people in the Founding Era. They note that both "the enactors" and "an informed speaker of the language" would have expected that "the interpretive rules that were customarily applied to such a document" governed constitutional interpretation; as a result, they believe that they have unified the two major strands of originalist theory: original intent and original meaning.[8]

The idea that a legally authoritative document, composed in a lawyer-rich environment, would be interpreted according to the usual methods for interpreting other kinds of legal documents makes considerable sense. It is less clear that those methods were exclusively "originalist in the modern sense of the term."[9] To be sure, the history of eighteenth-century interpretation includes many examples of what we now call originalism, but updating interpretations appeared as well. More broadly, we can see that "interpretation" in the legal context has had fundamentally the same meaning for a millennium or more, and it has included a cluster of related approaches to interpretation: objective and subjective, updated and original. What connects these approaches to one another – and separates them from noninterpretive judicial policymaking – is that they are all consciously rooted in the common goal of discerning and applying the will of the lawmaker.

BLACKSTONE, COKE, AND THE TRADITION THE FRAMERS INHERITED

Blackstone was undoubtedly "one of the greatest influences on ... American law,"[10] but his views are considerably broader than the textualism for which he has often been invoked. In fact, Blackstone and other influential legal commentators of that era embraced an impressively wide range of interpretive approaches, including evolving ones. Blackstone began the interpretation sections of his *Commentaries* with the statement that the "fairest and most

6 McGinnis and Rappaport, 786.

7 McGinnis and Rappaport, 786.

8 McGinnis and Rappaport, 752; see also McGinnis and Rappaport, "Unifying Original Intent." Lee J. Strang makes a similar argument in Lee J. Strang, *Originalism's Promise: A Natural Law Account of the American Constitution* (Cambridge: Cambridge University Press, 2019).

9 McGinnis and Rappaport, "Original Methods Originalism," 786.

10 David H. Flaherty, "An Introduction to Early American Legal History," in *Essays in the History of Early American Law*, ed. David H. Flaherty (Chapel Hill: University of North Carolina Press, 1969), p. 19.

rational method to interpret the will of the legislator is by exploring his intentions at the time when the law was made."[11] Identifying the "will of the legislator" through "his intentions" is thus the ultimate goal of interpretation. The next question is how best to determine what those lawmaker's intentions were.

Blackstone specified several "signs" that point to the lawmaker's will, the first of which has been a primary inspiration for original public meaning originalists: the words "in their usual and most known signification."[12] Blackstone did not stop there, however. In cases where the words are "dubious," he also cited the context, the subject matter, the "effects and consequence" and the "reason and spirit" of the law.[13] To these various signs, he added a focus on what the law had previously been, "the mischief, and the remedy."[14] He also described the power of judges to employ the notion of the "equity of the statute" to "disregard" the text when "some collateral matter arises" that would lead to an "unreasonable" outcome.[15] In those cases, judges can "conclude that this [unreasonable] consequence was not foreseen" by the lawmaker unless the "intent of the legislature [was] couched in such evident and express words, as leave no doubt [that] it was the intent of the legislature."[16]

In light of this litany of potential sources for ascertaining and applying the will of the lawmaker, Blackstone's *Commentaries* do not support the argument that the objective meaning of a text as of the time of enactment was the *only* recognized and acceptable method of legal interpretation. Even beyond Blackstone's pluralistic approach to identifying the will of the lawmaker, later in the *Commentaries*, he engaged in a dynamic interpretation in his description of the Magna Carta, which he cites in connection with the "personal liberty of individuals."[17] Blackstone's interpretation of the Great Charter as a font of individual rights departs from the meaning of the text at the time it was adopted in the thirteenth century, and requires an updating approach to language that originally protected under 20 percent of the population.[18] In summary, the extensive collection of Blackstone's "signs"

[11] William Blackstone, *Commentaries on the Laws of England: In Four Books; With an Analysis of the Work*, eds. Edward Christian et al., 19th ed. (New York, 1846), vol. 1, p. 40.

[12] Blackstone, *Commentaries*, vol. 1, p. 40.

[13] Blackstone, vol. 1, pp. 40–41.

[14] Blackstone, vol. 1, p. 60, citing Co. Litt. 11, 42.

[15] Blackstone, vol. 1, pp. 63–4.

[16] Blackstone, vol. 1, p. 64.

[17] Blackstone, vol. 1, p. 97.

[18] The great charter made essentially no provision for women or the vast majority of the population below the class of "Freemen." See, for instance, Jocelynne A. Scutt, *Women and Magna Carta: A Treaty for Rights or Wrongs?* (Basingstoke: Palgrave Macmillan, 2016), p. 14.

provides interpreters with considerably more flexibility to consult a range of sources of evidence of meaning than simply looking at the objective meaning of the text at the time it was adopted. But, in his view, they all relate to discerning and applying the lawmaker's intent.

If there were any English legal commentator who rivaled or exceeded Blackstone's influence on early American jurisprudence, it was Lord Coke, who, like Blackstone, focused on the intention of the lawmaker. Legal historian Charles Mullett's florid description of Coke includes the image of him as "the lamp by which young Aladdins of the law secured their juristic treasures. Six weeks with him alone was sufficient to secure Patrick Henry's admittance to the Virginia bar."[19] Similarly, John Adams called him "our judicial oracle,"[20] and Mullett notes that "in revolutionary days" Jefferson preferred "the whiggish virtues of Coke to ... Blackstone."[21] Charles McManis, in his analysis of the training of American lawyers in the constitutional era, calls Coke's *Institutes*, written about 150 years before the Constitution, the "universal text for 'reading at law,'" which was the primary method of legal education in eighteenth-century America.[22]

Coke begins by saying that: "[E]very statute ought to be interpreted according to the intent of them that made it."[23] He puts added emphasis on the original meaning, especially for foundational documents, such as the Magna Carta. That document "and the like were the forms of ancient acts" and must, therefore, "be construed and taken as the law was holden at that time when they were made."[24] Lord Coke has articulated here the principle of "contemporary expression," or *contemporanea expositio*, which, according to the often-cited compiler of maxims, Herbert Broom, means: "the best and surest mode of expounding an instrument is by referring to the time when, and circumstances under which, it was made."[25] Despite that affirmation of the meaning at the time the text became law, Lord Coke was also willing to embrace an

19 Charles F. Mullett, "Coke and the American Revolution," *Economica*, 38 (November 1932): 458.
20 Quoted in Mullet, "Coke and the American Revolution," 458.
21 Mullet, 458.
22 Charles R. McManis, "The History of First Century American Legal Education: A Revisionist Perspective," *Washington University Law Quarterly* 59, 3 (1981): 605 n52.
23 Edward Coke, *The Fourth Part of the Institutes of the Laws of England: Concerning the Jurisdiction of Courts* (London, 1809), p. 330.
24 Edward Coke, *The Second Part of the Institutes of the Laws of England: Containing the Exposition of Many Ancient and Other Statutes* (London, 1797), p. 1.
25 Herbert Broom, *A Selection of Legal Maxims: Classified and Illustrated* (London, 1845), p. 300. Broom says the Latin sentence reads: "Contemporanea expositio est optima et fortissima in lege," appearing in Coke, *Second Part of the Institutes*, p. 10.

evolving interpretation of the Great Charter. In Volume 2 of the *Institutes*, Coke described the updated meaning of *domini* as follows: "No demean, or proper cart . . . of any lord, . . . ought to be taken for the kings carriage, " which, Coke said, "extendeth to all degrees, and orders of the lesser, and greater nobility . . ., for albeit there were no dukes, marquesses, or viscounts within England at the making of the statute, yet this statute doth extend to them, for they are all *domini*."[26] For Lord Coke, even this "ancient Act" had to be interpreted to account for forms of nobility that could not have been considered by the thirteenth-century framers of the Magna Carta.

To put Coke's and Blackstone's views in historical perspective, we need to realize that what I have described as a related cluster of interpretive approaches can be seen well before the time at which the Magna Carta was framed. According to Peter Stein, interpretive jurisprudence had been developing since the time of the Roman Empire, where jurists served essentially as "custodians of the law."[27] Even though they did not play an official role in legal proceedings, they would explain the law to "the main players in the legal drama."[28] In these ancient legal contests, various "stock arguments" appeared with some regularity, one of which concerned the question: "Should the strict letter of the text or rather its spirit prevail? Should the actual intention . . . be decisive . . . and, in that case, how should [that] intention be ascertained?"[29]

Individual jurists developed reputations, and over time, "the opinions . . . of the more authoritative jurists were collected together in Digests, for reference in similar cases that might arise in the future."[30] Several centuries after the Digests began to be compiled, the Emperor Justinian converted those juristic writings, which had previously had only persuasive power, into "statutory form,"[31] creating essentially the First Restatement of Everything. At the same time, Justinian, anxious to crack down on any early enthusiasm for the notion of a separation of powers, instituted severe penalties for anyone who might try

[26] Coke, *Second Part of the Institutes*, p. 35. According David Carpenter, in "the thirteenth century, lords retained most of their manors in hand – 'in demesne' – rather than renting them out. . . . A new chapter [of the Magna Carta] in the Charter of 1217 safeguarded the demesne carts of lords from seizure, which meant the carts that they had on their demesne manors." David Carpenter, "Magna Carta and Society: Women, Peasants, Jews, the Towns and the Church," chap. 4 in *Magna Carta*, trans. David Carpenter (London: Penguin, 2015).

[27] Peter Stein, *Roman Law in European History* (Cambridge: Cambridge University Press, 1999), p. 13. See Peter Stein, "Interpretation and Legal Reasoning in Roman Law," *Chicago-Kent Law Review* 70, 4 (1995): 1539–56. See also W. W. Buckland, *A Text-Book of Roman Law*, 3rd ed. revised by Peter Stein (Cambridge: Cambridge University Press, 2007), pp. 25–32.

[28] Stein, *Roman Law*, p. 13.

[29] Stein, p. 17.

[30] Stein, p. 13.

[31] Stein, p. 35.

to interpret the enacted Digests in the future. Henceforth, any aspects of the law needing clarification beyond the text of the *Corpus Juris Civilis* should be referred to "imperial authority, to which alone is granted the right both to make and to interpret laws"; otherwise, except in very limited circumstances, all interpretation "is forbidden on pain of deportation and confiscation of all property" to prevent, in Ian Maclean's wonderful semi-translation, "'verbosi' from generating further 'discordia'."[32] Jurists could recite the words of the Digest, or summarize them, but could not "produc[e] any other interpretations, or rather, perversions, of [the] laws."[33] Surprisingly, scholars have failed to find a subsequent imperial relaxation of this prohibition, at least for lawyers and judges. Not surprisingly, disputes over interpretation, and the outpouring of accompanying legal commentary, has continued unabated.[34]

For a variety of complicated geopolitical reasons, Roman law influenced European law long after the end of the Roman Empire, and "Justinian's Digest came to be used in Western Europe as a source of rules and arguments."[35] In the sixteenth and seventeenth centuries, the application and "adaption of Roman law had gone on uninterrupted since the twelfth century," according to J. G. A. Pocock, with "glosses and commentaries upon glosses replacing the original texts as the sources of authority."[36] There was, however, always the

[32] Ian Maclean, *Interpretation and Meaning in the Renaissance: The Case of Law* (Cambridge: Cambridge University Press, 1992), p. 51. Justinian's words, as translated by Maclean, are: "It seems now appropriate for us to decree that no one – neither those who presently practise jurisprudence, nor those who will practise it in future – may presume to compose commentaries on these laws, except only in the case of those who wish to translate them into Greek by the method known to the Greeks as 'foot by foot' (that is in the same order and form as the Latin words), and those who might wish to annotate the titles to explain any fine points, or compose what are called paratitla (summaries). We hereby prohibit [jurists] from producing any other interpretations, or rather perversions, of our laws: lest their verbosity should bring dishonour to our laws by its confusion, as was done by the commentators on the Perpetual Edict, who by extracting new senses from one or another part of this well-made edict, reduced it to a multitude of meanings, causing confusion to arise in nearly all Roman decrees." Maclean, *Interpretation and Meaning*, p. 52.

[33] Maclean, p. 52.

[34] See Maclean, p. 53, which may bring some comfort to professors: "As well as being an embarrassment to jurists themselves, Justinian's prohibition has been an embarrassment to historians. More than one attempt has been made to find a convenient medieval imperial edict releasing jurists from the interdict . . . . Among the significant moments in this process, there has been cited . . . most recently, [a privilege] granted by Frederick I Barbarossa to academics which he caused to be inserted in the Code . . . in 1159."

[35] Stein, *Roman Law*, p. 43.

[36] J. G. A. Pocock, *Political Thought and History: Essays on Theory and Method* (Cambridge: Cambridge University Press, 2009), p. 165. Harold Berman notes that "the author (or authors) of the great thirteenth-century summa on English law, Bracton's *Treaties on the Laws and Customs of England*, quoted something like five hundred passages from Justinian's Digest,

"possibility of a fundamentalist revolt, a return to the original sources."[37] One school of thought, paralleling today's originalists, the "legal humanists[,] were predominantly philological," and they wanted to "establish the exact meaning which each word in the text of the law had borne in the minds of its original [Roman] users."[38] In this legal environment, François Hotman, whose writings were known to American lawyers – constitutional Framer James Wilson called him "the famous Hottoman" – argued that the "law must be appropriate to the circumstances and character of the people among whom it is to be employed," and he "insist[ed] 'que l'estat de la Republique Romaine est fort different de celuy de France.'"[39] The state of affairs existing in France in the 1500s was, as Hotman suggested, considerably different from that of the Roman Republic. But it is clear that, long before the US Constitution was written, interpreters were wrestling with many of the same kinds of issues that appear to divide twenty-first-century originalists and living constitutionalists.

Ian Maclean's *Interpretation and Meaning in the Renaissance* shows just how much Renaissance thinking about the interpretation of legal texts anticipated many of the issues faced by judges and scholars today, so much so that the "problems which most preoccupy Renaissance jurists can have a remarkably modern ring to them."[40] Maclean's book not only translates numerous valuable legal commentaries otherwise unavailable in English, but, on a broader level, operates as something of a Rosetta Stone by which we can see many of our own interpretative controversies being played out half a millennium or more ago by thoughtful scholars whose work is largely lost to today's lawyers and judges. To show how these issues repeat themselves, Maclean refers to Justice Felix Frankfurter describing in 1963 a cartoon in which a senator says: "I admit this new bill is too complicated to understand. We'll just have to pass it to find out what it means," which Maclean then links to a 1586 statement by French legal scholar Pierre Rebuffi: "[T]he law had first to be written and afterwards the meaning of the words of the law and the rules . . . elicited from it."[41] Almost exactly halfway in between, James Madison

without attribution, simply taking it for granted that they were 'the law' in England, even though many of them might not have been applicable in the king's courts." Harold J. Berman, *Law and Revolution: The Formation of the Western Legal Tradition* (Cambridge, MA: Harvard University Press, 1983), p. 123.

37 Pocock, *Political Thought and History*, p. 165.

38 Pocock, p. 165.

39 Wilson's opinion in *Chisholm v. Georgia*, 2 US 419, 459 (1793); Pocock, *Political Thought and History*, p. 166.

40 Maclean, *Interpretation and Meaning*, p. 65.

41 Ian Maclean, "Responsibility and the Act of Interpretation: The Case of Law," in *The Political Responsibility of Intellectuals*, eds. Ian Maclean, Alan Montefiore, and Peter Winch

said the same thing in Federalist 37, where he observed that "new laws" were "more or less obscure and equivocal, until their meaning be liquidated and ascertained by a series of particular discussions and adjudications."[42]

Maclean points to several alternative approaches to interpretation that have consistently recurred throughout the centuries. These core interpretive methodologies have experienced "little radical change although many shifts in emphasis" from the time of "their earliest methodical exposition [in the fourteenth century]" to recent works, including Ronald Dworkin, Stanley Fish, Paul Grice, and Robert Alexy.[43] The first two of these familiar categories of legal interpretation essentially represent competing approaches to ascertaining the original meaning. One focuses on what we tend to call the subjective understandings or intentions of the Framers: "the interpretation which accepts the historical will of the legislature as binding." The other concerns the original, "objective" semantic meaning of the words in context.[44] The remaining two categories fall into the realm of dynamic or evolving interpretations, again divided into whether the interpreter should look primarily at the people's "present usage" of the words or "the hypothetical will of the legislature," if it were "apprised of present conditions."[45]

Some contemporary commentators are inclined to doubt that "living" or "updated" meaning methods enjoy such a lengthy pedigree. As Howard Gillman has argued, it took "intellectual currents that were not available to the framers' generation – including Darwinism, historicism, and pragmatism – [to enable] judges and scholars [to] argue ... that the provisions of the Constitution were designed to adapt to changing environments and social purposes."[46] Similarly, Scalia and Garner argue that what counts is what kind

(Cambridge: Cambridge University Press, 1990), p. 170; Maclean, *Interpretation and Meaning*, p. 60.

42 *The Federalist Papers*, no. 37 (James Madison), in *The Avalon Project: Documents in Law, History and Diplomacy*, http://avalon.law.yale.edu/18th_century/fed37.asp.

43 Maclean, "Responsibility," 178. In particular, he cites Ronald Dworkin, *Law's Empire* (Cambridge, MA: Harvard University Press, 1986); Stanley Fish, "Working on the Chain Gang: Interpretation in the Law and in Literary Criticism," *Critical Inquiry* 9, 1 (September 1982): 201–16; H. P. Grice, "Logic and Conversation," in *Syntax and Semantics*, eds. Peter Cole and Jerry L. Morgan, vol. 3, *Speech Acts* (New York: Academic Press, 1975); and Robert Alexy, *Theorie der juristischen Argumentation: Die Theorie des rationalen Diskurses als Theorie der juristischen Begründung* (Frankfurt, Germany: Suhrkamp Verlag, 1978).

44 Maclean, "Responsibility," 177. Maclean notes that he has adopted these four positions from Ralf Dreier, "Interpretation," in *Staatslexikon*, 7th ed. (Freiburg, Germany: Herder, 1987), vol. 3, p. 181.

45 Maclean, "Responsibility," 177–8.

46 Howard Gillman, "The Collapse of Constitutional Originalism and the Rise of the Notion of the 'Living Constitution' in the Course of American State-Building," *Studies in American Political Development* 11, 2 (Fall 1997): 193.

of interpretation the Framers expected, and "[t]here were no 18th century textual evolutionists."[47] Instead, they argue, "Blackstone made it very clear that original meaning governed, and the supporters of evolving meanings in legal texts can point to no contemporaneous commentators who differed with him."[48] Some originalists have therefore argued that the notion of a dynamic, evolving approach to interpreting legal documents was only invented fairly recently as a way to justify the expansions of the federal government in the Progressive Era and the New Deal, and perhaps even later. For Scalia and Garner, "the notion of a Living Constitution, or at least general acceptance of that notion, is pretty new, dating from [as late as] the time of the Warren Court (1953–1969)."[49] Since these modern interpretive innovations did not arise until a century or more after the Constitution was written, Scalia and Garner conclude that "the idea that legal texts might be subject to semantic drift was alien to [the Framers'] modes of thought." The Constitution was never meant by the Framers to be living, but, as Justice Scalia would regularly proclaim at public lectures, "dead, dead, dead!"[50]

Such an argument misses the Renaissance jurists, where the concept that "the semantic content of words changes over time" is "regarded as a permanent process."[51] As Rebuffi noted: "[C]ustom and word usage can change the meanings of words and confer new ones on them."[52] Citing sources as early as the Roman Era, Maclean concludes that the many discussions concerning the changes of meaning through custom or the community's use of words demonstrates that jurists have long been aware of the possibility that legal meaning can evolve: "*consuetudo* [Rebuffi's Latin for "custom"] or *usus communis loquendi* [word usage] is not in itself remarkable in showing historicist features, but rather symptomatic of a feature of legal studies which until

47 Antonin Scalia and Bryan A. Garner, *Reading Law: The Interpretation of Legal Texts* (St. Paul, MN: Thomson/West, 2012), p. 404.

48 Scalia and Garner, *Reading Law*, p. 404.

49 Scalia and Garner, p. 405. See also William H. Rehnquist, "The Notion of a Living Constitution," *Texas Law Review* 54, 4 (May 1976): 693–706; and Gillman, "Collapse of Constitutional Originalism," 191–247.

50 Quoted in Clare Kim, "Justice Scalia: Constitution Is 'Dead,'" MSNBC, January 29, 2013, updated October 2, 2013, www.msnbc.com/the-last-word/justice-scalia-constitution-dead.

51 Maclean, *Interpretation and Meaning*, p. 133. This description parallels what Maclean describes as being "generally assumed" by many scholars today – that is, that "until the writing of German eighteenth-century philosophers, ideas or concepts were not thought themselves to have a history, but only words," and that, at least through the Renaissance, words themselves "began their life as full of meaning, and gradually declined or degenerated." Maclean, p. 133.

52 Quoted and translated in Maclean, p. 133. Maclean also cites Bolognetti, Wittenberg, and de Federicis on this point, showing that this observation of semantic shifts was widely shared during the Renaissance. Maclean, p. 133 n139.

recently had been associated only with more modern developments in jurisprudence."[53]

In short, legal scholars had written about the evolution of legal texts for centuries before the time of the Constitution, as they have done since then, as noted in Story's *Commentaries*: "No person can fail to remark the gradual deflections in the meaning of words from one age to another."[54] It is not necessary to try to draw detailed parallels between twenty-first-century America and Renaissance Europe – or, indeed, the Roman Empire – to show that some version of dynamic as well as original meaning methods of interpretation were known to and employed by lawyers, judges, and legislators through the ages, including by the American Founding generation. Of course, there is a multitude of differences in how the peoples in various times and places conceived of politics, philosophy, law, language, and the like. Nevertheless, this lengthy historical background speaks with impressive clarity: the essential arguments about the relative merits of these four basic methods have been largely unchanged for centuries, and probably millennia.

In light of these historical practices, rather than seeing updated meanings as a nineteenth- or twentieth-century American innovation, we need to bear in mind that, over many centuries, the same basic approaches have consistently existed side-by-side and have continually competed for dominance. Maclean's multi-century study emphasizes that there have been "many shifts in emphasis."[55] Lord Coke, for example, could slide easily from extolling the original meaning in one paragraph to enthusiastically updating the *Magna Carta* in another. Sometimes the arguments have been primarily hermeneutical, with academic commentators focusing on which approach is, in theory, the superior one. At other times, the arguments have been bound up in particular cases and controversies, as in sixteenth-century land disputes, when an essentially originalist view of Roman law might support one set of claimants, which would be countered by someone such as Hotman arguing that "a French lawyer entering a French court, equipped only with a knowledge of Roman rules of property and succession, would be as well qualified as if he had arrived among the American savages."[56]

[53] Maclean, p. 134.

[54] Joseph Story, *Commentaries on the Constitution of the United States: With a Preliminary Review of the Constitutional History* [...] (Boston, 1833), vol. 1, p. 437.

[55] Maclean, "Responsibility," 178.

[56] Stein, *Roman Law*, p. 79, citing Hotman, *Antitribonianus sive dissertatio de studio legum*, "written in 1552 but published posthumously in 1603." Hotman's title, *Antitribonianus*, refers to Tribonian, the official charged by the Emperor Justinian to create what became the *Corpus Juris Civilis*. Stein, p. 33.

ORIGINAL METHODS IN THE AMERICAN SETTING

We do not have an American treatise from the Founding Era that can rival the influence of Blackstone and Coke. To the extent that scholars have cited Founding Era sources, they typically come from arguments for and against particular outcomes in specific controversies. That record turns out to be mixed. Those favoring an adaptable, common law-like Constitution can cite Madison: "All new laws, though penned with the greatest technical skill, and passed on the fullest and most mature deliberation, are considered as more or less obscure and equivocal, until their meaning be liquidated and ascertained by a series of particular discussions and adjudications."[57] As Johnathan O'Neill points out, however, Madison had a somewhat different view during the national bank debate. In fact, "Madison attempted to establish the original meaning of the 'necessary and proper' clause by invoking the Philadelphia convention,"[58] an example that shows Madison's focus not only on the original meaning, but also on the use of the debates at the Convention to determine that meaning. In doing so, he took an approach that O'Neill has described as "the prevailing rules of interpretation"[59] in which interpreters "regularly referred to the 'intent' and 'purpose' of the framers, the ratifiers, and the Constitution."[60] They "occasionally consulted extrinsic sources," such as the Philadelphia convention or state ratifying conventions, but "the usual practice, following Blackstone ..., sought the originally intended meaning by examination of the constitutional text."[61]

Alexander Hamilton said that the Constitution "must speak for itself. Yet to candid minds, the ... explanation of it, by men, who had had a perfect opportunity of knowing the views of its framers, must operate as a weighty collateral reason for believing the construction agreeing with this explanation to be right, rather than the opposite one."[62] Lest those of us interested in returning the Framers to these discussions gain too much confidence from

57 *Federalist*, no. 37.

58 Johnathan O'Neill, *Originalism in American Law and Politics: A Constitutional History* (Baltimore, MD: Johns Hopkins University Press, 2005), p. 17. O'Neill also observes that "few at the time thought interpretation was anything other than the ascertainment and application of original intent." O'Neill, *Originalism*, p. 17.

59 O'Neill, p. 17.

60 O'Neill, p. 15.

61 O'Neill, p. 15.

62 Alexander Hamilton, "The Examination Number XV," March 3, 1802, in *The Papers of Alexander Hamilton*, ed. Harold C. Syrett, vol. 25, *July 1800–April 1802* (New York: Columbia University Press, 1977), p. 558. I am grateful to Brad Wilson for passing along this Hamiltonian reference. See also *Federalist*, no. 83, where Hamilton says, "The rules of legal interpretation are rules of common sense, adopted by the courts in the construction of the

Hamilton's statement, he took a somewhat different view in connection with national bank debate. He argued: "[W]hatever may have been the intention of the framers of a constitution, or of a law, that intention is to be sought for in the instrument itself, according to the usual & established rules of construction. Nothing is more common than for laws to *express* and *effect*, more or less than was intended."[63] Meanwhile, some Antifederalists, including the well-known "Brutus," anticipated the concern of modern critics of flexible interpretations that Article III would allow courts, under the guise of construing the Constitution, to be "the final lawgivers of the system, and in the end its absolute rulers."[64]

Although Scalia and Garner argue forcefully that the Framers were unfamiliar with semantic drift, Americans often enthusiastically claimed rights under the Magna Carta, which necessitated both updating and a transatlantic semantic drift. Patriot leader James Otis famously voiced a "living" approach to the Magna Carta when he cited it in opposition to the Stamp Act, as did the Massachusetts Assembly, when it "declared the [Stamp] Act invalid, [and] stated that because the Act was against the Magna Carta . . . it was . . . null and void."[65] Similarly, "Pennsylvania's assembly unanimously resolved that the vesting of jurisdiction in courts of admiralty to hear cases arising under the Stamp Act was 'highly dangerous to the Liberties of his Majesty's American Subjects, contrary to Magna Carta, the Great Charter and Fountain of English Liberty'."[66] Even more broadly, A. E. Dick Howard comments that "[t]hroughout the colonial period, Americans . . . repeatedly invoked Magna Carta, especially in their resistance to British policies in the years leading up to the revolution."[67]

laws . . . . In relation to such a subject [a constitution of government], the natural and obvious sense of its provisions, apart from any technical rules, is the true criterion of construction." *Federalist*, no. 83 (Alexander Hamilton), in *The Avalon Project: Documents in Law, History and Diplomacy*, http://avalon.law.yale.edu/18th_century/fed83.asp.

63 Alexander Hamilton, "Opinion on the Constitutionality of an Act to Establish a Bank," February 23, 1791, in *The Papers of Alexander Hamilton*, ed. Harold C. Syrett, vol. 8, *February 1791–July 1791* (New York: Columbia University Press, 1965), p. 111.

64 H. Jefferson Powell, "The Original Understanding of Original Intent," *Harvard Law Review* 98, 5 (March 1985): 909.

65 George P. Smith II, "*Marbury v. Madison, Lord Coke and Dr. Bonham*: Relics of the Past, Guidelines for the Present; Judicial Review in Transition?," *University of Puget Sound Law Review* 2 (1979): 260. See also James R. Ferguson, "Reason in Madness: The Political Thought of James Otis," *William and Mary Quarterly* 36, 2 (April 1979): 194–214.

66 A. E. Dick Howard, "Rights of Englishmen in British America: Magna Carta's American Journey," in *Magna Carta: Muse and Mentor*, ed. Randy J. Holland (Toronto: Thomson Reuters, 2014), chap. 8, Kindle.

67 Howard, "American Journey," chap. 8, Kindle.

The colonists' references to the Magna Carta were distinctly evolutionary. Much of the original charter did not actually have the force of law, its provisions were far from clear, and an agreement between the King and numerous barons long before Columbus sailed to North America did not, by its terms, encompass the later colonial empire. Sir John Baker explains: "Even in medieval times Magna Carta was not easy to interpret. Parliament was sometimes asked to explain it, usually without result, while the law schools tied themselves in knots exploring its intricacies."[68] In the occasional cases where the Magna Carta appeared clear, applying it to the American colonials' complaints about the Stamp Act involved an impressive degree of legal evolution. The Pennsylvania Assembly's argument, for example, was based on the idea that the use of admiralty courts to try Stamp Act cases was "destructive of one of [Magna Carta's] most darling and acknowledged Rights, that of Trials by Juries,"[69] but, as Baker observes: "[T]here was no trial by jury in 1215, in criminal cases, and until well into the seventeenth century the word 'peers' ... was taken to mean temporal lords of Parliament."[70] As these and numerous other examples demonstrate, "drifting" legal texts, even foundational texts such as the Magna Carta, were well known to Founding Era American leaders.[71] More broadly, the Framers were well aware of most of the fixed and dynamic interpretive methods still being debated today.

In general, strong evidence and persuasive arguments can be found to support a variety of specific interpretive methods, although, in considering these Founding Era materials, it is important to keep in mind that the Constitution was generally too recent for eighteenth-century commentators to argue that its meaning had evolved since ratification. The materials in these interpretative debates, therefore, more commonly focused on commitments to a fairly strict textualism versus appeals to broader interpretations based on values outside the language itself, ranging from natural law to the common law notion of the equity of the statute. As Justice Story wrote in 1815, surveying many of these considerations in *Terrett v. Taylor*: "[W]e think ourselves standing upon the principles of natural justice, upon the fundamental laws of every free government, upon the spirit and the letter of the Constitution of the

68 John Baker, "The Legal Force and Effect of Magna Carta," in Holland, *Magna Carta*, chap. 6, Kindle.

69 Quoted in Howard, "American Journey," chap. 8, Kindle, citing Edmund S. Morgan, ed., *Prologue to Revolution: Sources and Documents on the Stamp Act Crisis, 1764–1766* (Chapel Hill: University of North Carolina Press, 1959), p. 52.

70 Baker, "Legal Force," chap. 6, Kindle.

71 As textualist John Manning concedes, Blackstone wrote that judges can interpret statutes "'by the reason and spirit' of them." John F. Manning, "Textualism and the Equity of the Statute," *Columbia Law Review* 101, 1 (January 2001): 36.

United States, and upon the decisions of most respectable judicial tribunals."[72]

Scholars have also disagreed about how American courts and commentators interpreted statutes.[73] John Manning and William Eskridge, two of the most prominent and widely cited scholars in the debate over the Founding Era methods of interpretation, look at the same kinds of materials, written during essentially the same time period, yet reach opposing conclusions.[74] Taken together, these scholars provide abundant and persuasive evidence that lawyers and judges in the Founding Era employed the range of interpretive methods that had developed over the centuries. Both Manning and Eskridge begin with the context of English common law, under which, they agree, judges had the power, through the concept of "the equity of the statute," or "correction of that wherein the law (by reason of its universality) is deficient," to go beyond the meaning of the text as of its enactment.[75]

Manning concedes that the modern debates over statutory interpretation may be "largely beside the point" if the Framers' understandings generally followed Blackstone's view, which holds that judges can interpret a statute "by considering the *reason* and *spirit* of it."[76] Yet a major point of dispute between Manning and Eskridge is whether Blackstone was primarily making a retrospective comment reflecting the historical position of English judges vis-à-vis other branches of government. While "reason and spirit" might have been adequate guidance in the English courts in earlier times, interpretive methods would need to change as judges (in both America and England) were increasingly separated from the kinds of legislative functions that they had performed in eighteenth-century Britain.[77] The adoption of the US Constitution provided an opportunity

[72] *Terrett v. Taylor*, 13 US 43, 52 (1815).

[73] As Powell notes: "The public debate over the adoption of the Constitution ... revealed that Americans of all political opinions accepted the applicability to constitutional interpretation of hermeneutical views developed in relation to quite different documents – the Bible, parliamentary statutes, and private contracts. But there were sharp disagreements over which interpretive approach was acceptable." Powell, "Original Understanding," 912.

[74] Manning, "Textualism and the Equity of the Statute," 1–127; and William N. Eskridge Jr., "All about Words: Early Understandings of the 'Judicial Power' in Statutory Interpretation, 1776–1806," *Columbia Law Review* 101, 5 (June 2001): 990–1106.

[75] Manning, "Textualism and Equity," 35, citing Blackstone, *Commentaries*, vol. 1, p. 42, quoting Hugo Grotius, *De aequitate*, §3.

[76] Blackstone, *Commentaries*, vol. 1, p. 41. Manning writes, however, that Blackstone counseled that such an approach should not "be indulged too far, lest thereby we destroy all law, and leave the decision of every question entirely in the breast of the judge." Blackstone, vol. 1, p. 42, quoted in Manning, "Textualism and Equity," 36.

[77] "The relative fluidity of governmental functions," concludes Manning, "fits tightly with an interpretive method that minimizes the distinction between legislative and judicial functions." Manning, "Textualism and Equity," 46. Manning's extensive argument also focuses on

to break from the common law tradition that had included the concept of the equity of the statute, for the Constitution, in Manning's words, "explicitly disconnects federal judges from the legislative power and, in so doing, undercuts any judicial claim to derivative lawmaking authority."[78]

Portraying the Constitution as signaling a sharp break in an otherwise lengthy and well-established interpretive tradition is a difficult task, especially since references to the equity of the statute nevertheless continued to appear, even as governmental powers were increasingly separated into the different branches. To gather sufficient evidence to support his argument, Manning has to base his argument on what he perceives to be a trend. While a "shift away . . . had become perceptible during the eighteenth century," Manning concludes that "the trend was unmistakable" through the nineteenth.[79] Ultimately, he argues that, in the nineteenth century, "the 'plain meaning' rule . . . supplanted the equity of the statute as hornbook law in England,"[80] with perhaps a "narrow exception for 'an absurdity so great as to make perfectly clear that the Legislature did not intend it'."[81] He cites two late nineteenth-century treatises on statutory interpretation in the United Kingdom in support of his conclusion, but does not continue his analysis into the twentieth century, where he would find that the trend shifted back in the other direction. As a leading commentary on statutory interpretation stated in 1995, just as "the U.S. Constitution is regarded as 'a living Constitution,' so an ongoing British Act is regarded 'a living Act',"[82] citing another well-known twentieth-century commentary by barrister and legal scholar, Francis Bennion.

the degree to which Parliament and the Crown each claimed to possess legislative authority, and as time passed, the Crown at least had the "prerogative of dispensation – that is, the power to dispense with . . . laws of Parliament where equity so required." Manning, 48–9. Since at least through the seventeenth century, judges were seen as "executive officials," and the notion of the equity of the statute could be seen as essentially executive-branch powers that "were to become obsolete after the political struggles of the seventeenth century forged the modern English state." But, even on this account, Manning admits that "aspects of the complex historical record cast doubt on this explanation for the equity of the statute." Manning, 49–50.

78 Manning, 59.

79 Manning, 53–4.

80 Manning, 55, citing G. A. Endlich, *A Commentary on the Interpretation of Statutes* (Jersey City, NJ, 1888), pp. 444–6; and William Feilden Craies, *A Treatise on Statute Law: With Appendices Containing Statutory and Judicial Definitions* [. . .], 2nd ed. (London: Stevens & Haynes, 1911), p. 73: "If the words of the statute are . . . precise and unambiguous, then no more can be necessary than to expound those words in their ordinary and natural sense. The words themselves alone do in such a case best declare the intention of the lawgiver."

81 Manning, 55, citing discussions of the literal rule and the golden rule in statutory interpretation.

82 Rupert Cross, *Statutory Interpretation*, eds. John Bell and George Engle, 2nd ed. (London: Butterworths, 1987), p. 49, citing §288 of Francis Bennion, *Statutory Interpretation*, 3rd ed. (London: Butterworths, 1997), p. 617. See also J. F. Burrows, "The Problem of Time in

Although textualism was not necessarily the preferred (or only proper) methodology at the time of the Constitution, Manning argues that the Court clearly moved in that direction after John Marshall was appointed Chief Justice in 1801. While again conceding that the evidence is "not all of a piece," Manning notes that one of the Marshall Court's primary interpretative themes was, as Marshall said in an 1818 case, "when the legislature manifests [a] clear understanding of its own intention, which intention consists with its words, courts are bound by it."[83] Despite these strong statements by the Chief Justice, the concept of the equity of the statute continued to appear in American courts. By the middle of the nineteenth century, however, "American treatise writers had begun to criticize [this concept] in strong and explicit terms as incompatible with the appropriate role of the judiciary."[84] Nevertheless, more flexible approaches continued to appear throughout the century, and Manning distinguishes the classic "atextualis[t]" decision in the 1892 *Holy Trinity Church* case by noting that "the Court felt constrained to justify its departures from the text as a superior way to discover the legislature's true intent."[85] In short, he argues, textualism ultimately prevailed, but not all of the time, by late in the nineteenth century. That may be true, but it is important to note that it took over 100 years to arrive, which means that the late nineteenth-century textualism certainly does not represent a strong "original methods" argument. Nor was textualism universally embraced as hornbook law in the late nineteenth century. That was when University of Pennsylvania Law School Dean George Sharswood had written, in an updated edition of Blackstone's *Commentaries*, that "the intention of the makers of a statute is to govern, even though the construction grounded upon such intention may appear to be contrary to the literal import of the words."[86] Even if textualism were the majority rule in that era, exceptions would continue to appear, and hornbook law would also change again when it caught up with the mid-

Statutory Interpretation," *New Zealand Law Journal* (1978); D. J. Hurst, "The Problem of the Elderly Statute," *Legal Studies* 3, 1 (March 1983): 21–42; and D. J. Hurst, "Palm Trees in the House of Lords: Some Further Thoughts on Boland's Case," *Statute Law Review* 4, 3 (Autumn 1983): 142–65. Bennion states: "It is presumed that Parliament intends the court to apply to an ongoing act a construction that continuously updates its wording to allow for changes since the Act was initially framed (an updating construction)." Bennion, *Statutory Interpretation*, p. 617.

83 Manning, "Textualism and Equity," 90–91, citing *United States v. Palmer*, 16 US 610, 630 (1818). See also *United States v. Fisher*, 6 US 358, 386 (1805): "Where the intent is plain, nothing is left to construction."

84 Manning, "Textualism and Equity," 102.

85 Manning, 104, citing *Church of the Holy Trinity v. United States*, 143 US 457 (1892); see also *United States v. Goldenberg*, 168 US 95 (1897).

86 George Sharswood, ed., *Commentaries on the Laws of England: In Four Books*, by William Blackstone (Philadelphia, 1893), vol. 1, p. 60 n19.

twentieth-century living constitution trend that, in turn, inspired the most recent originalist "counter revolution."

Eskridge looks essentially at the same materials that Manning reviewed but finds a considerable amount of support for more flexible or dynamic interpretations. The fundamental dispute is the question of which approach to legal interpretation is the rule and which is the exception. Eskridge argues that many "American judges in the founding period interpreted statutory words more equitably than English judges ... in the same period."[87] Citing a 1796 case, he writes: "As Virginia's Justice Carrington put it, the lodestar in applying statutes was not 'strict rules of grammatical construction,' but rather 'the spirit, as well as the just exposition of the words of the law.'"[88] Eskridge also points to a series of "ameliorative" holdings: "Minor judicial surgery was the norm in cases such as *Respublica v. Keppele*, where the Pennsylvania Supreme Court refused to allow a parent to indenture his son to serve another family, notwithstanding the authorization of indentured servitude in an old law."[89]

To these examples of equitable interpretations focusing on the "spirit" of the law, we need to add the colonists' evolutionary interpretations of the Magna Carta, such as James Otis' updating approach in his declaration that the Stamp Act was "null and void,"[90] and the Pennsylvania Assembly's similar unanimous declaration about admiralty courts.[91] The notion of a living charter was very much in existence in Revolutionary America. Ultimately, all of the examples show that no single aspect of the traditional interpretive approaches was the only correct choice of jurists and political leaders during the Founding Era.

In summary, judges and commentators of the Founding Era were not completely devoted to any single approach, even if *some* judges or commentators were consistent in favoring one or another method in their own writings.[92] They had generally been well schooled in Coke and Blackstone, and they continued the interpretive tradition found in those volumes,

[87] Eskridge, "All About Words," 1013. For English judges, Eskridge cites William D. Popkin, *Materials on Legislation: Political Language and the Political Process*, 3rd ed. (New York: Foundation Press, 2001); and William D. Popkin, *Statutes in Court: The History and Theory of Statutory Interpretation* (Durham, NC: Duke University Press, 1999). For the American context, Eskridge "read the reported decisions of the courts in Connecticut, New Jersey, Pennsylvania, Virginia, North Carolina, and South Carolina between 1783 and 1795, as well as the eight reported decisions of the federal court of appeals." Eskridge, 1011–12.

[88] Eskridge, 1020.

[89] Eskridge, 1022.

[90] Smith, "*Marbury v. Madison*," 260. See also Ferguson, "Reason in Madness."

[91] Howard, "American Journey," chap. 8, Kindle.

[92] As Saul Cornell has written, the "suggestion that constitutional meaning is derived by elaborating the public meaning of the Constitution's text ... is not a neutral philosophical or historical claim that stands above the political fray; rather, it is simply one of the many

including a core commitment to ascertaining the lawmaker's intent, and an openness, in some circumstances, to embracing updated or flexible interpretations. Philip Hamburger, looking at somewhat different materials, has reached a similar conclusion:

> Americans could make use of very mixed intellectual traditions on social and legal change – traditions which assumed at least two general approaches. Having been exposed to the older ideas of natural law, the notion of the ancient constitution, and civic humanist concerns for permanence, Americans were familiar with the concept of permanent, immutable law.

That tradition – then and now – sounds like a strong support for some version of originalism. But Hamburger then continues:

> On the other hand, a significant number of Americans, including many who played prominent roles in the framing and ratifying of the Constitution, had become acquainted with the theories of Hale and the Scots that society undergoes change – change that requires or causes a corresponding development of legal and governmental institutions.[93]

Many of the debates among contemporary constitutional theorists generally map very well onto the eighteenth-century context. By engaging in original vs. dynamic, objective vs. subjective debates, we are citing the same methods, and repeating the same arguments as the Founding generation and many earlier generations. There is, however, one very notable difference in our current debates, an approach to constitutional decision making that is a twentieth-century invention. How that new concept relates to the way the Supreme Court decides constitutional cases brings us to the question of the limits of the concept of interpretation.

WHAT IS INTERPRETATION?

The novel twentieth- and twenty-first-century concept is the idea that interpretation is really just a function of getting the right result. Maclean points out

possible interpretative stances in political play at the time of the Founding." Saul Cornell, "The People's Constitution vs. The Lawyer's Constitution: Popular Constitutionalism and the Original Debate over Originalism," *Yale Journal of Law and the Humanities* 23, 2 (Summer 2011): 296–7.

[93] Philip A. Hamburger, "The Constitution's Accommodation of Social Change," *Michigan Law Review* 88, 2 (November 1989): 258. For a thoughtful analysis of how the common law tradition provides evidence supporting the claims of both textualists and dynamic interpreters, see Jeffrey A. Pojanowski, "Reading Statutes in the Common Law Tradition," *Virginia Law Review* 101, 5 (September 2015): 1357–424.

that some "modern commentators have claimed that . . . the criterion of truth may be abandoned altogether in favor of plausibility and successful . . . argument."[94] He says that "this would not have been conceded by . . . Renaissance jurists," nor can we find evidence of such an argument in the Founding Era. Although the reality of semantic drift has been well known for centuries, the notion that the ends justify the meanings is a very recent phenomenon.[95] I will argue on historical grounds that these solely results-oriented constitutional decisions – irrespective of whether we agree with them – fall outside the bounds of the concept of interpretation. Whether the Supreme Court should have the power to make constitutional decisions that are noninterpretive, that is, those that are not based on one of those well-established approaches to interpretation, is a different question. Chapter 9 will show, however, that the Court is not necessarily well equipped to make good decisions on that basis.

For now, it is important to be able to say what interpretation is, and is not. This effort is complicated by the fact that the question of what should count as *interpretive* judicial decision making has itself been a contested concept over the past fifty years or so, and different theorists employ different definitions. In summarizing the recent intellectual history on this issue, Keith Whittington notes that for Thomas Grey, "a purely interpretive approach was . . . limited to what could be found within the 'four corners' of the text of the Constitution," whereas John Hart Ely would unfavorably describe a "clause-bound" interpretivism that roughly parallels modern originalism.[96] Then Ronald Dworkin challenged the noninterpretive/interpretive distinction by showing "that non-interpretive methods are actually particular forms of interpretive argument,"[97] opening the definition up to a broad range of methods.

If we take the view that, at least in the abstract, the meaning of words is defined by the conventional linguistic practices of the relevant community, we can see that the word "interpretation" in the legal context means one of the four approaches identified by Maclean as being consistent for centuries. I will therefore divide judicial decision making into the two major categories of

94 Maclean, "Responsibility," 178.

95 Donald L. Drakeman, "Consequentialism and the Limits of Interpretation: Do the Ends Justify the Meanings?," *Jurisprudence* 9, 2 (2018): 300–318.

96 Keith E. Whittington, *Constitutional Interpretation: Textual Meaning, Original Intent, and Judicial Review* (Lawrence: University Press of Kansas, 1999), pp. 164–6. See also Thomas C. Grey, "Do We Have an Unwritten Constitution?," *Stanford Law Review* 27, 3 (February 1975): 710–14; and John Hart Ely, *Democracy and Distrust: A Theory of Judicial Review* (Cambridge, MA: Harvard University Press, 1980).

97 Whittington, *Constitutional Interpretation*, 165, citing Ronald Dworkin, *A Matter of Principle* (Cambridge, MA: Harvard University Press, 1985).

interpretive and noninterpretive based on the history of the methods described in this chapter. The term "interpretive" will refer to the four traditional approaches to interpretation that Maclean and others have described as being in constant use for many centuries, all of which were present at the time of the adoption of the Constitution, and all of which are focused on how best to determine the will of the lawmaker. These four approaches are the objective or subjective meaning of the text at the time of enactment, and the objective or subjective meaning at the time of the judicial decision.[98] That is, interpretive decisions can involve either updated meanings or original ones, but, in both cases, the interpretation is based on the Framers' intentions (the "will of the lawmaker").

Noninterpretive judicial decisions are all the rest, including those that the justices make as a result of pragmatic, consequentialist, philosophical, or any other forms of reasoning to the extent that such reasoning does not fairly fall within one of the four historically defined interpretive categories. Essentially, noninterpretive decisions are those in which the justices have decided on the best national policy rather than applying the policy chosen by the lawmaker. In noninterpretive decisions, the Court lives up to Brian Leiter's description as "a kind of super-legislature,"[99] or the justices follow Cass Sunstein's injunction to render decisions based on what they believe will "make … our constitutional system better rather than worse."[100] In this environment, as Eric Segall suggests: "Supreme Court constitutional law is best seen as common law where prior decisions and the justices' personal values writ large generate the decisions."[101]

A good, fairly noncontroversial, example of such a noninterpretive decision is *Bolling v. Sharpe*,[102] in which the Supreme Court essentially said that the Fourteenth Amendment's Equal Protection Clause, which, by its terms, applies specifically to the states, is also applicable to the federal government. *Bolling* was a companion case to *Brown v. Board of Education*,[103] and it held

98 See Maclean, *Interpretation and Meaning*, as discussed in Chapter 2.

99 Brian Leiter, "Constitutional Law, Moral Judgment, and the Supreme Court as Super-Legislature," *Hastings Law Journal* 66, 6 (2015): 1602: "All political actors know that the Supreme Court often operates as a super-legislature, and thus that the moral and political views of the Justices are decisive criteria for their appointment."

100 Cass R. Sunstein, "There Is Nothing that Interpretation Just Is," *Constitutional Commentary* 30, 2 (2015): 194.

101 Eric J. Segall, "Originalism as Faith," *Cornell Law Review Online* 102 (2016): 37, citing David A. Strauss, "The Supreme Court 2014 Term: Foreword; Does the Constitution Mean What It Says," *Harvard Law Review* 129, 1 (November 2015): 52–5.

102 *Bolling v. Sharpe*, 347 US 497 (1954).

103 *Brown v. Bd. of Educ.*, 347 US 483 (1954).

racial discrimination in the public schools in the District of Columbia to be unconstitutional. Chief Justice Warren's short opinion was based on a very simple noninterpretive argument: "[I]t would be unthinkable that the ... Constitution would impose a lesser duty on the Federal Government."[104] Although the Court referred to the Fifth Amendment's Due Process Clause as embodying "our American ideal of fairness,"[105] the opinion's rationale was very much in keeping with Story's "natural justice"[106] or Wilson's "principles of general jurisprudence."[107] As Peter Rubin writes: "[I]t is widely accepted, by those who defend the decision as well as those who attack it, that this doctrinal innovation cannot be easily justified by the Fifth Amendment's text or its history .... The conventional account is that the decision was ... essentially political rather than judicial."[108]

It is worth noting that I am not taking a position here on whether certain principles of natural law – or other bases for moral decision making – are inherent or implied in the Constitution itself. As Robert George has pointed out: "Throughout the Twentieth century ... a lively debate ... existed regarding the question of whether the Constitution incorporates natural law in such a way as to make it a source of judicially enforceable, albeit unwritten, constitutional rights and other guarantees."[109] A successful argument that the documentary record shows that the will of the lawmaker, in adding a particular provision to the Constitution, included certain substantive elements of a particular understanding of natural law would be an interpretive decision (as defined here),[110] whereas a noninterpretive reference to the

[104] *Bolling*, 347 US at 500.

[105] *Bolling*, 347 US at 499.

[106] *Terrett*, 13 US at 52.

[107] *Chisholm*, 2 US at 453.

[108] Peter J. Rubin, "Taking Its Proper Place in the Constitutional Canon: *Bolling v. Sharpe*, *Korematsu*, and the Equal Protection Component of Fifth Amendment Due Process," *Virginia Law Review* 92, 8 (December 2006): 1880. Although Rubin takes a somewhat different view, it remains the case, as he notes, that "the Court's opinion itself certainly did not justify" its constitutional conclusion. Rubin, "Taking Its Proper Place," 1880.

[109] Robert P. George, "Natural Law, the Constitution, and the Theory and Practice of Judicial Review," *Fordham Law Review* 69, 6 (2001): 2270. See also Philip A. Hamburger, "Natural Rights, Natural Law, and American Constitutions," *Yale Law Journal* 102, 4 (1993): 907–60. See, generally, George Duke and Robert P. George, eds., *The Cambridge Companion to Natural Law Jurisprudence* (Cambridge: Cambridge University Press, 2017); John Finnis, *Natural Law and Natural Rights*, 2nd ed. (New York: Oxford University Press, 2011); and Robert P. George, *In Defense of Natural Law* (Oxford: Oxford University Press, 1999); and numerous others.

[110] See, as a potential example, Vincent Phillip Muñoz, "Two Concepts of Religious Liberty: The Natural Rights and Moral Autonomy Approaches to the Free Exercise of Religion," *American Political Science Review* 110, 2 (May 2016): 369–81.

natural law would be similar to Justice Wilson's, where the consideration of the natural law in *Chisholm* was entirely independent of the "question before us [under] the Constitution."[111]

Along similar lines, the moral or philosophical reading of particular constitutional provisions, as advocated by Dworkin and others, could be interpretive or not, based on the best evidence of the nature of the Framers' intentions. Whether the Constitution states "abstract moral and political principles" will therefore depend on what the record shows about the Framers' choice in adopting the provision. Research into the arguments for and against the choices made by the Convention (or the First Congress with respect to the Bill of Rights) is likely to show that some do, and some do not. If they do state such a principle, an interpretive decision will focus on the understanding of that principled policy choice either as of ratification or as updated at the time of the decision. A noninterpretive decision in the same case would be one in which the justices are, in James Fleming's words, "thinking for themselves" rather than "engaging in ... living constitutionalist talk about 'updating,'" or seeking to avoid "responsibility for our constitutional choices by taking refuge in originalism."[112]

UPDATING VS. NONINTERPRETIVE JUDICIAL DECISION MAKING

Perhaps because Justice William Brennan seized the rhetorical highground with his call for an "aspirational" and "living" constitution, many originalists have tended to oppose any approach to dynamic or adaptable constitutional interpretations. This across-the-board opposition is virtually impossible to sustain as the Courts need to apply an over 200-year-old Constitution to the twenty-first century. By the same token, the need to adapt the Constitution's meaning to changing circumstances does not mean that the concept of interpretation must stretch as far as some nonoriginalists have suggested in their embrace of pragmatic and consequentialist judicial reasoning without reference to the original will of the lawmaker. The history of interpretation,

[111] *Chisholm*, 2 US at 453. Randy E. Barnett, for example, adopts both approaches: one in *The Structure of Liberty: Justice and the Rule of Law* (Oxford: Oxford University Press, 1998); and the other in *Restoring the Lost Constitution: The Presumption of Liberty* (Princeton, NJ: Princeton University Press, 2004). For arguments that the natural law points to originalism as an interpretive methodology, see Jeffrey A. Pojanowski and Kevin C. Walsh, "Enduring Originalism," *Georgetown Law Journal* 105, 1 (November 2016): 97–158; and Lee J. Strang, *Originalism's Promise: A Natural Law Account of the American Constitution* (Cambridge: Cambridge University Press, 2019).

[112] James E. Fleming, *Fidelity to Our Imperfect Constitution: For Moral Readings and Against Originalism* (New York: Oxford University Press, 2015), pp. 65, 80, 182.

which established the "original methods" inherited by the Founders from centuries of Western jurisprudence, shows how it is possible to distinguish between interpretive adaptation to new circumstances and results-oriented noninterpretive decisions. The next chapter will discuss an interpretive approach to adapting constitutional interpretation to twenty-first-century America by employing such a Framer-focused approach.

4

Original Methods Updating

The deep jurisprudential tradition that created the original methods that were in effect at the time of the Constitution provides the foundation for an interpretive approach for applying its fixed text to changing circumstances. Across the centuries, even commentators with strong preferences for following the lawmaker's original meaning have recognized that there are legitimate times for judges to adapt an old law to fit new circumstances.[1] Coke's *Institutes* specified that the Magna Carta was one of the "ancient Acts" that needed to be "construed and taken as the law was holden at the time when they were made," but also said that later-created classes of nobility required an adjustment to the meaning of "domini."[2] Chapter 3 showed how the American colonists claimed rights under the Magna Carta to which they were only entitled under an updated interpretation. Even originalist standard-bearer Justice Scalia has applied the Fourth Amendment to later-developed technology, concluding, in *Kyllo v. United States*, that a thermal-imaging device employed on a public street constituted an unreasonable search of a nearby private home: "It would be foolish to contend that the degree of privacy secured to citizens by the [Constitution] has been entirely unaffected by the advance of technology," argued Justice Scalia in the opinion for the Court.[3]

John Finnis, in a widely reported 2015 public lecture, excoriated judges for updated interpretations that have essentially turned courts into "roving law

[1] There are, of course, various schools of thought within both the updating and the original meaning camps. Unless otherwise indicated, my uses of "originalism," "original meaning," *contemporanea expositio*, and the like are meant to refer generally to an interpretive method focusing on the meaning at (or around) the date of enactment, and my uses of "living," "ambulatory," "always speaking," "dynamic," and similar phrases are meant to refer to an updated rather than an original meaning.

[2] Edward Coke, *The Second Part of the Institutes of the Laws of England: Containing the Exposition of Many Ancient and Other Statutes* (London, 1797), pp. 1, 35.

[3] *Kyllo v. United States*, 533 US 27, 33–34 (2001).

reform commissions."[4] Especially concerning, he noted, was the way in which the European Court of Human Rights began to use the phrase "living instrument" in the 1970s to justify the creation of rights "the signatory states 'definitely did not intend to grant,' or 'positively intended not to grant'."[5] Finnis, who teaches at law schools in both the United States and the United Kingdom, extended his critique not only to the European Court of Human Rights, but also to the European Court of Justice, the Supreme Court of United States, the Supreme Court of Canada, and the Supreme Court of the United Kingdom.[6] At the same time, however, Finnis also acknowledged that updated interpretations can, in fact, have a proper role in judicial decisions if the new "situation or condition falls within the categories picked out by the propositions expressed" at the time of enactment.[7] The critical question is how to apply an old law to new facts in a way that is rooted in what the lawmaker was originally seeking to accomplish.

The history and practice of interpretation shows that updated constructions will remain central, and likely essential, elements of judicial practice.[8] In light of that history, I will point to a principled approach to adapting laws to changing circumstances that has its foundation in Coke and Blackstone, and was developed over the centuries in the UK courts, where they had to consider, as just one example, whether a nineteenth-century law giving the

4 John Finnis, "Judicial Power: Past, Present and Future" (lecture, Gray's Inn, London, UK, October 20, 2015), 23, https://papers.ssrn.com/sol3/papers.cfm?abstract_id=2710880.

5 Finnis, "Judicial Power," 23.

6 Finnis, 23.

7 Finnis, 23.

8 The approach taken in this book is not meant to minimize the importance of what are sometimes called "grand" theories of statutory or constitutional interpretation that seek to focus interpreters on one specific aspect of the process. For an excellent analysis of the competing theories in the context of statutory interpretation, which fits constitutional interpretation as well, see Jeffrey A. Pojanowski, "Reading Statutes in the Common Law Tradition," *Virginia Law Review* 101, 5 (September 2015): 1357–424. Generally speaking, the advocates of original meaning as the primary approach to interpretation are, as described by Pojanowski, those inclined to "formalist approaches to interpretation [that] are ... more committed to treat the 'objective' meaning [of the] enacted statutory language ... or original legislative intent ... as precluding further independent judgment by the interpreter." Pojanowski, "Reading Statutes," 1363. Meanwhile, proponents of updating as a general rule are a subset of the antiformalists who, "while giving weight to original meaning or intention, affords the interpreter greater authority to broaden, narrow, or, in some cases, reject the most plausible available understanding of that original meaning or intention," to the extent that the statutes "conflict with contemporary public values." Pojanowski, 1363. Such theories, and the deep thinking in the philosophy of law that lies beneath them, continue to inform the types of questions, and the range of answers, that relate to the deceptively simple task of interpreting an authoritative text.

British government a monopoly over telegraphic communications covered the later-invented telephone. For Thomas Edison's telephone company, a court wedded to the principle of *contemporanea expositio* would result in an economic boon. (It favored updating instead.)[9] This disciplined approach to applying the original understanding to new circumstances, described in greater detail later in this chapter, was articulated most recently in cases decided by the United Kingdom's highest court.

Looking to the United Kingdom to see how judicial approaches to updating have developed from the time of Coke and Blackstone offers an opportunity to view something of a parallel legal universe, where the interpretive questions have been similar, and the resulting judicial responses provide a rich context for considering methods that might be appropriate for American constitutional interpretation. Accordingly, with all the customary caveats about making compare-and-contrast generalizations across centuries and continents, I will propose not only that we need a principled updating methodology for American constitutional interpretation – irrespective of whether interpreters are otherwise inclined to favor static or flexible readings of the text – but also that the experience in the United Kingdom, from Lord Coke to the modern UK courts, has identified one that has the potential to create considerably more clarity and consistency than the record of Supreme Court decision making that Attorney General Meese called a "jurisprudence of idiosyncracy."[10]

The framework discussed in this chapter is based on a set of criteria by which judges first assess the nature of the changing circumstances, and then consider how those changes relate to the original end–means decision represented by the text. Updating, as distinguished from noninterpretive decision making (as defined in Chapter 3), is fundamentally a matter of considering the new facts in light of the lawmaker's original design and rationale. Describing this method thus emphasizes how important it is for interpreters to understand the rationale that motivated the Framers to adopt the constitutional text in the first instance. Comprehending that rationale, not just the objective meaning of the words in context, is essential for interpreters to be able to distinguish between noninterpretive judicial policymaking and applying a fixed text to changing conditions.

[9] See *Attorney-General v. Edison Tel. Co. of London* [1880] 6 QBD 244; Nathaniel C. Moak, *Reports of Cases Decided by the English Courts: With Notes and References to Kindred Cases and Authorities*, vol. 29 (Albany, NY, 1882).

[10] Quoted in Edwin Meese III, "The Supreme Court of the United States: Bulwark of a Limited Constitution," *South Texas Law Review* 27, 3 (Fall 1986): 458.

HOW THE LAW ADAPTS TO CHANGE

In contemporary democratic societies, when the public changes its mind about which policies should govern the country, those changes are most likely to take the form of enactments by lawmaking bodies, as elected representatives create new laws (including constitutional provisions) that better reflect the shifting desires of their constituents. The issues of judicial updating arise when the language of the law has not changed despite the fact – or at least the possibility – that potentially relevant scientific, semantic, social, moral, or political circumstances have changed in a significant way. The courts may thus be put in the position of deciding whether to interpret the existing laws in ways that may not have been contemplated at the time of enactment. These cases turn on whether the governing legal text should have a static or dynamic meaning, and they challenge courts to consider the proper role of the judiciary vis-à-vis the lawmaker in establishing and changing the law. This potential tension between old laws and new circumstances is likely to appear in any country with fixed, written laws, but perhaps none is more challenging than the United States with a difficult-to-amend Constitution that has endured over ten times longer than the average constitution around the world.

Once a constitutional provision has been ratified, a variety of types of changing circumstances can take place. Technology will certainly continue to evolve, and many of the updating cases revolve around the need to apply eighteenth- or nineteenth-century language to factual situations that far exceed the possibilities imaginable by those who enacted the laws. Then, there are the cases where the state of knowledge has largely remained constant, but people's attitudes or the meanings of words have changed. There are thus two basic types of updating case (to oversimplify to a considerable degree). Updating as a result of technological progress asks the courts to apply, as it were, old answers to new forms of the question. If the legislature has already decided that the government should have a monopoly on telegraphic communications, are telephones similar enough to telegraphs to be treated in the same way?

In the other major type of updating case, the activities in question are not substantially different today than they were at the time of enactment, and the court needs to consider whether society's understandings have shifted to such an extent that the result today should be different now than it would have been then. Those who advocate a robust use of updating methods to change the constitutional law so as better to reflect a new societal consensus – or perhaps the aspirations of some of society's members – may build their methodological cases on the need for courts to account for technological change. But these types of social-and-cultural-change cases are, in many respects, the opposite of the technology cases. Rather than applying old answers to new questions, judges are considering whether they should give a new answer to an old question because the meanings of the words, or the moral and political attitudes of society, have changed to such a great extent. This kind of case asks the courts to consider what conditions, if any, will permit them legitimately to interpret an authoritative text in a way that reaches the opposite interpretive conclusion than the one that judges at the time of enactment would have made under the same circumstances.

These last cases, the ones revolving around the question of changes in community values, public opinion, or other sources of the judges' conceptions of justice or fairness, raise the clearest concern that the courts could be usurping what should properly be the prerogative of the political branches of government to change the Constitution to reflect a new policy. As the US Supreme Court said in a twentieth-century case involving the constitutionality of anti-sodomy laws: "The Court is most vulnerable and comes nearest to illegitimacy when it deals with judge-made constitutional law having little or no cognizable roots in the language or design of the Constitution."[11] This concern was raised again by Chief Justice John Roberts in the 2015 case discussing whether state marriage laws were constitutionally required to recognize same-sex marriage. In that case, *Obergefell v. Hodges*, the Chief Justice said: "[T]his Court is not a legislature. Whether same-sex marriage is a good idea should be of no concern to us."[12] Then, echoing Chief Justice Marshall's famous statement in the 1803 *Marbury v. Madison* case, that it is the "duty of the judicial department to say what the law is," he argued: "Under the Constitution, judges have the power to say what the law is, not what it should be."[13] Yet, as the history of updating demonstrates, judges have regularly revised the meaning of laws to keep up with (or perhaps press ahead of) changes in public attitudes, and Chief Justice Roberts' separation of powers concerns were expressed in a dissenting opinion. The majority opinion in *Obergefell*, however, upheld the constitutional right to same-sex marriage, and Justice Kennedy's majority opinion spoke of the importance of recognizing

[11] *Bowers v. Hardwick*, 478 US 186, 194 (1986). This decision was overturned in *Lawrence v. Texas*, 539 US 558 (2003), where the Court said, after criticizing the historical discussion in *Bowers*: "In all events we think that our laws and traditions in the past half century are of most relevance here. These references show an emerging awareness that liberty gives substantial protection to adult persons in deciding how to conduct their private lives in matters pertaining to sex." *Lawrence*, 539 US at 571–2.

[12] *Obergefell v. Hodges*, 576 US, 2 (2015) (Roberts, C.J., dissenting).

[13] *Marbury v. Madison*, 5 US 137, 137 (1803); *Obergefell*, 576 US at 2 (Roberts, C.J., dissenting).

that the "history of marriage is one of both continuity and change." For Justice Kennedy, "That institution . . . has evolved over time," and so, then, should the Court's interpretation of the law.[14]

This need for judges to consider how to take evolving social attitudes into account was addressed by Lord Justice Thomas Bingham in a 1995 case involving a British military policy declaring that "homosexuality is incompatible with service in the Armed Forces."[15] The question presented was whether that administrative decision was "reasonable." Bingham was an especially influential jurist; he later became a Justice of the UK Supreme Court, and was the author of an award-winning book, *The Rule of Law*,[16] a volume likely to be read by every law student in Britain today. He wrote that "the progressive development and refinement of public and professional opinion at home and abroad [is] . . . an important feature of this case,"[17] which involved a policy whose roots were at least fifty years old. In considering how that progression might influence his decision, he noted: "A belief which represented unquestioned orthodoxy in Year X may have become questionable by Year Y and unsustainable by Year Z."[18] Ultimately, Bingham concluded that the policy was not irrational, noting that it "was supported by both Houses of Parliament and by those to whom the ministry properly looked for professional advice."[19]

Bingham's alphabetical updating analysis of the meaning of "reasonable" was invoked two years later by Lord Justice Ward in a case involving a question of semantic drift. Justice Ward argued that a 1920's tenancy statute employing the term "family" should include same-sex partners, even though the enacting legislature would likely have concluded otherwise, and despite the fact that an earlier case had reached a contrary decision. His 1997 judgment said: "I have come to a clear conclusion that [the earlier 1984 case] was decided in year X; [my Lords] . . . believe us to be in year Y whereas I have been persuaded that the discrimination would be thought by the broad mass of the people to be so unsustainable that this must by now be year Z."[20] Well aware that critics would say that this "is a matter for Parliament," Ward said: "If I am to be criticized – and of course I will be – then I prefer to be criticized . . . for being ahead of the

[14] *Obergefell*, 576 US at 6. Later, he argued, "The right to marry is fundamental as a matter of history and tradition, but rights come not from ancient sources alone. They rise, too, from a better-informed understanding of how constitutional imperatives define a liberty that remains urgent in our own era." *Obergefell*, 576 US at 18–19.

[15] Quoted in *R v. Ministry of Def., ex parte Smith* [1996] 1 All ER 257.

[16] Tom Bingham, *The Rule of Law* (London: Allen Lane, 2010).

[17] *R v. Ministry of Def.*, 1 All ER.

[18] *R v. Ministry of Def.*, 1 All ER.

[19] *R v. Ministry of Def.*, 1 All ER.

[20] *Fitzpatrick v. Sterling Hous. Ass'n Ltd.* [1997] 4 All ER 991.

times, rather than behind the times. My hope ... is that I am in step with the times." Ultimately, he decided that "to conclude otherwise would be to stand like King Canute, ordering the tide to recede when the tide in favour of equality rolls relentlessly forward and shows no sign of ebbing."[21]

These "progressive development" cases raise a series of closely linked methodological questions. How can judges observe and measure that progression, and how should they determine whether the tides of public opinion are ebbing or flowing? Compare, for example, Bingham's and Ward's focus on progressive development with Justice Scalia's anti-updating arguments. As Scalia has argued, especially in connection with constitutional cases: "It certainly cannot be said that a constitution naturally suggests changeability; to the contrary, its whole purpose is to prevent change – to embed certain rights in such a manner that future generations cannot readily take them away." Society's changes, according to Scalia, do not always lead to a brighter future. "A society that adopts a bill of rights," he posits, "is skeptical that 'evolving standards of decency' always 'mark progress,' and that societies always 'mature,' as opposed to rot."[22]

Bingham also spoke of "public and professional opinion" without commenting further on whether there may be times when those are two different things – that is, legal or academic elites (in other words, professional opinion) may hold different views than the public at large – nor did he explain whether judges should consider opinion polls or other independent sources of data that could provide information about how various political and professional groups assess the relevant issues. Again, Justice Scalia has provided the opposing view, asking rhetorically: "What is it that the judge must consult to determine when, and in what direction, evolution has occurred? Is it the will of the majority, discerned from newspapers, radio talk shows, public opinion polls, and chats at the country club? Is it the philosophy of Hume, or of John Rawls, or of John Stuart Mill, or of Aristotle?"[23]

Finally, as Ward said in his judgment in the tenancy rights case, how can the courts make these updating interpretations without "exceeding the limits of the judicial function"? On this point, both Ward, who would opt to be ahead of the times, and Scalia, who, no doubt, would have stood with King Canute, share a deep concern over the proper role of the judiciary in a modern democracy. As Justice Scalia has argued, in connection with both statutory and constitutional

[21] *Fitzpatrick*, 4 All ER.

[22] Antonin Scalia, *A Matter of Interpretation: Federal Courts and the Law* (Princeton, NJ: Princeton University Press, 1997), p. 40.

[23] Scalia, *A Matter of Interpretation*, p. 45.

interpretation: "It is simply not compatible with democratic theory that laws mean whatever they ought to mean, and that unelected judges decide what that is."[24] Even outspoken advocates of updating acknowledge that the courts must be sensitive to issues of "sociological legitimacy"[25] and the separation of powers Lady Hale, recently President of the UK Supreme Court, describes herself as a supporter of the European Convention on Human Rights and the work of the Strasbourg Court (also known as the European Court of Human Rights, or ECtHR), but she, at the same time, has urged the ECtHR judges "to accept that there are some natural limits to the growth and development of the living tree [approach to updating]. Otherwise I have a fear that their judgments, and those of the national courts which follow them, will increasingly be defied by our governments and Parliaments."[26]

Hale's comment is rooted in the concern that legal judgments, even those rendered by our highest courts, are not self-executing, and require the cooperation of other arms of political governance. If citizens and their elected representatives believe that the courts have exceeded their proper boundaries, those other branches may not only refuse to enforce their decisions, but may also look for opportunities to push the boundaries back, and thus diminish the power of the courts. In fact, the degree to which the ECtHR has affected UK jurisprudence is one of the reasons a number of legal scholars and politicians have supported Brexit, the United Kingdom's withdrawal from the European Union. Even before Brexit, in 2014, Conservatives in Britain, angered by the jurisprudence of the Strasbourg Court as it had affected the interpretation of UK laws, proposed to adopt legislation to ensure that "the UK courts will interpret legislation based upon its normal meaning and the clear intention of Parliament, rather than having to stretch its meaning to comply with Strasbourg case law."[27]

COMMON UPDATING THEMES: STATUTES, CONSTITUTIONS, AND CONVENTIONS

Basically, the same issues arise whether judges are interpreting the Magna Carta and other genuinely "ancient Acts," or the United States Constitution,

[24] Scalia, p. 22.

[25] See Chapter 8.

[26] Baroness Hale, "Beanstalk or Living Instrument? How Tall Can the European Convention on Human Rights Grow?" (lecture, Gray's Inn, London, June 16, 2011), www.gresham.ac.uk/lecture/transcript/print/beanstalk-or-living-instrument-how-tall-can-the-european-convention-on-human/.

[27] Conservative Party, *Protecting Human Rights in the UK: The Conservatives' Proposals for Changing Britain's Human Rights Laws* (London: Alan Mabbutt, 2014), p. 6, www.conservatives.com/~/media/files/downloadable%20Files/human_rights.pdf.

or, indeed, considerably more recent statutes, treaties, and international conventions. These interpretive debates are unlikely to be completely resolved in favor of either end of the methodological spectrum. As Lord Coke, Professor Finnis, Justice Scalia, and Lady Hale have all said in one fashion or another, updating can sometimes be the proper interpretative approach, but it should not necessarily be applied in every case. The critical issues, then, are how to know when the time is right, and to what degree the meaning should change over time, especially in light of the original end–means decision of the lawmaker.

It is worth noting that these issues of "when" and "how" to update arise irrespective of whether a broad-based commitment to updating becomes the dominant mode of interpretation in a particular jurisdiction. Some legislatures, as in Canada, for example, have adopted interpretation acts that require courts to take an "always speaking" or "ambulatory" approach, thus providing an apparently carte blanche legislative blessing for judicial updating.[28] Yet that interpretation act itself needs to be interpreted, as courts consider the extent to which the legislature's original understandings and policy choices should contribute to determining, in the words of the Canadian statute, the law's "true spirit, intent and meaning." By the same token, even though Justice Scalia has written extensively about the perils of updating, his opinion in the *Kyllo* search-and-seizure case involving an infrared heat detector appeared to go well beyond simply acknowledging technological advancements.[29] Not only has heat-detecting technology evolved since the eighteenth century, but so have our expectations of privacy, as compared to the fear of "door-breaking" invasions to which the Fourth Amendment was a response.[30] As Michael

[28] Interpretation Act, RSC 1985, c. I-23, s. 10 (Can.): "The law shall be considered as always speaking, and where a matter or thing is expressed in the present tense, it shall be applied to the circumstances as they arise, so that effect may be given to the enactment according to its true spirit, intent and meaning." Peter Hogg has pointed out that the Supreme Court of Canada has taken the same methodological approach when it interprets the Canadian constitution. He has written that "the principle of progressive (or dynamic) interpretation, as articulated in the metaphor of the 'living tree,' has become the dominant theory of interpretation in Canada. Under this theory, the language of the Constitution is applied to contemporary conditions and ideas without regard for the question whether the framers would have contemplated such an application." Peter W. Hogg, "Canada: From Privy Council to Supreme Court," in *Interpreting Constitutions: A Comparative Study*, ed. Jeffrey Goldsworthy (Oxford: Oxford University Press, 2006), p. 87.

[29] See *Kyllo*, 533 US at 33–4.

[30] For a summary of the historical background, see David E. Steinberg, "The Original Understanding of Unreasonable Searches and Seizures," *Florida Law Review* 56, 5 (December 2004): 1051–96; Thomas Y. Davies, "Recovering the Original Fourth Amendment," *Michigan Law Review* 98, 3 (December 1999): 547–750; and sources cited therein.

Ramsey observes: "[T]he Kyllo approach does not fit the new technology into a category defined by the text . . . . Rather, the level of privacy . . . required creation of a new category (unduly intrusive observations made from the public street)."[31] Updating will be a fact of judicial life, and the key question is how it can be done with reference to the lawmaker's intentions. As discussed in Chapter 3, it is that commitment to the will of the lawmaker that distinguishes an updating interpretation from judicial policymaking.

MODEL FOR UPDATING

The approach outlined here grows out of the classical approach to interpretation described by Coke and Blackstone, but its specific form has been recently developed by judges in the United Kingdom. I am proposing a model from the United Kingdom's highest court with some trepidation. Judges and scholars who are opposed to an updated, living Constitution are often equally opposed to using foreign law to interpret the US Constitution.[32] Especially for originalists, it is hard to see how contemporary foreign law can provide any insights into the original meaning of constitutional language ratified in eighteenth-century America. In response to the use of foreign law to justify Supreme Court decisions,[33] Republican lawmakers introduced a bill titled "The Constitution Restoration Act of 2005," which read in part:

> In interpreting and applying the Constitution of the United States, a court of the United States may not rely upon any constitution, law, administrative rule, Executive order, directive, policy, judicial decision, or any other action of any foreign state or international organization or agency, other than English constitutional and common law up to the time of the adoption of the Constitution of the United States.[34]

This provision never actually became law, but it is interesting that, at least for these Republicans, use of "English constitutional and common law" prior to

[31] Michael D. Ramsey, "Beyond the Text: Justice Scalia's Originalism in Practice," *Notre Dame Law Review* 92, 5 (2017): 1963–4.

[32] See Michael C. Dorf, "The Use of Foreign Law in American Constitutional Interpretation: A Revealing Colloquy between Justices Scalia and Breyer," FindLaw, January 19, 2005, https://supreme.findlaw.com/legal-commentary/the-use-of-foreign-law-in-american-constitutional-interpretation.html. See also Steven G. Calabresi and Stephanie Dotson Zimdahl, "The Supreme Court and Foreign Sources of Law: Two Hundred Years of Practice and the Juvenile Death Penalty Decision," *William and Mary Law Review* 47, 3 (December 2005): 743–909.

[33] See *Atkins v. Virginia*, 536 US 304 (2002); *Roper v. Simmons*, 543 US 551 (2005).

[34] Constitution Restoration Act of 2005, HR 1070, 109th Cong., § 201 (2005). See also Ronald Kahn, "The Constitution Restoration Act, Judicial Independence, and Popular Constitutionalism," *Case Western Reserve Law Review* 56, 4 (Summer 2006): 1083–118.

the time of the US Constitution is perfectly appropriate, including the long history of interpretation described in Chapter 3. As for this chapter's consideration of updating methods, it will be helpful to keep in mind that I am not proposing that the Supreme Court look to or adopt the law of the United Kingdom. Instead, I am suggesting that a methodical approach to updating, developed by thoughtful judges in a country whose legal system has also been deeply influenced by Coke's and Blackstone's writings, may help US courts to consider how to make decisions that can account for changing circumstances but are also consistent with the Framers' choices about constitutional policy.

The House of Lords itself (acting for the Queen in Parliament) traditionally served as the final court of appeal in the United Kingdom, with that role fulfilled, as of the turn of the twenty-first century, by the twelve Lords of Appeal in Ordinary, commonly known as the Law Lords. In 2009, a separate institution, the Supreme Court of the United Kingdom, was established to take over that judicial role.[35] Although the Law Lords, and now the Supreme Court justices, have occasionally considered cases dealing with non-statutory governmental policies, the updating cases in the United Kingdom have generally involved laws adopted by Parliament. Some of those statutes are "ancient Acts," such as the Magna Carta and the Bill of Rights of 1689, which are typically treated as being of constitutional status; otherwise, the United Kingdom famously has an "unwritten," or at least uncodified, constitution.[36]

UK judges and commentators have tended to lean in one direction or the other over time. As discussed in Chapter 3, Lord Coke demonstrated that both updating and the originalist rule of *contemporanea expositio* have coexisted for well over 300 years. Original meanings appear to have been dominant throughout much of the twentieth century but were then overtaken by a trend towards more frequent uses of evolutionary or "ambulatory" interpretive approaches. This shift may be seen in Rupert Cross' influential work on statutory interpretation. While his 1976 edition had highlighted the centrality

[35] The foundation for the establishment of the Supreme Court was the Constitutional Reform Act, 2005, c. 4.

[36] Lord Neuberger explains: "Some people say that the United Kingdom has a constitution – in documents such as Magna Carta and the Bill of Rights, and in constitutional conventions as developed in practice. But these are merely a collection of provisions which developed somewhat haphazardly to deal with specific historical events or crises. Anyway, they can all be revoked or altered by a simple majority in parliament – indeed, all but three of the sixty or so provisions of the original 1215 Magna Carta, despite being promulgated on several occasions by successive Kings . . . have been repealed by simple parliamentary statute over the past three hundred years." David Neuberger, "The UK Constitutional Settlement and the Role of the UK Supreme Court" (lecture, Legal Wales Conference, Bangor, Wales, October 10, 2014), 8–9, www.supremecourt.uk/docs/speech-141010.pdf.

of the meaning as of the date of enactment, in the 1987 revised edition, the editors said that they "share[d] the views of leading commentator [Francis] Bennion, [et al.] that there is a general rule in favour of an 'updating' or 'ambulatory' approach, rather than an historical one."[37] A more recent text has announced that, in the United Kingdom: "[T]he constitutional orthodoxy which has developed is that statutes should (generally) be presumed to be 'always speaking'," and, as a result, "'the interpreter is to make allowances for any relevant changes that have occurred, since the Act's passing, in law, social conditions, technology, the meaning of words and other matters'."[38]

As that late-twentieth-century interpretive orthodoxy developed in the United Kingdom, judges had to wrestle with the methodological when-and-how issues of judicial updating. By contrast, in the United States, justices have often been vocal proponents of either the living or "dead" schools of constitutional interpretation, but they have not necessarily explicitly engaged with the specific methodological issues involved in how to account for changing circumstances. In the *Obergefell* case, Justice Kennedy simply declared that, as "the institution of marriage ... has evolved," so, then, should the Court's interpretation of the law.[39] In Justice Scalia's opinion in the *Kyllo* case, he brushed the methodological issue aside, saying simply that "it would be foolish" to argue against our current expectations of privacy.[40]

Rather than leaving unstated the arguments about what kind of updating is appropriate, the Court could consider, as a model, an approach that appeared in a case before the UK Law Lords in 1981. This was a transitional time in interpretive thinking and practice, halfway between the publication of the first edition of Cross' text, which had emphasized the original meaning, and the second edition, which embraced updating. The analytical framework for

37 Rupert Cross, *Statutory Interpretation*, eds. John Bell and George Engle, 2nd ed. (London: Butterworths, 1987), p. 49, citing §288 of Francis Bennion, *Statutory Interpretation*, 3rd ed. (London: Butterworths, 1997), p. 617. See also J. F. Burrows, "The Problem of Time in Statutory Interpretation," *New Zealand Law Journal* (1978); D. J. Hurst, "The Problem of the Elderly Statute," *Legal Studies* 3, 1 (March 1983): 21–42; and D. J. Hurst, "Palm Trees in the House of Lords: Some Further Thoughts on Boland's Case," *Statute Law Review* 4, 3 (Autumn 1983): 142–65. Bennion states: "It is presumed that Parliament intends the court to apply to an ongoing act a construction that continuously updates it wording to allow for changes since the Act was initially framed (an updating construction)." Bennion, *Statutory Interpretation*, p. 617. For the prior view, see Rupert Cross, *Statutory Interpretation* (London: Butterworths, 1976), p. 47, citing, for example *The Longford* (1889) 14 PD.

38 Ian Loveland, *Constitutional Law, Administrative Law, and Human Rights: A Critical Introduction*, 7th ed. (Oxford: Oxford University Press, 2015), p. 64, quoting Bennion, *Statutory Interpretation*, p. 686.

39 *Obergefell*, 576 US at 8.

40 *Kyllo*, 533 US at 33–4.

updating put forth in the 1981 case by Lord Wilberforce, and rooted in the common law tradition of Coke and Blackstone, was deemed "authoritative" over twenty years later in a leading judgment by Lord Bingham.[41] Interestingly, as discussed further below, although the US Supreme Court has not spelled out a similarly authoritative method for updating the meaning of constitutional provisions, the rationale in one of the Court's most prominent updating cases, *Brown v. Board of Education*, implicitly follows the logic of Wilberforce's approach.

Wilberforce's commentary on judicial updating appeared in *Royal College of Nursing v Department of Health and Social Security*,[42] where he ultimately concluded that the statute in question should not be given an updated meaning. That statute, the Abortion Act 1967, provided for pregnancies to be lawfully terminated under certain conditions "by a registered medical practitioner." After the law was enacted, a new procedure for terminating pregnancies was developed that allowed nearly all of the work to be performed by a nurse, with a physician performing just a portion of the steps, and otherwise being on call.

Wilberforce's speech began with a focus on the facts and circumstances surrounding the original enactment:

> In interpreting an Act of Parliament it is proper, and indeed necessary, to have regard to the state of affairs existing, and known by Parliament to be existing, at the time. It is a fair presumption that Parliament's policy or intention is directed to that state of affairs.

This initial inquiry resonates with the approach to interpretation articulated by Coke and Blackstone, with the latter invoking the authority of Lord Coke to say: "There are three points to be considered" in statutory interpretation, "the old law, the mischief, and the remedy."[43]

41 *R (Quintavalle) v. Sec'y of State for Health* [2003] UKHL 13, 15. Surprisingly, Lord Wilberforce's authoritative approach was not explicitly followed in a considerably more recent case that was widely reported as being an updating case: *Yemshaw v. London Borough of Hounslow* [2011] UKSC 3. See Richard Ekins, "Updating the Meaning of Violence," *Law Quarterly Review* 129 (2013): 19. It is not clear that updating was involved, however. I have shown that, if the legislative record had been consulted, no updating would have been required. Donald L. Drakeman, "Constitutional Counterpoint: Legislative Debates, Statutory Interpretation and the Separation of Powers," *Statute Law Review* 38, 1 (February 2017): 116–24.

42 *Royal Coll. of Nursing v. Dep't of Health & Soc. Sec.* [1981] 1 All ER 545.

43 William Blackstone, *Commentaries on the Laws of England: In Four Books; With an Analysis of the Work*, eds. Edward Christian et al., 19th ed. (New York, 1846), vol. 1, p. 60, citing Co. Litt. 11, 42. See also Coke's opinion in *Heydon* [1584] EWHC Exch. J36.

The updating question arises some time later in light of new circumstances, or what Lord Wilberforce called "a fresh set of facts bearing on policy": "[W]hen a new state of affairs, or a fresh set of facts bearing on policy, comes into existence, the courts have to consider whether they fall within the Parliamentary intention." The key question is whether those new facts are "within the same genus of facts as those to which the expressed policy has been formulated." Moreover, even if the new situation does not necessarily fit within "the same genus of facts," it can be deemed to do so "if there can be detected a clear purpose in the legislation which can only be fulfilled if the extension is made."

Where Wilberforce addresses the positive case in which new facts might fall within the lawmaker's intended outcome (that is, the appropriate remedy for the "mischief" in Blackstonian terms), Blackstone posits instead the negative, but with essentially the same interpretive outcome, which is for the judge's decision to apply the lawmaker's intention to the unforeseen circumstances. Blackstone rejected the notion that courts could declare a legislative act void if it was "contrary to reason," but, "where some collateral matter arises out of the general words, and happens to be unreasonable," judges may "conclude that this consequence was not foreseen by the parliament, and therefore ... disregard it."[44] In either the Wilberforce or Blackstone version, then, there are cases in which judges may need to consider how to maintain a focus on the will of the lawmaker in light of unforeseen circumstances. As Finnis argues, it can be appropriate for "judges to apply old ... statutes, constitutions or treaty conventions to new situations and conditions" if it "falls within the categories picked out by the propositions expressed" in the text, even if those situations were "not envisaged at the time of enactment."[45]

Wilberforce then added one additional consideration whether a statute can appropriately be judicially updated, namely, how broadly the approach should be applied. The courts need to look to the text for a signal:

> How liberally these principles may be applied must depend upon the nature of the enactment, and the strictness or otherwise of the words in which it has been expressed. The courts should be less willing to extend expressed meanings if it is clear that the Act in question was designed to be restrictive or circumscribed in its operation rather than liberal or permissive. They will be much less willing to do so where the new subject matter is different in kind or dimension from that for which the legislation was passed.

[44] Blackstone, *Commentaries*, vol. 1, pp. 63–4.
[45] Finnis, "Judicial Power," 23.

For Wilberforce, the judicial authority to update the meaning of a text does not include gap filling or asking what Parliament might have done had it been confronted with the new circumstances; it is limited to "the terms of the Act itself." The remainder of the quotation later deemed authoritative is:

> [T]here is one course which the courts cannot take, under the law of this country: they cannot fill gaps; they cannot by asking the question, "What would Parliament have done in this current case – not being one in contemplation – if the facts had been before it?" attempt themselves to supply the answer, if the answer is not be found in the terms of the Act itself.[46]

In the *Royal College of Nursing* case, Wilberforce thought that the issue of whether to update the application of the Abortion Act was one for the legislature to decide. As he put it, the Act "is, if ever an Act was, one for interpreting in the spirit that only that which Parliament has authorised on a fair reading of the relevant sections should be held to be within it."[47] Especially since the Act dealt "with a controversial subject involving moral and social judgments on which opinions strongly differ," he declined to extend the statute to the newly developed procedure because it was "clearly not just a fresh species or example of something already authorised."[48] In short, where controversial political and moral issues are at stake, any question about whether the "fresh set of facts" belongs to the same genus should be "left for Parliament's fresh consideration."[49]

Wilberforce's method would ultimately become authoritative, although, in this case, his conclusion did not convince a majority of the court. Nevertheless, in reviewing the judgments of the other Law Lords, it is not clear that they believed that *Royal College of Nursing* actually represented a case for judicial updating. Although there had been a significant technological change between the time of the statute and its judicial interpretation, the three Law Lords in the majority took considerable pains to interpret the text and purpose of the Act as it was at the time of enactment, not as the meanings of words or the social conditions may have changed thereafter. Irrespective of the outcome, the importance of Wilberforce's analysis lies in the value of explaining how courts can consider – and, equally importantly, explain – the issue of updating in a manner that is consistent with the will of the lawmaker, the text, and the role of judges in a constitutional democracy.

46 *Royal Coll. of Nursing*, 1 All ER at 565.
47 *Royal Coll. of Nursing*, 1 All ER at 565.
48 *Royal Coll. of Nursing*, 1 All ER at 565.
49 *Royal Coll. of Nursing*, 1 All ER at 565.

Wilberforce's approach requires judges to devote considerable efforts to demonstrating that they are not simply replacing the lawmaker's views with their own. The judges need to explain their reasoning in the light of a series of questions focusing on the lawmaker's original decision, what was known at that time, how things have changed, and the degree to which the lawmaker used language that pointed towards an expansive interpretation. Wilberforce also urged courts to be especially thoughtful about all of these issues when considering controversial cases. In summary, this updating framework contains essentially four basic questions:

(1) What "state of affairs" existed at the time of enactment that led to the lawmaker's end–means decision?
(2) What "fresh set of facts" bearing on that policy have arisen?
(3) Do the new circumstances "fall within the same genus of facts" as the ones originally addressed by the lawmaker? Or, if not, can the purpose of the provision (that is, the policy chosen by the lawmaker) be fulfilled only if extended to the new facts and circumstances?
(4) Does the language of the text signal that its interpretation should either be "restrictive" or "liberal"?

These criteria represent a potentially useful framework for considering updating cases in the interpretation of the US Constitution as well. It is important to recognize, however, that this set of questions is merely a framework, not a formula. It begins by asking the court to develop a full understanding of the lawmaker's intention in light of the circumstances that existed at the time. It then asks how circumstances have changed, and whether that "fresh set of facts" is "within the same genus" as those considered at the time of enactment, or if there are other factors that would potentially defeat the goal of the original policy choice. Finally, the Court needs to ask whether the Framers signaled in the constitutional language whether it should be read expansively. The value of this framework is that it focuses the justices not on whether their decision necessarily leads to what they believe to be a good outcome for society, but on the degree to which a proposed updated interpretation is consistent with the decision the Framers believed they were making when the provision was framed and ratified.

A LITMUS TEST?

Finally, although the Equal Protection Clause does not otherwise feature prominently in this book, it has become something of a "litmus test for theories of constitutional interpretation."[50] As Jack Balkin has written: "It is often said that no theory of constitutional interpretation is sound if it cannot explain and justify *Brown v. Board of Education*."[51] The decision in *Brown* declaring racial discrimination in education unconstitutional arguably could not have been reached by an originalist methodology, for example.[52] Having the Supreme Court reach what it believes to be the correct decision, at least on issues as important as the one the Court faced in *Brown*, appears to animate many contemporary constitutional theorists. As Randy Barnett has written: "For most [constitutional scholars], regardless of ideology, any theory of interpretation that does not get *Brown* correct, is unacceptable, almost by definition."[53]

It is interesting to see that the analysis in the Supreme Court's unanimous opinion in *Brown* implicitly followed the four-part updating method proposed in this chapter.[54] How the Framers themselves interpreted the clause represents a reasonable beginning of the updating inquiry, but not necessarily the end. Chief Justice Warren acknowledged (perhaps optimistically) that the evidence was "inconclusive" as to whether the Framers and ratifiers of the Fourteenth Amendment expected it to eliminate racial segregation in the schools. But even if the evidence clearly showed that the Congress that framed the Fourteenth Amendment permitted segregated schools, and,

[50] Jack M. Balkin, preface to *What* Brown v. Board of Education *Should Have Said: The Nation's Top Legal Experts Rewrite America's Landmark Civil Rights Decision*, ed. Jack M. Balkin (New York: New York University Press, 2002), p. x.

[51] Balkin, preface, pp. x–xi.

[52] See Alexander M. Bickel, "The Original Understanding and the Segregation Decision," *Harvard Law Review* 69, 1 (November 1955): 1–65, which was originally drafted as a memorandum for one of the justices for whom Bickel was clerking at the time. See also Jack Balkin, who writes that "the general consensus has been that most of the framers and ratifiers of the Fourteenth Amendment did not expect that it would outlaw segregation of the public schools … . Even the galleries of Congress were segregated." Jack M. Balkin, "Rewriting *Brown*: A Guide to the Opinions," in *What* Brown v. Board of Education *Should Have Said*, p. 53. For a contrary, pro-originalism view of the *Brown* case, see Michael W. McConnell, "Originalism and the Desegregation Decisions," *Virginia Law Review* 81, 4 (May 1995): 947–1140.

[53] Randy Barnett, "Originalism and *Brown*," *Volokh Conspiracy* (blog), May 12, 2005, www.volokh.com/posts/1115921115.shtml. See also Jack M. Balkin, "What *Brown* Teaches Us about Constitutional Theory," *Virginia Law Review* 90, 6 (October 2004): 1537: "Most law professors agree that any serious normative theory of constitutional interpretation must be consistent with *Brown v. Board of Education* and show why the case was correctly decided." Similarly, Will Baude notes: "In practice almost every constitutional theorist feels the need to say that Brown is right." Will Baude, "Does Originalism Justify Brown, and Why Do We Care So Much?" *Volokh Conspiracy* (blog), *Washington Post*, January 24, 2014, www.washingtonpost.com/news/volokh-conspiracy/wp/2014/01/29/does-originalism-justify-brown-and-why-do-we-care-so-much.

[54] *Brown v. Bd. of Educ.*, 347 US 483 (1954).

therefore, may have believed that separate-but-equal was a legitimate attribute of equality at that time, Warren pointed to dramatic growth of public education and recent research in psychology and sociology. These changes could well be seen as providing a relevant "fresh set of facts," namely, the conclusion from the social science data that educational equality was inherently incompatible with segregated schools.[55] These facts, relating to a key assumption underlying the separate-but-equal decision in *Plessy v. Ferguson*[56] – namely, that separate could, in fact, be equal – would seem fairly to demonstrate why the application of the concept of equality, especially as it related to the rights of African Americans, would lead to a different result now than it would have at the time of ratification. Finally, there is nothing in the language of the Fourteenth Amendment – "No state shall … deny to any person within its jurisdiction the equal protection of the laws" – signaling that the language should be interpreted in a restrictive manner. There is, therefore, a good argument that the decision in *Brown* is compatible with a consistently applied, Framer-centric updating methodology in light of the nature of the language, the Framers' end–means choices, and the relevant circumstances.

CONCLUSION

Even agreement on this type of interpretive framework will not necessarily mean that the justices will also agree on the outcome. But it will provide a foundation for analyzing constitutional issues that maintains a focus on the Framers' intentions rather than the justices' own preferences, or on the attitudes that the justices believe people may (or should) hold, either at present or in the future. Such a Framer-centric approach is consistent with the nature of interpretation as it has been discussed and debated for centuries. Another value of this four-step approach is that it would point the justices' attention towards the nature of the Framers' original decision and the reasons for it – that is, what state of affairs the policy was addressing, and how was it designed to do so – rather than encouraging them simply to look for a convenient quotation from a friendly Framer at the eighteenth-century constitutional cocktail party. To achieve these goals, interpreters need to explore the drafting history (to the extent that it is accessible) in an effort to comprehend, as much as possible, the reasoned arguments, disagreements, and negotiations that led

[55] See Kenneth B. Clark, Isidor Chein, and Stuart W. Cook, "The Effects of Segregation and the Consequences of Desegregation: A (September 1952) Social Science Statement in the *Brown v. Board of Education of Topeka* Supreme Court Case," *American Psychologist* 59, 6 (September 2004): 495–501.

[56] *Plessy v. Ferguson*, 163 US 537 (1896).

to the final form of the constitutional text. As the next three chapters will show, a search for the original public meaning may be insufficient to provide interpreters enough evidence of the Framers' end–means choice to be able to consider how it should – or should not – adapt to changing circumstances.

Proponents of noninterpretive judicial decision making have questioned the reliability of evidence about original intent/meaning, while originalists have countered that judges embracing a living constitution cannot reasonably measure the stage of society's evolution except by reference to their own political preferences, an argument bolstered by, among other things, a wealth of political science scholarship on judicial choice.[57] These are questions whose answers can be rooted in factual inquiries, which is one of the messages of this chapter. What the Framers set out to do can potentially be discoverable from diligent inquiry, as are the answers to the question of what "fresh set of facts" exist, and whether they belong in the same "genus" as the original ones. The key questions ask for factual answers, and assessing the strength of the evidence for reaching a particular factual conclusion is well within the traditional realm of judicial competence. Much as originalists will need to work hard to show that they have convincingly identified the meaning at the time of the Constitution, justices proposing updated applications will need to clear equally high epistemological barriers where it comes to the fresh set of facts and how they fit within the limits of the original policy choice. Meanwhile, the next chapter will include a detailed factual analysis to show that a search for the objective public meaning alone can be insufficient either to reach a determination of the original meaning or to provide a basis for considering how to apply the provision to changing circumstances.

[57] See, for example, Eileen Braman, *Law, Politics, and Perception: How Policy Preferences Influence Legal Reasoning* (Charlottesville: University of Virginia Press, 2009), noting that "the dominant assumption in social science literature [is] that judges are primarily motivated by policy"; Braman instead proposes "an alternative characterization of motives based on the idea that those who are trained in the legal tradition come to internalize legal norms and 'accuracy' goals consistent with idealized notions of decision making." Braman, *Law, Politics, and Perception*, p. 7. See, generally, Michael A. Bailey and Forrest Maltzman, *The Constrained Court: Law, Politics, and the Decisions Justices Make* (Princeton, NJ: Princeton University Press, 2011).

5

The Semantic Summing Problem

The preceding chapters have centered on the goal of interpretation, which is, according to Blackstone, "interpret[ing] the will of the legislator . . . by exploring his intentions at the time."[1] Blackstone then directs us to "signs" of those intentions, the first of which is the words "in their usual and most known signification."[2] This chapter will show the degree to which the words, even in context, have the potential to leave matters "dubious," in his terms, hence the need for other evidence of the will of the lawmaker. In particular, this chapter will show that the "summing problem," which has most often been associated with the difficulty of determining a single intention of the Framers' "many myndes," is matched by its semantic equivalent: the fact that the evidence of objective public meaning can lead to a multitude of potential meanings. To describe the nature of the problem, I will analyze two clauses of the Constitution that have generated a great deal of litigation and interpretive controversy. This analysis will show that there are multiple equally strong candidates for the meanings of the words "in their most usual and most known significance," in Blackstone's terms. In the next chapter, I will show that the new capabilities offered by searches in corpus linguistics databases will not offer a "Big Data" solution to the semantic summing problem, and may well exacerbate it. Then, Chapter 7 will demonstrate how seeking the Framers' intentions in a review of the debates and drafting history leading to the final versions of the Constitution can resolve the semantic summing problem, at least in the case of these highly contested and frequently litigated clauses.

The first example focuses on the tax clauses. Article I, Section 8, Clause 1, specifies that "Congress shall have Power to lay and collect Taxes, Duties,

[1] William Blackstone, *Commentaries on the Laws of England: In Four Books; With an Analysis of the Work*, eds. Edward Christian et al., 19th ed. (New York, 1846), vol. 1, p. 40.

[2] Blackstone, *Commentaries*, vol. 1, p. 40.

Imposts and Excises . . . ; but all Duties, Imposts and Excises shall be uniform throughout the United States." Section 2 mandates that "Representatives and direct taxes shall be apportioned among the several states . . . according to their respective numbers."[3] Whether a levy imposed by the federal government is an excise, a direct tax, or not a tax at all has animated the constitutional debates surrounding two large and expensive governmental programs: Social Security and the Affordable Care Act. The critical question arising under these clauses is whether the federal levy in question is a "direct tax," which must be apportioned among the various states in the same manner as congressional representatives, or an excise, which needs only to be uniform throughout the states. These tax provisions have led to Supreme Court decisions affecting healthcare and retirement programs that are responsible for over one-third of the federal budget, and thus have had enormous real world impact.

The second of the two clauses discussed in this chapter is the Establishment Clause of the First Amendment: "Congress shall make no law respecting an establishment of religion." This clause is the subject of a breathtakingly large interpretive literature. As I have noted elsewhere: "[T]here have been serious scholarly disputes over the meaning of at least seven of the ten words in the clause, including 'an'."[4] Because of the multiplicity of good arguments about the Establishment Clause's original meaning, combined with the continuing vitality and political salience of church–state disputes in America, the clause has been the source of literally dozens of Supreme Court cases in the twentieth and twenty-first centuries, with justices often widely split on the meaning of the clause even when, as has generally been the case, they appear to share a common commitment to finding an interpretation based on its original meaning.

Perhaps the best reason for concentrating on these two provisions – one drafted by the Constitutional Convention and the other by the First Federal Congress – is that it is possible to trace the meanings of the key terms virtually to their origins in the English language. That research offers an opportunity to compare the formal definitions that can be found in dictionaries and commentaries with a considerable amount of evidence of how people in the Founding Era actually used the words in the relevant contexts. The semantic

[3] US Const. Art. I, § 8, cl. 1; Art. 1, § 2, cl. 3. See also the Sixteenth Amendment, ratified in 1913, providing that "Congress shall have power to lay and collect taxes on incomes . . . without apportionment . . . and without regard to any census or enumeration." US Const. Amend. XVI.

[4] Donald L. Drakeman, "Which Original Meaning of the Establishment Clause Is the Right One?," in *The Cambridge Companion to the First Amendment and Religious Liberty*, eds. Michael D. Breidenbach and Owen Anderson (Cambridge: Cambridge University Press, 2020), p. 366.

evidence will show that, in both cases, there were, at the time of ratification, at least two – and possibly more – equally strong candidates for the original public meaning, an array of textual "plain meanings" that persists today.

THE TAX CLAUSES

Several years ago, Joel Alicea and I had the opportunity to delve deeply into the historical evidence relating to the meaning of the term "excise" in Article I.[5] We consulted a wide range of sources, from dictionaries and commentaries to statutory language in Britain and America. We were especially interested in the 150-year period from when the concept of an excise tax was brought from Holland to England, through Congress' enactment in 1794 of a purported excise tax on the ownership of carriages, as recommended by Secretary of the Treasury, Alexander Hamilton.[6] The tax was challenged by a Virginian named Daniel Hylton, who claimed that it was a direct tax requiring apportionment, rather than an excise that needed only to be uniform.[7] *Hylton v. US* would be the Supreme Court's first opportunity to pass on the constitutionality of a federal statute, and for those who might think that the use of strategically positioned federal cases to influence the direction of the law is a relatively recent phenomenon, it is worth noting that the *Hylton* "case was trumped up, the facts were bogus, the procedure was defective, and the Court lacked a quorum."[8] The goal was to get the Supreme Court to rule on the question of whether the carriage tax was an excise tax or a direct tax, in which case it would have required apportionment under the Constitution. Because the tax was a fairly modest one, in order to meet the necessary amount in controversy set by the Judiciary Act of 1789, Mr. Hylton agreed to be sued for the taxes due on an alleged ownership of 125 carriages, more than probably existed in the entire state of Virginia, on the

[5] Joel Alicea and Donald L. Drakeman, "The Limits of New Originalism," *University of Pennsylvania Journal of Constitutional Law* 15, 4 (April 2013): 1161–219.

[6] Julius Goebel Jr. and Joseph H. Smith, eds., *The Law Practice of Alexander Hamilton: Documents and Commentary* (New York: Columbia University Press, 1980), vol. 4, p. 299; and An Act Laying Duties upon Carriages for the Conveyance of Persons, 1 Stat. 373–5 (1794, repealed 1802). Attorney General William Bradford indicated that "it was Hamilton who fathered the proposal of the 1794 carriage tax." Goebel and Smith, *Law Practice of Alexander Hamilton*, vol. 4, p. 300.

[7] Compare US Const. Art. I, § 2, cl. 3, with US Const. Art. I, § 8, cl. 1.

[8] Alicea and Drakeman, "Limits of New Originalism," 1162–3. See also *Hylton v. United States*, 3 US 171 (1796). For a description of these and other defects in the case, see David P. Currie, *The Constitution in the Supreme Court: The First Hundred Years, 1789–1888* (Chicago: University of Chicago Press, 1985), pp. 32–7.

condition that, if he lost, he would actually only owe the tax on the one carriage he likely owned.[9]

The evidence supporting both sides of this definitional debate is so strong that my coauthor Joel and I were simply unable to agree on the answer to the question of whether the original semantic meaning of the term "excise" included an annual tax on the ownership of an item, such as a carriage. Hylton's argument that the term "excise" was not correctly applied to the tax was supported by several notable Virginians, including Edmund Pendleton and James Madison, who had opposed the tax in Congress on the grounds that it was unconstitutional.[10] Citing numerous dictionaries and commentaries, they argued that an "excise" is a "duty on articles manufactured for sale."[11] Excises are thus limited to taxes on sales of goods (or making goods destined for sale), including what consumers today would typically call a sales tax. In commentaries and dictionaries around the time of the Constitution, this type of classic definition appeared regularly. Adam Smith wrote in the *Wealth of Nations*: "The duties of excise are imposed chiefly upon goods of home produce destined for home consumption. They are imposed only upon a few sorts of goods of the most general use."[12] Similarly, Noah Webster's dictionary defined excise as involving "consumption" or "on the retail," which is consistent with Blackstone, who wrote: "Directly opposite in its nature to [imposts on merchandise] is the excise duty, which is an inland imposition, paid sometimes upon the consumption of the commodity, or frequently upon the retail sale, which is the last stage before the consumption."[13] This definition carries forward to modern dictionaries, as well. A recent edition of Webster's calls an excise a "tax levied on domestic goods during manufacture or before sale."[14]

If excises were limited to these well-known definitions, there could be an excise tax on the manufacture or sale of a carriage, but, as Hylton and his supporters argued, an annual tax on the ownership of a carriage is not an excise

9 See Edward B. Whitney, "The Income Tax and the Constitution," *Harvard Law Review* 20, 4 (February 1907): 283 n1.

10 4 Annals of Cong. 630–730 (1794).

11 Edmund Pendleton, "United States against Hilton: Some Remarks on the Argument of Mr. Wickham," *Aurora General Advertiser*, February 11, 1796, quoted in Goebel and Smith, *Law Practice of Alexander Hamilton*, vol. 4, p. 332.

12 Adam Smith, *An Inquiry into the Nature and Causes of the Wealth of Nations*, ed. Edwin Cannan (London: Methuen, 1904), vol. 2, p. 362.

13 Noah Webster, *An American Dictionary of the English Language*, 1st ed. (1828), s.v. "excise"; Blackstone, *Commentaries*, vol. 1, p. 237.

14 *Webster's New Dictionary of the English Language: Revised and Updated* (2002), s.v. "excise." See also *Oxford English Dictionary*, new edition (2000), s.v. "excise."

but a direct tax, which would need to be apportioned. Because the term "direct tax" was not clearly defined in dictionaries, commentaries, or elsewhere (although Adam Smith had used it without defining it), the Virginians argued essentially that if the tax did not qualify as an excise, then it must be a direct tax.[15]

Whereas the Virginians pointed to dictionaries, Hamilton argued that usage was a better guide to the meaning of excise. In particular, he "suggested the utility of seeking the constitutional meaning . . . 'in the statutory language of [England], from which our Jurisprudence is derived'."[16] There it is clear, as even Hylton's counsel admitted, that if "the meaning of the word excise is to be sought in the British Statutes, it will be found to include the duty on carriages, which is there considered as an excise."[17] Similar taxes were considered excises in New England as well. Massachusetts had an annual "duties of excise" on carriages (which it instituted in 1781), as did Rhode Island, which described its annual taxes on carriages, horses, dogs, and billiard tables as "excises."[18] Irrespective of the formal definitions that appeared to limit "excises" to taxes on manufacturing for sale or on sales transactions, regular usage in England and New England showed that the practice of imposing excise taxes was considerably broader.

Since excises were more common in the Northern states at the time of the Constitution, it is likely that there was a genuine difference in how Americans understood the taxation provisions based on where they lived. When James Madison argued in the Congress that the tax was unconstitutional, Massachusetts representative Fisher Ames responded: "It was not to be wondered at if he [that is, Madison], coming from so different a part of the country, should have a different idea of this tax." Ames said that in Massachusetts, however, "this tax had been long known; and there it was called an excise."[19] At the same time, it is easy to see why the Virginians would opt for the dictionaries' definition over one determined by how the word was used in English and

[15] Charles J. Bullock, "Direct and Indirect Taxes in Economic Literature," *Political Science Quarterly* 13, 3 (September 1898): 456–9.

[16] Alexander Hamilton, "Statement of the Material Points of the Case," quoted in Goebel and Smith, *Law Practice of Alexander Hamilton*, vol. 4, p. 335.

[17] Hamilton, "Statement of the Material Points," vol. 4, pp. 351, 355.

[18] An Act Laying Certain Duties of Excise on Certain Articles therein Mentioned, for the Purpose of Paying the Interest on Government Securities, Mass. Acts 525–33 (1781); An Act Laying Duties of Excise on Certain Articles therein Described, R.I. Acts & Resolves 23–32 (1786). For the Massachusetts law, see generally Paul S. Boyer, "Borrowed Rhetoric: The Massachusetts Excise Controversy of 1754," *William and Mary Quarterly* 21, 3 (July 1964): 328–51.

[19] 4 Annals of Cong. 730 (1794).

American state statutes. As Hylton's lawyer pointed out, the issues in this case reached far beyond horses and buggies. In the South, "they possess a species of property . . . upon which, if this law stands, the whole burden of government may be exclusively laid . . . [because under] the English precedent . . . servants constitute an article in the catalogue of their excises."[20] In other words, *Hylton* was a test case to determine whether the federal government could impose an annual tax on the ownership of slaves, especially since, as Hylton's attorney argued, "an American majority exists, who might inflict [such a tax] without feeling the imposition."[21]

When the case reached the Supreme Court, Justice William Paterson concluded that the "argument on both sides turns in a circle . . . . What is the natural and common, or technical and appropriate, meaning of the words 'duty' and 'excise' is not easy to ascertain."[22] From all the evidence, he concluded that "[d]ifferent persons will annex different significations to the terms."[23] The manner in which Justice Paterson resolved this case of semantic circling is described in Chapter 7 as an example of how seeking and finding evidence of the Framers' intentions can resolve instances in which the language seems genuinely ambiguous. Identifying the will of the lawmaker in this case thus allows the Court to reach a decision based on a shared understanding of the nature of the Framers' end–means decision even when individual Framers as prominent as Hamilton and Madison had differing opinions on the clause's expected application.

THE ESTABLISHMENT CLAUSE[24]

Judging by today's voluminous Establishment Clause literature, we would expect the eighteenth-century constitutional debates to have been equally vigorous, pitting advocates for the view that religion must be "be separated from the jurisdiction of the state" against those who believed that the state's encouragement of religion would promote civic virtue and "good order."[25] That is, in fact, exactly what had happened in Virginia and Massachusetts

[20] John Taylor, *An Argument Respecting the Constitutionality of the Carriage Tax* (Richmond, 1795), p. 20 (emphasis omitted).
[21] Taylor, *An Argument*, p. 20.
[22] *Hylton*, 3 US at 176.
[23] *Hylton*, 3 US at 176.
[24] For much more along the lines of this section, see Donald L. Drakeman, *Church, State, and Original Intent* (New York: Cambridge University Press, 2010).
[25] For the first view, see Isaac Backus, *An Appeal to the Public for Religious Liberty, Against the Oppressions of the Present Day* (Boston, 1773). For the second view, see Massachusetts Constitution, 1780, in *The Sacred Rights of Conscience: Selected Readings on Religious*

when they had recently decided whether to have broad-based taxes for the support of ministers (Massachusetts) or churches (Virginia). These two states were home to a quarter of the American population (not to mention all six of its first presidents), and support for these two opposite church–state policies was divided almost exactly in half.[26] Through these lively and lengthy debates, we can see the shape and tenor of the arguments, and appreciate the degree to which citizens of both states took these church–state issues very seriously.

Thomas Jefferson was one of the leaders of the opposition to the tax in Virginia, which was very narrowly defeated. Later in life, he portrayed the conflict as "the severest contests in which I have ever been engaged."[27] Petitions from both sides flooded into the legislature, including one signed by 10 percent of the adult male residents, and an even more famous one, the "Memorial and Remonstrance Against Religious Assessments," by James Madison, which opposed a contribution of even as little as "three pence" to what he described as an establishment of religion. Ultimately, it took some clever procedural maneuvering by Madison finally to defeat the tax.[28]

After a similar degree of public disagreement and debate in the constitutional convention and the newspapers, Massachusetts ultimately ratified a constitution in 1780 that included, in Article III, a requirement that towns impose taxes for the support of "public Protestant teachers of piety, religion, and morality" in order to foster "the good order and preservation of civil government."[29] As Theophilus Parsons subsequently said, religion is necessary in a republic because it makes everyone "a better . . . parent, child, neighbor, citizen, and magistrate."[30] Parsons, who became the state's Chief Justice, was responsible for ensuring that Article III, which had not actually received sufficient votes, was deemed to be ratified along with the rest of the constitution.[31]

Liberty and Church–State Relations in the American Founding, eds. Daniel L. Dreisbach and Mark David Hall (Indianapolis: Liberty Fund, 2009). For a comparison of the attitudes of three of the first four presidents, see Vincent Phillip Muñoz, *God and the Founders: Madison, Washington, and Jefferson* (New York: Cambridge University Press, 2009).

26 Drakeman, "Which Original Meaning?," 367.

27 *The Autobiography of Thomas Jefferson, 1743–1790*, ed. Paul Leicester Ford (Philadelphia: University of Pennsylvania Press, 2005), p. 62.

28 See, generally, Thomas E. Buckley, *Church and State in Revolutionary Virginia, 1776–1787* (Charlottesville: University Press of Virginia, 1977).

29 Massachusetts Constitution, 1780, in Dreisbach and Hall, *Sacred Rights of Conscience*, p. 246.

30 *Barnes v. First Parish in Falmouth*, 6 Mass. 400, 406 (1810).

31 Samuel Eliot Morison, A *History of the Constitution of Massachusetts* (Boston: Wright and Potter, 1917), pp. 400–401. Article III had received a majority of affirmative votes, but not the two-thirds that was required.

Supreme Court justices faced with deciding whether the Establishment Clause permits prayer and Bible reading in the schools, aid to religious education, and similar issues have most often read the clause's history as if all of these important issues had been settled by the adoption of the First Amendment, and they have typically awarded the victory to the views Madison and Jefferson had previously expressed in Virginia.[32] The "Memorial and Remonstrance" petition Madison wrote during the Virginia conflict, along with "[a]ll the great instruments of the Virginia struggle," became, as Justice Wiley Rutledge put it, "the warp and woof of our Constitutional tradition."[33] Yet, at the same time, other justices and scholars have studied the identical text and historical context, and instead have come to the conclusion reached by Chief Justice Rehnquist: "The Establishment Clause did not require government neutrality between religion and irreligion nor did it prohibit the Federal government from providing nondiscriminatory aid to religion."[34]

In light of the background of these battles over church–state interactions in the states – and in the context of our own ongoing public debates and disagreements over many of the same concepts – it is tempting for interpreters to assume that the Establishment Clause was added to the Constitution to adopt a broad-based principle about how the government should relate to religion. The question is: which principle? Those favoring a strict separation of church and state find a "wall of separation" principle, while "nonpreferentialists" have read the clause in a way that allows the government to support religion as long as it does so evenhandedly. A third group has pointed to the language specifically forbidding Congress from making law *respecting* an establishment of religion, and argues that a commitment to federalism is at the heart of the Establishment Clause, one that grants jurisdiction over church–state issues exclusively to the states. To put the language of the Establishment Clause in its original semantic context, we need to start with the origins of the terms in England prior to the Constitution.

The Church By Law Established: The Linguistic Background

It is not necessary to recount Henry VIII's marital and other problems to draw attention to the King's bold (at least at the time) assertion of sovereign power over the church in the 1534 Act of Supremacy, its repeal and the brief return of

[32] See *Everson v. Bd. of Educ.*, 330 US 1 (1947); and *Abington Sch. Dist. v. Schempp*, 374 US 203 (1963).

[33] *Everson*, 330 US at 39 (Rutledge, J., dissenting).

[34] *Wallace v. Jaffree*, 472 US 38, 106 (1985).

the Catholic Church under Mary, and Elizabeth's second Act of Supremacy in 1559, "restoring to the crown the ancient jurisdiction over the state ecclesiastical and spiritual."[35] The result of placing civil power over all things ecclesiastical meant that the state would henceforth appoint the bishops and codify the Church's theological doctrines in statutes that would also specify approved modes of worship. At least by 1603, the Church of England's "Constitutions and Canons" would refer to itself as "the Church ... by law established" under the Crown, the denial of which would be grounds for excommunication.[36]

None of this statutory language kept the English Reformation free from tumult, and, in 1628, King Charles I, "Defender of the Faith and Supreme Governor of the Church," issued a Declaration in conjunction with a republication of the statutorily defined Articles of Faith by his appointed bishops. Its purpose was "for the avoiding of Diversities of Opinions" expressed "in either of our Universities," Oxford and Cambridge – especially Cambridge, where Puritanism seemed to be getting out of hand. Among other things, Charles decreed that no one "shall ... put his own sense or comment to the meaning of the [Articles of Faith], but shall take it in the literal and grammatical sense." All university faculty not "submit[ting] to it in the plain and full meaning thereof" shall be, in the King's words, "liable to our displeasure," a very meaningful threat in the era of the Star Chamber.[37] These efforts were part of a broader "crackdown against Puritanism," and, two years after this royal declaration of a theological and statutory plain meaning rule, a Puritan group established the Massachusetts Bay Colony.[38]

35 Act of Supremacy, 1558, 1 Eliz. 1, c. 1. See also Act of Uniformity, 1662, 14 Car. 2, c. 4; and *The Thirty Nine Articles of Religion, Established in the Church of England: With Expository Observations* [...], ed. William Beveridge (London, 1757).

36 "The Church of England a True and Apostolicall Church," chap. 3 in *Constitutions and Canons Ecclesiasticall: Treated upon by the Bishop of London, President of the Convocation of the Province of Canterbury, and the Rest of the Bishops and Clergie of the Said Province* (London, 1604), D2r.

37 *Articles Agreed upon by the Archbishops and Bishops of Both Provinces* [...] (London, 1629), p. 5. See generally Patrick Collinson, *The Religion of Protestants: The Church in English Society, 1559–1625* (Oxford: Clarendon Press, 1982).

38 J. David Hoeveler, *Creating the American Mind: Intellect and Politics in the Colonial Colleges* (Lanham, MD: Rowman & Littlefield, 2002), pp. 3, 18. The Puritans were not always welcome on the other side of the Atlantic either. A similar effort to eliminate troubling diversities of religious opinions came in Virginia in 1642, when the New England Puritans had sent a minister to preach there. The Virginia House of Burgesses, which, in 1619, had mandated that "[a]ll ministers shall duely read divine service, and exercise their ministerial function according to the Ecclesiastical lawes and orders of the Churche of Englande," responded with the following: "For the preservation of the puritie of doctrine and unitie of the church, It is

Multiple Meanings in America

Based on the King's English, as it were, the *Oxford English Dictionary* ("OED") provides, as one of the definitions of the noun "establishment," a summary of what the 1603 canons had described as "the church by law established": the "'establishing' by law (a church, religion, form of worship)," including in "early use, the settling or ordering in a particular manner, the regulating and upholding of the constitution and ordinances of the church recognized by the state."[39] In support of this definition, the OED cites a speech from Lord Digby in 1640: "A Man . . . that made the Establishment by Law the Measure of his Religion."[40] It is this approach to defining an "establishment of religion" that led to a statement by New Hampshire's Chief Justice Jeremiah Smith, in the 1803 case of *Muzzy v. Wilkins*, that the Granite State had no religious establishment, in spite of the provision in New Hampshire's constitution authorizing the towns to provide financial support for "public protestant teachers of piety, religion and morality." (This New Hampshire constitutional language was very similar to Article III of the 1780 Massachusetts Constitution.) "No one sect is invested with any political power much less with a monopoly of civil privileges and civil offices," wrote Justice Smith, and "[a]ll denominations are equally under the protection of the law, are equally the objects of its favor and regard, and, therefore, there is no establishment."[41]

In the same vein, Connecticut Judge Zephaniah Swift in 1796 linked the meaning of establishment to an exclusive statutory relationship between the state and a particular set of theological tenets. He concluded that Connecticut had no establishment despite a system of ecclesiastical taxes that resembled the ones in New Hampshire and Massachusetts. Swift argued that a religious establishment had only existed earlier in Connecticut's history when the law gave a "civil endorsement to the Savoy Confession of Faith."[42] The Connecticut legislature had adopted the Savoy Confession in 1708, along

enacted that all ministers whatsoever which shall reside in the collony are to be conformable to the orders and constitutions of the church of England, and the laws therein established, and not otherwise to be admitted to teach or preach publickly or privatly, And . . . all nonconformists upon notice of them shall be compelled to depart the collony with all conveniencie." William Waller Hening, *The Statutes at Large: Being a Collection of All the Laws of Virginia, from the First Session of the Legislature in the Year 1619* (Richmond, 1809), vol. 1, p. 277.

39 *Oxford English Dictionary Online*, s.v. "establishment," accessed June 15, 2018, www.oed.com/view/Entry/64536.

40 *OED Online*, s.v. "establishment."

41 William G. McLoughlin, *New England Dissent, 1630–1833: The Baptists and the Separation of Church and State* (Cambridge, MA: Harvard University Press, 1971), vol. 2, pp. 863–70.

42 McLoughlin, *New England Dissent*, vol. 2, pp. 923–4.

with "regulations in the administration of church discipline," with the proviso that doing so would not prevent churches "who soberly ... dissent from the united churches hereby established" from worshiping "according to their consciences."[43] Swift pointed out that the revision of the law in 1784 had eliminated that endorsement of the Savoy Confession, and thus ended the establishment.[44]

This is also the usage reflected in Georgetown Law Professor George W. Paschal's nineteenth-century treatise, *The Constitution of the United States Defined and Carefully Annotated*, which defines "establishment" with a quotation from Worcester's 1860 Dictionary as "a system of religion recognized and supported by the State; as the ... Established Church of England."[45] Interestingly, the much more recent 2007 edition of Webster's Dictionary employs essentially the same definition of an "established church": "church officially recognized as national institution."[46] Today, the Supreme Court could certainly choose this well-provenanced definition of an establishment of religion as the original semantic meaning, although doing so would upend much of the Establishment Clause jurisprudence of the past eighty years.

Despite these guides as to what an establishment of religion may have meant not only in the early national period but also for quite some time thereafter, the linguistic terrain at that time was considerably more complicated than the dictionaries suggest. As Thomas Curry notes: "On this matter, [Connecticut's Judge] Swift was out of touch with the religious system of his state," since "throughout the revolutionary period ... Connecticut made no bones about the fact of its Congregationalist establishment of religion."[47] Theophilus Parsons similarly saw Massachusetts' system of religious taxes as an establishment. Parsons was a leader in the 1780 Massachusetts Convention that had adopted Article III, and he later became a judge in a case involving those religious taxes. He wrote a lengthy opinion extolling the benefits of Massachusetts's establishment of religion, at just about the same time that the

43 "Act of Assembly Adopting the Saybrook Platform, Oct. 1708," in Benjamin Trumbull, *A Complete History of Connecticut: Civil and Ecclesiastical* [...] (New Haven, CT, 1818), vol. 1, pp. 486–7. On the Savoy Confession, see David A. Weir, *Early New England: A Covenanted Society* (Grand Rapids, MI: Wm. B. Eerdmans, 2005), p. 196.

44 McLoughlin, *New England Dissent*, vol. 2, pp. 923–4.

45 George W. Paschal, *The Constitution of the United States Defined and Carefully Annotated* (Washington, DC, 1868), p. 254. See Joseph E. Worcester, *Dictionary of the English Language* (Boston, 1860), s.v. "establishment."

46 *Collins Webster's Dictionary, Revised and Updated* (2007), s.v. "established church."

47 Thomas J. Curry, *The First Freedoms: Church and State in America to the Passage of the First Amendment* (New York: Oxford University Press, 1986), pp. 183–4.

Connecticut and New Hampshire courts were denying that the same system of religious taxation had created one in their states. In the 1810 Massachusetts case *Barnes v. Falmouth*, Justice Parsons took the opportunity to "consider the motives which induced this people to introduce into the constitution a religious establishment, the nature of the establishment introduced, and the rights and privileges it secured to the people, and to their [Protestant] teachers."[48] Ultimately, he concluded that "the people of Massachusetts ... adopted and patronized a religion, which, by its benign and energetic influences, might cooperate with human institutions, to promote and secure the happiness of the citizens."[49]

Parson's use of the term "establishment" to describe the taxes that allowed the state to "patronize ... a religion," coincided with the usage James Madison had employed in his "Memorial and Remonstrance Against Religious Assessments." Not all Virginians agreed with Madison's broad definition, however. In his edition of Blackstone's *Commentaries*, St. George Tucker took the more traditional route: "a civil establishment of a particular mode of religion ... is, where a predominant sect enjoys exclusive advantages, and makes the encouragement of its own mode of faith and worship a part of the constitution of the state."[50] On the definitional question, both Madison and Parsons affirmed what Swift and Smith had denied, which is that a general assessment form of religious tax constituted an establishment of religion.

This exact definitional point had been actively debated in the Massachusetts newspapers when the adoption of Article III was under consideration, since it was essentially codifying the same town-based approach to religious taxes that had been in place for a long time. Isaac Backus, a leading Baptist opposed to the taxes, had called the Massachusetts approach to funding public Protestant teachers of religion an establishment of religion.[51] In response, an anonymous writer adopting the name "Hieronymus" scoffed that "Backus ... displayed 'his ignorance' in defining a religious establishment

[48] *Barnes*, 6 Mass. at 404.

[49] *Barnes*, 6 Mass. at 406.

[50] St. George Tucker, "Note G" of the appendix to *Blackstone's Commentaries: With Notes of Reference, to the Constitution and Laws, of the Federal Government of the United States; and of the Commonwealth of Virginia*, ed. St. George Tucker (Philadelphia, 1803), vol. 2, p. 7.

[51] McLoughlin, *New England Dissent*, vol. 1, p. 615. McLoughlin notes that Hieronymus was answering "Backus's tract, Government and Liberty Described." McLoughlin, vol. 1, p. 614. Other influential Baptists agreed. Curry notes that, "In 1790 John Leland specifically stated that 'a general assessment (forcing all to pay some preachers) amounts to an establishment.'" Thomas John Curry, "The First Freedoms: The Development of the Concepts of Religion and Establishment" (PhD diss., Claremont Graduate School, 1983), 698.

simply in terms of religious taxation,"[52] whereas Hieronymus was certain that a "religious establishment by law is the establishment of a particular mode of worshipping God, with rites and ceremonies peculiar to such mode, from which the people are not suffered to vary."[53] In a separate letter, Hieronymus reiterated: "I am not able to find anything that has the appearance of establishment. All the various denominations of Protestants are treated alike."[54] Pursuing the same line of argument that Connecticut's Judge Swift would adopt, he admitted that Massachusetts had an establishment in the past – "when the state established the Cambridge Platform as the creed of the colony" – but, "since ... 1692 the Congregational churches had been disestablished."[55] John Adams, who, together with his second cousin Samuel, drafted much of the 1780 Constitution, may have best summarized the conflicting usages of the term in Massachusetts when he hailed the state's laws as "the most mild and equitable establishment of religion that was known in the world, if indeed they could be called an establishment."[56]

Taken together, this evidence of how the term "establishment of religion" appeared in prominent public documents – petitions, pamphlets, judicial opinions, legal commentaries, and the like – points in multiple directions. Michael McConnell argues that "virtually every American – and certainly every educated lawyer or statesman – knew from experience what those words meant."[57] These examples show that McConnell is right in the sense that they had strong views about what "establishment of religion" meant, but that does not mean that they all shared the same understanding. Nondenominational religious taxes were an establishment for Parsons, who celebrated them, as well as for both Madison and Backus, who did not. Yet only a formal, exclusive state church with statutorily defined rites and creed would constitute an establishment for judges Smith and Swift, as well as Hieronymus and St. George Tucker.

In looking only at the evidence relating to the last four words of the Establishment Clause ("an establishment of religion"), a court seeking the original public meaning could reach two very different conclusions.

52 McLoughlin, vol. 1, p. 615.

53 McLoughlin, vol. 1, p. 614.

54 McLoughlin, vol. 1, p. 616.

55 McLoughlin, vol. 1, pp. 616–17. On the Cambridge Platform, see Weir, *Early New England*, p. 195.

56 Quoted in Thomas J. Curry, *First Freedoms*, p. 131. See John Witte Jr., "'A Most Mild and Equitable Establishment of Religion': John Adams and the Massachusetts Experiment," *Journal of Church and State* 41, 2 (Spring 1999): 213–52.

57 Michael W. McConnell, "Establishment and Disestablishment at the Founding, Part I: Establishment of Religion," *William and Mary Law Review* 44, 5 (2003): 2107.

Following Madison's "Memorial and Remonstrance," which is, in fact, what the Supreme Court has done most often, any governmental financial support for religion, even if it were done in an evenhanded, nonpreferential way, would constitute an establishment. As Justice Hugo Black wrote in the Court's opinion in the landmark *Everson* case: "The 'establishment of religion' clause of the First Amendment means at least this: Neither a state nor the Federal Government can set up a church. Neither can pass laws which aid one religion, aid all religions, or prefer one religion over another .... No tax in any amount, large or small, can be levied to support any religious activities or institutions."[58] Such a definition would mean that New Hampshire and Connecticut would have the kinds of religious establishment identified in the First Amendment's Establishment Clause, even though the courts in those states had reached the opposite conclusion, and the definitions to which those judges pointed are well supported by multiple examples of historical usage in public documents at the time of the Founding. Meanwhile, it is much more difficult to find eighteenth-century support for the more expansive definition adopted by Justice Black. When it comes to finding the original public meaning, it is not clear – at least from a methodological point of view – that older usages should necessarily be privileged over more recent ones if both were regularly employed in public discourse at the time of ratification, which is certainly the case for these various definitions of "establishment of religion."

What Does "Respecting" Add to the Clause?

So far, just from the examples of word usage already described, we cannot tell from evidence supporting the strongest candidates for semantic meaning whether nonpreferential tax support for religion would constitute an establishment of religion, and there are even more complexities to come. What Congress is actually forbidden to do is to make a law "respecting an establishment of religion." The word "respecting" could perform three different functions, at least two of which have substantial definitional support from Founding Era word usage. The first possibility is that "respecting" somehow enlarges the meaning of establishment. As Phillip Muñoz observes, "Justice Rutledge in *Everson* and Justices John Paul Stevens and Souter, more recently, have interpreted the First Amendment's words '*respecting an* establishment' to mean that the government may not make any law remotely resembling or

[58] *Everson*, 330 US at 15–16. Interestingly, Justice Black here has adopted, almost verbatim, language from historian Charles Beard. Charles A. Beard, *The Republic* (New York: Viking Press, 1943), p. 165. See also Drakeman, *Church, State, and Original Intent*, p. 118.

tending towards an establishment."[59] This definition lacks Founding Era support, however. I have found it difficult to locate eighteenth-century sources using "respecting" essentially as a synonym for "tending towards." In a review of twenty examples of the word "respecting" in a database of American publications between 1750 and 1770, the only use of the word that I found was as a synonym for "regarding" or "on the subject of."[60]

There are still two possible remaining functions for "respecting" to play, and each relies only on the well-documented definition of "on the subject of."[61] One is that the Congress is prohibited from making laws regarding a nationally established religion. That is, Congress will not create whatever it is that we have decided constitutes a religious establishment. Perhaps that means prohibiting a formal Church of England style of establishment, or maybe it refers to any "three pence" allocated by Congress in support of religion – that definitional question remains open, as discussed already.

The other possible reading of "respecting" has been proposed by several scholars, including Phillip Muñoz, who has argued: "The key to unlocking the meaning of the Establishment Clause lies in understanding the words 'respecting an'," which he reads as making the concept of federalism in church–state matters the central theme of the clause.[62] Muñoz thus introduces another potential principle in the Establishment Clause – that is, the general concept of federalism found throughout the Constitution was specifically enhanced in the First Amendment by prohibiting Congress from making laws "respecting an establishment of religion," including any law that might affect religious establishments in the various states. Justice Clarence Thomas focused on this

59 Vincent Phillip Muñoz, "Block that Metaphor," review of *Church, State, and Original Intent*, by Donald L. Drakeman, *Claremont Review of Books* 10, 4 (Fall 2010): 51.

60 Drakeman, *Church, State and Original Intent*, p. 262. John Witte has collected dictionary definitions in John Witte Jr., *God's Joust, God's Justice: Law and Religion in the Western Tradition* (Grand Rapids, MI: Wm. B. Eerdmans, 2006), pp. 196–7. Later in life, after his presidency, James Madison wrote a few unpublished notes, which scholars now call the Detached Memoranda, in which he said, "The Constitution of the U.S. forbids everything like an establishment of a national religion." He was recanting his earlier support of chaplains and national days of prayer. Not only were these notes unpublished, but he did not link his conclusion about "everything like" to the use of the word "respecting." Elizabeth Fleet, "Madison's 'Detached Memoranda,'" *William and Mary Quarterly* 3, 4 (October 1946): 534–68.

61 Webster, *An American Dictionary* (1828), s.v. "respecting." "Respecting: regarding; having regard to; relating to." The *OED* defines "respecting" as "with reference or regard to," citing, among others, Thomas Paine's letter to the Abbé Raynal. *Oxford English Dictionary Online*, s. v. "respecting," accessed November 6, 2017, www.oed.com/view/Entry/275489.

62 Vincent Phillip Muñoz, "The Original Meaning of the Establishment Clause and the Impossibility of its Incorporation," *University of Pennsylvania Journal of Constitutional Law* 8, 4 (August 2006): 630.

interpretation of the Establishment Clause in *Town of Greece v. Galloway* (2014), where he concluded: "Congress could not interfere with state establishments, notwithstanding any argument that could be made … under the Necessary and Proper Clause." He argued that, because "the relationship between church and state in the fledgling republic was far from settled at the time of ratification," such a "lack of consensus … suggests that the First Amendment was simply agnostic on the subject of state establishments." Therefore, deciding whether "to establish or disestablish religion was reserved to the States." His focus on the importance of the federalism principle led him to say that the clause only "*probably* prohibits Congress from establishing a national religion."[63]

Of the three candidates for the original public meaning of "respecting" in the Establishment Clause, only the one chosen most often by the Supreme Court – "respecting" as an expander or amplifier of the term "establishment of religion" – is hard to justify in light of the evidence from eighteenth-century American linguistic usage. But, after discarding that one (at least for the sake of argument), it is virtually impossible to decide between the other two, both of which employ the same definition of "relating to." Since there are also two well-supported definitions of the phrase "establishment of religion," we are left with a two-by-two matrix: four equally good original public meanings of the text (Table 5.1).

All four of these possibilities are well-supported by documentary evidence of the usage of the words of the Establishment Clause in context – that is, how these words were being used at that time by knowledgeable speakers of the language who were talking about the relationship of church and state. Moreover, all four represent potentially rational policy choices in light of well-known church–state issues of the time. Yet, they point to different answers to constitutional questions under a provision of the Bill of Rights that has been responsible for many, many Supreme Court cases.

Once again, as with the tax clauses, seeking the intentions of the Framers in the debates in the First Congress can point with considerable clarity to a shared understanding of the end–means decision made by the Framers. That analysis is found in Chapter 7, but first it is important to consider whether

[63] *Town of Greece v. Galloway*, 572 US 1, 1 (2014) (emphasis added). The opinion references Muñoz, "Original Meaning," 605. *Town of Greece*, 572 US at 3. For additional scholarly support for this reading of the clause, see Steven D. Smith, "The Jurisdictional Establishment Clause: A Reappraisal," *Notre Dame Law Review* 81, 5 (2006): 1843–94; Steven D. Smith, *Foreordained Failure: The Quest for a Constitutional Principle of Religious Freedom* (New York: Oxford University Press, 1995); and Akhil Reed Amar, *The Bill of Rights: Creation and Reconstruction* (New Haven, CT: Yale University Press, 1998), pp. 33–42.

TABLE 5.1 *The establishment clause and the semantic summing problem*[64]

	Narrow reading of "**establishment**" No established church	**Broad** reading of "**establishment**" No public funding of religion
National reading of "**respecting**"	Congress is prohibited from making laws relating to a formal national church with statutes specifying the official rites and doctrines The clause would not relate to any other federal interaction with religion The clause would have nothing to do with any church–state activities in the states	Congress is prohibited from making laws providing broad-based tax support for religion (or, a fortiori, setting up a national church) This reading would simply be unclear as to whether other federal activities in support of churches other than taxes would constitute an establishment of religion, although a reasonable position would be to say that, if Americans were divided between two specific definitions, it would be difficult to turn this into as strict a separationist view as the Court has taken in some cases
Federal reading of "**respecting**"	Congress is prohibited from making laws on the subject of formal Church of England- style establishments in the states, and presumably, Congress could not create a national church. (While Justice Thomas' use of the word "probably" suggests that the clause may have been so single-mindedly animated by a commitment to federalism that it would have no applicability to federal church–state activities, that reading would be hard to reach from an exclusive focus on the original textual meaning)	Congress is prohibited from making laws on the subject of broad-based religious taxes in the states, and, presumably, by the federal government as well

[64] I would like to thank Lynn Uzzell for this table, and for suggesting that it would show the complexity of multiple meanings better than a series of very long sentences.

new technological tools can resolve these semantic challenges. The preceding analysis of the meaning of an establishment of religion was based on public documents to which church–state constitutional scholars have had ready access for a long time. That well-trod research pathway has recently been augmented by the digital search tools associated with the field of corpus linguistics.[65] The recent creation of a Corpus of Founding Era American English (COFEA), combined with modern digital searches and data analysis, offers the promise of a data-driven solution to these kinds of semantic issues. Unfortunately, as discussed in the next chapter, computer-aided digital searches will not resolve the conundrum of having four, or even two, viable candidates for the original meaning. But a Framer-focused search for the rationale and meaning can provide the necessary clarity, as seen in Chapter 7.

65 See Thomas R. Lee and James C. Phillips, "Data-Driven Originalism," *University of Pennsylvania Law Review* 167, 2 (January 2019): 261–335. See also James C. Phillips, Daniel M. Ortner, and Thomas R. Lee, "Corpus Linguistics and Original Public Meaning: A New Tool to Make Originalism More Empirical," *Yale Law Journal Forum* 126, 101 (May 2016): 23, where they write: "We cannot hope to accurately reconstruct the hypothetical, objective, reasonably well-informed reader in the United States in 1788 unless we look at a host of examples of the English language produced by ordinary, reasonably well-informed Americans of that time."

6

Is Corpus Linguistics Better than Flipping a Coin?

Chapter 5 described a semantic summing problem that can arise as interpreters search for the objective public meaning of constitutional terms. Paralleling the summing problem long associated with identifying a single intention of a multimember lawmaking body, the semantic summing problem appears when there are competing potential meanings for constitutional words or phrases. This chapter will address the question of whether the new digital tools of corpus linguistics have the potential to provide scientific solutions to disputes over the objective public meaning of constitutional provisions.

"Originalism is on the cusp of its own Big Data revolution," declares Lee Strang, noting that "[f]or the first time, both a body of data of the Constitution's original meaning and the technology to utilize that data are becoming available."[1] Legal scholars started this revolution by borrowing a fascinating tool from their colleagues in language, literature, and history – large digital compendia of written texts associated with the field of corpus linguistics[2] – with the aim of using targeted digital searches to discover the meaning of constitutional terms in the Founding Era. Rather than relying on the limited information available in the few relevant dictionaries, or going through the painstaking process of finding and reading the statutes, legislative debates, newspapers, legal cases, novels, almanacs, and other materials

[1] Lee J. Strang, "How Big Data Can Increase Originalism's Methodological Rigor: Using Corpus Linguistics to Reveal Original Language Conventions," *UC Davis Law Review* 50, 3 (February 2017): 1184.

[2] See Thomas R. Lee and James C. Phillips, "Data-Driven Originalism," *University of Pennsylvania Law Review* 167, 2 (January 2019): 261–335. See also James C. Phillips, Daniel M. Ortner, and Thomas R. Lee, "Corpus Linguistics and Original Public Meaning: A New Tool to Make Originalism More Empirical," *Yale Law Journal Forum* 126, 101 (May 2016): 21–32.

making up the documentary record of the latter half of eighteenth-century America, scholars can perform computer searches in databases consisting of thousands of texts and millions of words. Originalism now has the potential to be "data-driven,"[3] "scientific,"[4] "rigorous," and "empirical."[5]

With these tools, Strang argues that it should be possible – or at least far more possible than ever before – to accurately identify "the [constitutional] text's conventional meaning at the time of ratification."[6] Doing so is valuable because "[o]riginal meaning originalism's interpretive core is language conventions."[7] Utah Supreme Court Justice Thomas R. Lee and colleagues also emphasize the importance of a Big Data approach to interpretation, saying: "We cannot hope to accurately reconstruct the hypothetical, objective, reasonably well-informed reader in the United States in 1788 unless we look at a host of examples of the English language produced by ordinary, reasonably well-informed Americans of that time."[8] Along the same lines, Lawrence Solum, in his recent turn towards developing an originalist methodology, includes corpus linguistics as one of the three independent approaches comprising the "triangulation" method of identifying original public meaning, along with analyzing the constitutional record and immersion "in the linguistic and conceptual world of the authors and readers of the constitutional provision being studied."[9]

Strang is certainly right about two things: we have digitized collections of texts representing language use in the constitutional era, and the technology to access them on a word-by-word basis. The remaining essential questions are whether those collections are genuinely representative, and whether we have the necessary data analysis tools to make sense of all of the resulting information in a way that clearly points towards an accurate understanding of the objective meaning of the text. As Strang observes, there are some cases where the technological approach may not eliminate the possibility of

3 Lee and Phillips, "Data-Driven Originalism," 261.

4 Clark D. Cunningham and Jesse Egbert, "Scientific Methods for Analyzing Original Meaning: Corpus Linguistics and the Emoluments Clauses," Georgia State University College of Law, Legal Studies Research Paper, No. 2019–02 (February 2019), https://ssrn.com/abstract=3321438.

5 Phillips, Ortner, and Lee, "Corpus Linguistics," 21.

6 Strang, "Big Data," 1188.

7 Strang, 1189. He expands this point as follows: "The language conventions contemporary with the Framing and Ratification are the building blocks of original meaning. Computer-assisted research permits – in a way unassisted techniques do not – the relatively easy and relatively accurate recovery of these language conventions." Strang, 1189.

8 Phillips, Ortner, and Lee, "Corpus Linguistics," 23.

9 Lawrence B. Solum, "Triangulating Public Meaning: Corpus Linguistics, Immersion, and the Constitutional Record," *Brigham Young University Law Review*, 6 (2017): 1621.

inaccuracy,[10] and whether tools of corpus linguistics can deliver a single clear original public meaning will need to be evaluated on a clause-by-clause basis.

In practice, corpus linguistics searches for the Constitution's original meaning have often sought to select one of two possible meanings. Is "religion" in the First Amendment limited to theism or not?[11] Are the terms "commerce"[12] and "emoluments"[13] broad or narrow? The goal has been to determine the answer objectively and empirically through a Big Data analysis of language use in the Founding Era. For the sake of argument, and to highlight the key role of assumptions in applying this methodology to constitutional interpretation, I will propose an alternative approach to resolving lawsuits that has the advantage of being equally or more objective, while also being faster, cheaper, and a great deal less complicated: flipping a coin, for which the odds of an accurate answer to these kinds of binary questions is 50 percent. Moreover, as with other approaches to the search for original meaning, coin flipping would go a long way towards addressing one of the jurisprudential issues frequently cited by advocates of originalism – that is, the need to restrain judges from making decisions based on their own preferences. Despite its numerous advantages, coin flipping in cases of constitutional interpretation is

[10] In particular, he mentions "four situations: (1) the facets of the originalist interpretative process to which CART [computer-assisted research techniques] is inapplicable; (2) when CART's necessary conditions do not occur; (3) human error utilizing CART; and (4) the word or phrase was new, or the word or phrase's conventional meaning was in flux." Strang, "Big Data," 1235. For a critique of the use of corpus linguistics in legal interpretation, see, for example, John S. Ehrett, "Against Corpus Linguistics," *Georgetown Law Journal Online* 108 (Spring 2019): 50–73. On the subject of when it does and does not make sense, see Neal Goldfarb, "Corpus Linguistics in Legal Interpretation: When Is It (In)appropriate?" (lecture, BYU Law School, Provo, UT, February 6–8, 2019), https://papers.ssrn.com/sol3/papers.cfm?abstract_id=3333512. For a history of the use of linguistics in legal interpretation and some proposed guidelines, see Lawrence M. Solan, "Legal Linguistics in the US: Looking Back, Looking Ahead," Brooklyn Law School, Legal Studies Paper, No. 609 (July 2019), https://papers.ssrn.com/sol3/papers.cfm?abstract_id=3428489. See also Stephen C. Mouritsen, "Corpus Linguistics in Legal Interpretation: An Evolving Interpretive Framework," *International Journal of Language and Law* 6 (2017): 67–89; and Lawrence M. Solan and Tammy Gales, "Corpus Linguistics as a Tool in Legal Interpretation," *Brigham Young University Law Review*, 6 (2017): 1311–57.

[11] See Lee J. Strang, "The Original Meaning of 'Religion' in the First Amendment: A Test Case of Originalism's Utilization of Corpus Linguistics," *Brigham Young University Law Review*, 6 (2017): 1683–750.

[12] Randy E. Barnett, "New Evidence of the Original Meaning of the Commerce Clause," *Arkansas Law Review* 55, 4 (2003): 857–9.

[13] Cunningham and Egbert, "Scientific Methods," 16; and James Cleith Phillips and Sara White, "The Meaning of the Three Emoluments Clauses in the U.S. Constitution: A Corpus Linguistic Analysis of American English from 1760–1799," *South Texas Law Review* 59, 2 (Winter 2017): 191.

normatively weak compared to the promise of scientifically based results. It is hard to imagine that an interpretive theory would be adopted by the Supreme Court if cases involving the interpretation of texts with contested original meanings would be decided by a coin toss, or by any other method that could not make a better claim of accuracy than randomly being right half the time.

Is corpus linguistics likely to be accurate more than half the time? This chapter will show that, in a number of important ways, corpus linguistics may not be up to the assigned task (at least yet), despite the sophisticated constitutional analyses that have appeared so far. The problems are not rooted in the impressive research done by scholars to date, but in the historical and methodological assumptions they are making when they set out to use corpus linguistics databases for the purpose of constitutional interpretation.

THE KEY METHODOLOGICAL QUESTIONS

The central issues for those employing corpus linguistics as a tool for constitutional interpretation are the ones faced by everyone who tries to put data to work: how to set up the experiment/databases, what questions to ask, and how to analyze the resulting data, all with the goal of generating accurate, reliable, and useful information. This challenge – shared by experimental physicists, medical researchers overseeing clinical trials, and, now, constitutional theorists – requires careful attention at each stage to a series of questions about how the data was collected, how representative it is, how accurate our understanding of that data is, and what should count as a meaningful result.[14] In considering whether the tools of corpus linguistics are appropriate for addressing questions of constitutional interpretation, the specific issues include:

1. Are the documents in the database fairly representative of language use by the public at the time of the Constitution? Note that answering this question requires originalism theory to defend a particular definition of the "public." Is it the usage attributable, for example, to the specific group of people who served as ratifiers, or perhaps to how an average American citizen/voter/resident used the words? Alternatively, some originalists have suggested that we should identify how a hypothetical ratifier having a certain level of education or knowledge of the law or politics would

[14] There is a large literature addressing these issues in numerous fields. For a critical analysis, see Danah Boyd and Kate Crawford, "Critical Questions for Big Data: Provocations for a Cultural, Technological, and Scholarly Phenomenon," *Information, Communication & Society* 15, 5 (June 2012): 662–79.

have understood various constitutional terms.[15] Different databases, or at least different approaches to data analysis, may be necessary depending on who counts as the "public."

2. Has the search process been properly designed to identify all of the relevant uses of the language, and to exclude irrelevant uses? Note that answering this question requires the interpreter to make a cogent case for defining "relevant" and to design a search method based on the appropriate inclusion and exclusion criteria.
3. Has the interpreter (or, as seems to be the case in several corpus linguistics constitutional searches to date, the interpreter's research assistants), in reviewing and analyzing the examples of language use resulting from the search, correctly assigned a meaning to each use? At this critical step, note the risks of inadvertently introducing confirmation bias into the process. Initiating the research to answer a specific twenty-first-century legal question flowing from a legal environment defined by current Supreme Court doctrine and precedents may frame the issue in a manner that is quite unlike the eighteenth-century context.
4. Has the interpreter correctly interpreted the results to determine the objective public meaning? Note that addressing this issue requires a sound theory supporting a method for selecting only one of two or more competing meanings if more than one usage has been identified in the dataset.

Getting the correct answer to all of these questions is not impossible, but it is very hard, and it asks researchers to take methodological issues very seriously.[16]

IS THE DATABASE REPRESENTATIVE?

With an eye specifically towards constitutional cases, Brigham Young University has assembled the "Corpus of Founding-Era American English," or COFEA, covering written materials from 1760 to 1799.[17] As of this writing,

[15] See, for example, Vasan Kesavan and Michael Stokes Paulsen, "The Interpretive Force of the Constitution's Secret Drafting History," *Georgetown Law Journal* 91, 6 (August 2003): 1162. To avoid the temptation of equating that well-informed hypothetical ratifier with a twenty-first-century lawyer or law professor, it will be important to take into account literacy rates, the nature of eighteenth-century education, and the like.

[16] Among other things these questions encompass the "scientific standards of *generalizability*, *reliability*, and *validity*" cited in Cunningham and Egbert, "Scientific Methods," 6 (original emphasis).

[17] Corpus of Founding Era American English (COFEA), accessed September 13, 2019, https://lcl.byu.edu/projects/cofea/.

COFEA contains over 135 million words from 126,393 texts from the American Founding Era.[18] COFEA is essentially a compendium of compendia. Its sources have been available in searchable databases in the past, but this is the first time they have been assembled as a group and marketed as a Founding-Era repository of meaning that could be useful for constitutional interpretation.[19] Version 3.00, built on February 4, 2019, relies heavily on three principal sources of documents: the National Archives' Founders Online, Evans Early American Imprints, and HeinOnline's collection of legal treatises and orders. These three sources provide COFEA with over 90 percent of its words and texts.[20] The remainder comes from Farrand's *Records of the Federal Convention of 1787*, the United States Statutes at Large, and Elliot's *Debates in the Several State Conventions on the Adoption of the Federal Constitution*.

The nature of the documents in COFEA raises the question of whether it offers researchers a fair picture of language use in Founding-Era America or is better understood as a source for determining how a subset of elites communicated. (As noted earlier, whether the goal of the corpus linguistics exercise is to identify the usage patterns of one group of Americans or another is an issue for originalism theory that has become considerably more important in the context of corpus linguistics analyses.) Almost 30 percent of the words in the COFEA come from the Founders Online collection of the papers of just six people: the first four presidents – George Washington, John Adams, Thomas Jefferson, and James Madison – along with Benjamin Franklin and Alexander Hamilton. The large percentage of documents from these papers tends to skew the collection strongly towards elite communication patterns and word use.[21] Not only were four of these Founders college graduates, a rarity in an era in

[18] BYU Law & Corpus Linguistics, accessed August 27, 2019, https://lawcorpus.byu.edu. For a useful summary of resources, see Corpora of Historical English (1500s–Early/Mid 1900s), http://davies-linguistics.byu.edu/personal/histengcorp.htm. Brigham Young University has also assembled COEME, the Corpus of Early Modern English, covering texts written by authors in several countries and centuries prior to the nineteenth century. COEME contains over a billion words from 40,300 texts written during the 325-year period between 1475 and 1800.

[19] Corpus of Founding Era American English (COFEA), accessed September 13, 2019, https://lcl.byu.edu/projects/cofea/.

[20] Corpus of Founding Era American English (COFEA), accessed September 13, 2019, https://lcl.byu.edu/projects/cofea/.

[21] Since these collections include both outgoing and incoming letters, an analysis of the authors of the incoming letters would be a valuable exercise in the effort to determine the degree to which the Founders Online collection represents more than how these six people used the language. See, generally, National Archives and Records Administration, *The Founders Online: Open Access to the Papers of America's Founding Era; A Report to Congress* (Washington, DC: National Archives and Records Administration, 2008).

which competence in Latin and Greek was a requirement for admission, but the remaining two, George Washington and Benjamin Franklin, were far from being linguistically representative of the ordinary Americans whose rustic language use was the object of humor and scorn in England.[22] Similarly, the legal documents in HeinOnline and the US Statutes at Large were typically written by lawyers and public officials, and both Farrand's *Records of the Convention* and Elliot's ratification debates feature records generated by legal and political elites.

This focus on elite communication is a critical methodological issue. Historians have pointed out that the argument that ordinary people and elites might have a different understanding of the Constitution is as old as the Constitution itself. Saul Cornell observes that whether the Constitution was an elite document to be interpreted primarily by lawyers, or a "people's constitution," was a matter of great contention in the ratification debates.[23] Along similar lines, Jack Rakove worries about the "poverty of public meaning originalism," and points to the case of the ordinary Founding-Era citizen, whom he calls "Joe the Ploughman" (after the 2008 presidential campaign reference to "Joe the Plumber").[24]

Beyond these concerns about whether COFEA includes a reasonable representation of ordinary language use, it is not even clear that the COFEA collection fully represents elite American speech patterns. The 30 percent of the corpus derived from the Founders Online leaves out the Founders from North Carolina, South Carolina, Maryland, and Georgia in the South; New Jersey and Delaware in the middle colonies; and Connecticut, New Hampshire, and Rhode Island in New England.[25] At the same time, the New York, Massachusetts, and Pennsylvania Founders – Hamilton, Adams, and Franklin – were Eastern linguistic elites whose language use may have been substantially different than that of the agricultural and frontier settlers in

[22] "An English journalist ill-naturedly had warned as early as 1787 that the American language was already so different from the English that English dictionaries in the future might as well ignore Americanisms: 'If this is true, let us leave the inventors of this motley gibberish to make a Dictionary for themselves'." Peter Martin, *The Dictionary Wars: The American Fight over the English Language* (Princeton, NJ: Princeton University Press, 2019), p. 20.

[23] Saul Cornell, "The People's Constitution vs. The Lawyer's Constitution: Popular Constitutionalism and the Original Debate over Originalism," *Yale Journal of Law and the Humanities* 23, 2 (Summer 2011): 295–337.

[24] Jack N. Rakove, "Joe the Ploughman Reads the Constitution: Or, the Poverty of Public Meaning Originalism," *San Diego Law Review* 48, 2 (May–June 2011): 575–600.

[25] To the extent that the Founders Online collection includes inbound letters from residents of other states, it may reflect somewhat broader coverage than just the writings of six men. At the same time, however, inbound letters from foreign writers will make it more difficult to see the collection as representing just American patterns of speech and word use.

the western portions of their states. Even in Virginia, where Washington, Madison, and Jefferson owned large farms, it is not clear that these educated and sophisticated political leaders communicated in the same ways as their considerably less cosmopolitan agrarian and frontier neighbors.

Regional variations in language use were responsible for the Supreme Court's first opportunity to rule on the constitutionality of a federal statute. As Chapter 5 explained, the subject was an annual tax on the ownership of carriages, and the question was whether it was properly considered an "excise" tax, and, therefore, exempt from the apportionment required for direct taxes by Article I. In 1794, when Congress debated whether to adopt the tax, Virginia congressmen John Nicholas and James Madison argued that it was unconstitutional on the grounds that taxes on the ownership of property were direct taxes whereas indirect taxes such as excises related only to transactions involving the sale of goods.[26] Fisher Ames of Massachusetts disagreed, and he explained the regional linguistic roots of the dispute, saying, "[I]t was not to be wondered at if he [Madison], coming from so different a part of the country, should have a different idea of this tax."[27] In Massachusetts, he reported, "this [type of] tax had been long known; and there it was called an excise."[28] The Supreme Court ultimately upheld the tax, but Justice Paterson noted that, because both parties had presented strong evidence of different usages, "the [semantic] argument on both sides turns in a circle," and, as a result, "the natural and common ... meaning of the words 'duty' and 'excise,' ... is not easy to ascertain."[29] Corpus linguistics databases will need to demonstrate that they are geographically and demographically broad enough to encompass these kinds of regional variations.

The portion of COFEA most likely to compensate for the focus on just a handful of famous Founders is Evans Early American Imprints. Because that collection includes pamphlets, books, broadsides, and other types of texts, it would seem to reach more broadly into common patterns of American communication. Yet very few Americans wrote any of the published materials, which were typically the product of educated elites. Using Evans Imprints, Mary Ann Yodelis analyzed printed materials published in Boston between 1763 and 1775 and determined that religious printing, including lengthy sermons and collections of the psalms, constituted over half of all printed

26 4 Annals of Cong. 630–730 (1794).

27 4 Annals of Cong. 730 (1794).

28 4 Annals of Cong. 730 (1794).

29 *Hylton v. United States*, 3 US 171, 176 (1796). In the end, Justice Paterson based his decision on the Framers' intentions. Joel Alicea and Donald L. Drakeman, "The Limits of New Originalism," *University of Pennsylvania Journal of Constitutional Law* 15 (April 2013): 1183-5.

material, not all of which was written by people living in America, with the rest being primarily government documents, such as judicial opinions and legislative reports.[30] There were also some advertisements, editorials, and the like, but they constituted a small portion of the documents that were printed at the time. As a result, the Evans portion of COFEA does not extend the corpus's reach substantially beyond some aspects of late eighteenth-century word usage by highly educated religious and political elites, some of whom may never have set foot in North America. In fact, of the five largest documents in the Evans collection that were published during the years covered by COFEA (representing over 3.6 million words), only one was written by an American – Yale-educated minister and geographer, Jedidiah Morse.[31] The rest included works by an English clergyman; a first-century Jewish historian, whose book was written in Greek and translated by an Englishman; a Scottish minister; and a British politician.[32]

These issues about whether the database is broadly representative of language use at the time of the Constitution can be addressed. COFEA will undoubtedly expand over the years as more constitutional era resources are digitized. At each stage of that corpus development, researchers will need to be aware of the evolving nature of the materials and the degree to which they do, or do not, represent broader patterns of language use. At present, the net effect of COFEA's substantial reliance on the available digital collections of six Founders plus the materials in Evans Imprints is that constitutional scholars studying Founding-Era language use have to worry about the "lamppost problem" or "streetlight effect" often cited in the social sciences – that is, whether the search is rendered less accurate because of the tendency to look for answers where it is easiest to see, but not necessarily where the answers are most likely to be.[33] Finally, to determine whether COFEA genuinely represents public meaning, originalism theorists need to decide exactly who is the "public," and then researchers need to consider in detail whether COFEA fully represents the conventional language patterns of that group.

[30] Mary Ann Yodelis, "Who Paid the Piper? Publishing Economics in Boston, 1763–1775," *Journalism Monographs* 38 (February 1975): 8.

[31] Jedidiah Morse, *The American Universal Geography* [...], vol. 1 (Boston, 1793).

[32] John Foxe, *The New and Complete Book of Martyrs* [...], vol. 1 (New York, 1794); Flavius Josephus, *The Whole, Genuine, and Complete Works of Flavius Josephus* [...], trans. George Henry Maynard (New York, 1792); William Robertson, *The History of the Reign of Charles the Fifth* [...], vol. 1 (Philadelphia, 1770); and J[ames] Burgh, *Political Disquisitions* [...], vol. 1 (Philadelphia, 1775).

[33] See, for instance, Abraham Kaplan, *The Conduct of Inquiry: Methodology for Behavioral Science* (New York: Routledge, 2017).

DOES THE SEARCH PROCESS CAPTURE THE RIGHT INFORMATION?

After these historical and theoretical issues have been satisfactorily resolved, the real work begins: identifying the meaning of a word or phrase based on the computer search results. The search parameters must be designed to pick up alternate eighteenth-century spellings, which will require either prior knowledge of (or guesses about) likely variations, as well as plurals and other morphological forms associated with various parts of speech. That is the easy part. The hard part is the fact that, in the constitutional corpus linguistics literature to date, such a search has returned at least dozens,[34] if not hundreds[35] or thousands,[36] of "hits," that is, examples of the use of the term in the database. Whether there are only a few or many "hits" generates different methodological challenges. If the search identifies only a few examples of use, the researcher will need to be concerned about whether the search somehow missed instances of the word, and whether a handful of examples is sufficient to make a strong definitional case.

Perhaps more likely than cases where the constitutional term is rarely found in COFEA will be the research exercises yielding a very large number of hits, thus creating a significant workload for the researchers who will have to identify the meaning, in its relevant context, for each of the occurrences. At this point, the interpreter (and/or research assistants) can narrow the search to obtain what would seem to be the most relevant information, such as by looking for "collocates" – in other words, those cases where the term, say, "establishment," is found within a specified number of words of another potentially relevant word, such as "religion." Such a collocation search may eliminate uses relating to the establishment of a bank, but doing so can inadvertently bias the search in the direction of the interpreter's basic twenty-first-century question. There is no a priori linguistic reason that the use of the word "establishment" in the eighteenth century was different based on whether a bank or a religion were being established. To employ search parameters tending to exclude uses relating to banks, the interpreter has made the assumption that examples of the use of the word "establishment" in connection with a bank offer no relevant information about the use of the same word in the context of religion. Yet the only way to know if that assumption is correct is to do the linguistic analysis that has been excluded by the search criteria. Using collocation as a way to reduce the total number of

[34] Stephanie H. Barclay, Brady Earley, and Annika Boone, "Original Meaning and the Establishment Clause: A Corpus Linguistics Analysis," *Arizona Law Review* 61 (2019): 541.

[35] Strang, "Original Meaning of 'Religion,'" 1700.

[36] Barnett, "New Evidence," 857–9; Cunningham and Egbert, "Scientific Methods," 8.

hits could also exclude what may be important examples where the collocation term is either not present at all or occurs too many words away to be picked up under the revised search criteria. The conundrum facing researchers is that either valuable definitional information could be lost by narrowing the search, or, if the search is not narrowed in one way or another, the interpreter may need to take on an extremely lengthy process of deriving a definition of the constitutional word or phrase by reading many thousands of documents, and then studying each of the examples in its specific context to reach a determination about how the term was employed.

HOW TO CONVERT USES INTO MEANINGS?

The task of converting hits into meanings can be deceptively difficult, and it raises the methodological question of whether the people assigning those meanings have the necessary training for the job. To assess how the word is used in each instance, the researcher needs to examine the document carefully to make a subjective judgment about the objective meaning of the word in that particular context. Put differently, the people mining the linguistic data must perform, for each of the dozens, hundreds, or thousands of hits, exactly the same formidable interpretive task that generated the need for the corpus linguistics research in the first place. In trying to identify the meaning of a particular word in one specific context (in this case, the Constitution), they must correctly comprehend the meaning of that same word in many different contexts, such as sermons, advertisements, and newspaper stories. To date, this work has typically been done by law professors and their research assistants, not all of whom have otherwise devoted themselves to the study of eighteenth-century American history or literature.

For some corpus linguistics researchers, a deeper familiarity with the eighteenth-century environment seems to be unnecessary. They argue that "[w]ith 'a little background and training in the underlying methodology,' lawyers, judges, and others who seek to understand original meaning can employ this tool,"[37] even Supreme Court justices.[38] That suggestion may be overly optimistic, however, as the historical context for any particular usage may be considerably broader than the four corners of the document.[39] If researchers

[37] Barclay et al., "Original Meaning," 529, quoting Thomas R. Lee and Stephen C. Mouritsen, "Judging Ordinary Meaning," *Yale Law Journal* 127 (2018): 866.

[38] Barclay et al., 529, citing *Carpenter v. United States*, No. 16–402, 585 US 1, 7 n4 (2017) (Thomas, J., dissenting).

[39] Or, at least, it may be significantly broader than the initial picture generated by a COFEA search, which does not necessarily show the entire document but just a few words or lines on each side of the search term.

or their assistants are unfamiliar with the social and political context, they may miss nuances of usage visible only from a more comprehensive study of the issues being discussed.

Take, for example, a 1768 article in the *New York Gazette*, in which the author says, "every establishment of religion ... ought to be maintained ... by the infliction of temporal punishments on transgressors."[40] This document, found in COFEA via the Evans Early American Imprints collection, is one of the nine documents (of a total of eleven hits) cited by Barclay et al. to demonstrate that "establishment of religion" was understood as "a legal or official designation of a specific church or faith by a particular nation or colony."[41] But in categorizing that usage, a significant contextual issue may have been overlooked. The author (likely William Livingston, a Yale graduate and first governor of New Jersey) was arguing vehemently against the idea of allowing the Church of England to appoint a bishop in North America. One interpretative possibility is that he was merely using the "establishment" term in its well-understood, conventional meaning. That is how Barclay et al. read it. Alternatively, a fair reading of the document in context could conclude that he was exaggerating for effect, and actually making a *reductio ad absurdum* argument to the effect that having an Episcopal bishop in America was tantamount to laws punishing people for not being Episcopalians. My point is not that the interpretation by Barclay et al. of this document is necessarily wrong, but to show that assigning definitions to search terms by looking at corpus linguistics hits is a potentially complex task about which reasonable people could disagree, and for which specialized knowledge of the historical period may be important.

As a result of these complexities, the process of turning hits into quantifiable cases of one usage or another can potentially lead to different outcomes based on the fact that different researchers and their research assistants could make different subjective judgments about the meaning of the various hits. That possibility presents a challenge for one of the arguably scientific elements of using corpus linguistics to ascertain constitutional meaning: reproducibility. Several researchers have highlighted the role of reproducibility as a central element of the reliability of the method. Clark Cunningham and Jesse Egbert note that the "use of computers to analyze corpus data provides reliability in the form of stable and consistent results that can be replicated."[42] Similarly, Barclay et al. write that "'a key goal of corpus linguistics is to aim for

40 "'The American Whig,' XV" (1768), in *Church and State in American History: Key Documents, Decisions, and Commentary from Five Centuries*, eds. John F. Wilson and Donald L. Drakeman, 4th ed. (New York: Routledge, 2020), p. 69.

41 Barclay et al., "Original Meaning," 538.

42 Cunningham and Egbert, "Scientific Methods," 7.

replicability of results,' which provides greater generalizability and validity than other methods constitutional scholars have employed."[43]

Multiple aspects of reliability and reproducibility need to be considered in applying corpus linguistics to constitutional interpretation. The original source for the statement from Barclay et al. is a quotation from Tony McEnery's and Andrew Hardie's *Corpus Linguistics: Method, Theory and Practice*,[44] which discusses the ethics of corpus linguistics research generally (that is, not necessarily in connection with constitutional interpretation). Not only should "corpus users ... make the analyses on which their results were based available to future researchers ... in the interests of replicability," they argue, but the "analyses may be based on algorithms embedded in particular computer programs," which then need to be maintained for future researchers to use.[45] These points relate to the reproducibility of the search aspect of accessing the corpus, not the ultimate conclusions as to meaning derived by researchers assigning meaning to the various hits. Accordingly, it will be difficult to say, without further evidence, that corpus-based constitutional interpretation necessarily generates reproducible results. In fact, in two corpus linguistics analyses of the term "emoluments," both sets of authors cite the reliability and reproducibility of the method while coming to distinctly different conclusions about whether the term was understood at the time of the Constitution to be broad or narrow.[46]

As COFEA itself continues to evolve, the issue of the reproducibility of search results is likely to become even more difficult. From version 2.1 to version 3.0, the number of texts increased from 95,133 to 119,801, while the word count, following corrections, dropped from 138,892,619 to 133,488,113.[47] As a result, a search of COFEA version 2.1 could return a significantly different number of hits than the same search of version 3.0. Moreover, the fact that different researchers will convert the hits into meanings will

[43] Barclay et al., "Original Meaning," 530, quoting Tony McEnery and Andrew Hardie, *Corpus Linguistics: Method, Theory and Practice* (Cambridge: Cambridge University Press, 2012), p. 66.

[44] McEnery and Hardie, *Corpus Linguistics*.

[45] McEnery and Hardie, p. 66.

[46] Compare Phillips and White, "Meaning of the Three Emoluments Clauses," 233: "Using full-blown corpus linguistic analysis ... this Article finds that the Congressional and Presidential Emoluments Clauses would have *most likely* been understood to contain a narrow, office or public-employment sense of 'emolument,'" (original emphasis) with Cunningham and Egbert, "Scientific Methods," 16: "*emolument* had a broad meaning that included, but was certainly not limited to, profits related to an official office."

[47] Corpus of Founding Era American English (COFEA), accessed September 13, 2019, https://lcl.byu.edu/projects/cofea/.

continue to be a challenge for the reproducibility of the final determination of meaning. As future versions of COFEA emerge, and as new researchers attempt to replicate the assignments of meaning, the results could change in significant ways. In the end, none of these methodological issues makes it impossible to identify the objective meaning of a word or phrase via corpus linguistics in a manner that is reliable and reproducible, but they make it considerably more difficult.

HOW TO CHOOSE ONE MEANING FROM MULTIPLE CANDIDATES?

Finally, and perhaps most difficult of all, is the question of what interpreters should do when the results of the corpus linguistics search identify multiple meanings that are well attested in the eighteenth-century sources. As Lawrence Solan points out: "[B]etter empirical tools ... only get us so far, as a) there may be multiple original public meanings ... [and] b) we are lacking a coherent theory to justify when one original public meaning rather than another should be relied upon."[48] Solan's insights highlight major challenges to the effective use of corpus linguistics data for constitutional interpretation. One possible solution is to declare that any word or phrase for which there are two or more usages discernable in the database is irreducibly ambiguous, thus providing no answer as to a single original meaning. In other words, with no clear evidence that there was only one objective public meaning, the combination of corpus linguistics searches and originalism theory has run its course. That could happen very frequently, as studies to date have tended to find that there were at least two identifiable uses of the word in question.[49]

Alternatively, the most commonly used approach to decide what to do with multiple meanings has been a counting rule, often called the frequency thesis.[50] That is, the single meaning for constitutional purposes is the one appearing in the dataset the greatest number of times. Randy Barnett appears to adopt this approach in his 2003 analysis of the use of the term "commerce" in the *Pennsylvania Gazette*, which scholars often cite as the first example of corpus linguistics use for determining the public meaning of a constitutional

48 Lawrence M. Solan, "Can Corpus Linguistics Help Make Originalism Scientific?" *Yale Law Journal Forum* 126, 101 (May 2016): 57. See also Phillips, Ortner, and Lee, "Corpus Linguistics."

49 See, for example, Barnett, "New Evidence," 856–7; Strang, "Original Meaning of 'Religion'"; and Barclay et al., "Original Meaning."

50 The principal alternative to the frequency rule may simply be the conclusion that the data available from searches of corpus linguistics collections identifies more than one potential original public meaning.

term.[51] When Barnett did his research, COFEA did not yet exist, and he performed a statistical analysis of the occurrences of "commerce" in a Pennsylvania newspaper between 1728 and 1800. His methodological approach, which has been adopted by a number of subsequent corpus researchers, was to employ a team of research assistants to locate and categorize occurrences of the word "commerce," with Professor Barnett ultimately reviewing their analyses of whether the meaning was broad or narrow. In the course of this research, he identified "nearly 1,600 uses of the term," with only "a mere handful of candidates [a total of 31] for a broad usage."[52] He concluded that the narrow usage was correct, saying: "*Notwithstanding [a] few possible counterexamples*, this survey clearly establishes that ... the normal, conventional, and commonplace public meaning of commence ... was 'trade and exchange'."[53]

Strang has similarly used the frequency thesis in his recent corpus linguistics analysis of the original meaning of the word "religion,"[54] especially as to whether religion referred only to theistic beliefs. Strang summarizes his conclusions as follows:

> Approximately 74% of usages of the word religion in the data set were theistic. Less than 1% had instances of religion compatible with non-theistic definitions of religion. The raw numbers make this point more starkly: only an average of 13 instances out of 1335 total uses were non-theistic.

From a data analytics perspective, Strang likens these results to Barnett's earlier analysis of the word "commerce," saying that his conclusion "is similar to Professor Barnett's groundbreaking findings, where he determined that 31 out of 1594 instances of *commerce* fit the trade conception from Professor Barnett's stable of conventions."[55] In both studies, the authors deemed the more frequent of two uses of the term to be the constitutionally correct one.

Along the same lines, Barclay et al. have recently identified a meaning for the phrase "establishment of religion" based on a COFEA search and the

[51] Barnett, "New Evidence." Since Barnett's paper and before COFEA appeared, various scholars have used digital tools as one method of ascertaining the meaning of the constitution, including this author. See Donald L. Drakeman, *Church, State, and Original Intent* (New York: Cambridge University Press, 2010), p. 245 n153, in which I used the 1750–70 portion of the Sabin Americana collection. See also Jennifer L. Mascott, "Who Are 'Officers of the United States'?," *Stanford Law Review* 70, 2 (February 2018): 443–564, using the National Archives Founders Online.

[52] Barnett, "New Evidence," 859.

[53] Barnett, 862 (emphasis added).

[54] Strang, "Original Meaning of 'Religion,'" 1700–1703.

[55] Strang, 1703.

application of the frequency thesis.[56] Beginning at the broadest possible level of the "root word *establish*," they find that it "appeared 268.26 times per million within the COFEA database."[57] Then, they applied various coding and collocation methods to narrow the search, and they arrived at thirty-three total results in the COFEA database, most of which were merely quoting the Establishment Clause itself. After eliminating those cases and one "false hit" (they write that "one was discussing establishment in the purely ecclesiastic sense and was thus a false hit")[58], they ultimately identify eleven relevant results. Nine of these eleven hits employ "establishment of religion" in the context of a "legal or official designation of a specific church or faith by a particular nation or colony." Although the phrase "establishment of religion" was also discussed in association with other characteristics, they use the frequency thesis to settle on the one that appeared most often in the dataset.[59]

While it seems to be clear from the detailed research conducted by Barnett, Strang, and Barclay et al. that "commerce," "religion," and "establishment of religion" had some uses that were much more common than others in the specific databases involved in their searches, corpus linguistics-based originalism needs an argument supporting the claim that constitutional meaning should be equivalent to the most frequent use when there are clear examples of other uses. Phillips et al. say, for example: "To the extent the hypothetical average user of English in the late 1700s is operationalized to mean that the most frequent uses or senses of meaning are the most 'ordinary,' then frequency data is fundamental to discovering original public meaning."[60] They do not defend this frequency thesis, which appears in a passive construction ("is operationalized to mean that"), but simply note that if we decide to adopt an interpretive process based on that kind of numerical scoring, corpus linguistics can provide the numbers. Others have questioned the validity of the frequency thesis. For example, Herenstein writes: "A word might be used more frequently in one sense than another for reasons that have little to do with the ordinary meaning of that word. Specifically, a word's frequency will not necessarily reflect the 'sense of a word [or] phrase that is most likely implicated in a given linguistic context'."[61]

56 Barclay et al., "Original Meaning," 532.
57 Barclay et al., 533.
58 Barclay et al., 538.
59 Barclay et al., 538.
60 Phillips, Ortner, and Lee, "Corpus Linguistics," 25.
61 Ethan J. Herenstein, "The Faulty Frequency Hypothesis: Difficulties in Operationalizing Ordinary Meaning through Corpus Linguistics," *Stanford Law Review Online* 70 (December 2017): 114, quoting Lee and Mouritsen, "Judging Ordinary Meaning," 788. See also Carissa

Of the various moving parts involved in corpus-based constitutional interpretation, the frequency thesis may be the one most in need of both practical and theoretical justification. If constitutional meaning is determined by ordinary meaning, which, in turn, is "operationalized to mean that the most frequent uses or senses of meaning are the most 'ordinary'," [62] then how researchers count becomes extremely important. There are numerous issues involved in the how-to-count question. For example, how should researchers deal with a letter to George Washington by Alexander Hamilton that appears in both of their collections in the Founders Online portion of COFEA? Does that letter count as two uses or one? Although, on one hand, it would seem sensible to eliminate duplicates; on the other, perhaps it is important to count both the person who wrote the letter and the one who read it.

For that matter, since the search for public meaning is focused on how people read and understood the Constitution, perhaps corpus linguistics research needs be much more attentive to how many people read the words being counted. Should a document that was widely reprinted in newspapers and pamphlets be assigned a greater weight than a private letter that was only ever seen by one person? If widespread public usage (or exposure to usage) is an important consideration for the identification of original meaning (which goes back to the issue of how interpreters define "public"), researchers may need to find ways to estimate the number of people who read each document. Newspaper circulations could be tracked, the number of people signing petitions can be counted, reprintings can be totaled, and so on.

A study of printing in Boston during the period covered by COFEA shows, for example, that newspapers had around 2,000 subscribers, and a typical book sold about 500 copies, while over 60,000 almanacs were printed each year.[63] If one of the goals of the corpus search is to ascertain which meanings were in common and widespread use at the time of the Constitution, researchers need to consider whether to develop an algorithm for counting hits based not only on the number of times the word is used in the database but also on the number of times the relevant documents were reprinted. For example, total hits could be calculated along the lines of: N = [500 × hits in books] + [2,000 × hits in newspapers] + [60,000 × hits in almanacs] + [1 × hits in private letters], and so on. In short, merely counting occurrences of words in the

Byrne Hessick, "Corpus Linguistics and the Criminal Law," *Brigham Young University Law Review*, 6 (2017): 1503–30; and Daniel C. Tankersley, "Beyond the Dictionary: Why *Sua Sponte* Judicial Use of Corpus Linguistics Is Not Appropriate for Statutory Interpretation," (February 2018), http://dx.doi.org/10.2139/ssrn.3117223.

62 Phillips, Ortner, and Lee, "Corpus Linguistics," 25.

63 Yodelis, "Who Paid the Piper?," 22–37.

COFEA collection provides little, if any, guidance about the degree to which those words, and their various associated meanings, were actually in public circulation in the Founding Era.[64]

Along similar lines, we know from the 1790 census that the population of Virginia was about twice as large as that of Massachusetts. We have also seen that the constitutional term "excise" meant very different things in those two states. Should uses of the word by Madison and other Virginians count twice as much as uses by Ames and his Massachusetts neighbors? If not, the frequency thesis may lead to usages that were not actually used the most frequently. If so, interpreters will need to devise a population-weighted equation for calculating frequency; they will also be faced with complicated questions as to whether to count the large number of people who were not eligible to vote, or become citizens, in the states in which they lived.

Even with a more nuanced approach to gauging frequency, the basic methodological question remains: we currently lack a theoretical justification for the rule that constitutional meaning must be equated with the most frequent usage. To be sure, someone arguing in favor of a meaning that *never* appears in the documentary record of eighteenth-century America would have to bear a very heavy burden of proof, but that has not typically been the case in the corpus-based research to date. Instead, nearly all of the corpus linguistics searches show two or more usages. Constitutional corpus linguistics theorists employing the frequency thesis need to construct a persuasive argument for why constitutional meaning cannot be found in bona fide, well-attested usages simply because another usage occurs more frequently in documents having nothing to do with the Constitution.

THE ODDS OF SUCCESS

As we consider the various methodological challenges, it becomes clear that each of the researcher's assumptions and subjective judgments about how to compile the database, perform the search, analyze and classify the results, and turn those results into an interpretation of the Constitution raises questions about the degree of confidence we can have in any specific COFEA-derived

[64] For an example of how our perception of Founding-Era issues and arguments can change based on a consideration of how widely reprinted the documents were, see Saul Cornell, *The Other Founders: Anti-Federalism and the Dissenting Tradition in America, 1788–1828* (Chapel Hill: University of North Carolina Press, 1999); and Donald L. Drakeman, "The Antifederalists and Religion," in *Faith and the Founders of the American Republic*, eds. Daniel L. Dreisbach and Mark David Hall (New York: Oxford University Press, 2014), pp. 120–43.

determination of the original meaning. This brings us back to the original question: is corpus linguistics a better way of resolving lawsuits involving questions of constitutional meaning than flipping a coin? For the sake of argument, we can make a (generous) assumption that there is an 85 percent probability that each of the following steps has been completed correctly: (1) the database has been constructed fairly and comprehensively to represent the use of the constitutional words in the Founding Era by whoever constitutes the "public" in "original public meaning"; (2) the interpreter has selected the right search criteria to include all of the hits relevant to ascertaining the meaning of the word, and to exclude irrelevant ones; (3) the interpreter – or the interpreter's research assistants – has accurately defined, correctly categorized, and precisely counted every hit as to the meaning employed in that particular context; and (4) the interpreter has correctly reached a conclusion from analyzing the resulting data, via the frequency thesis or otherwise, as to the objective public meaning of that word or phrase as it is used in the Constitution. The likelihood of a correct outcome from this four-step process is .85 × .85 × .85 × .85, which is 52 percent. That is essentially equivalent to the coin flip method rejected earlier. If any one of these variables drops to 50 percent, as may be fair today regarding either the representative nature of the corpus or the validity of the frequency thesis, the likelihood drops to 30 percent, and flipping a coin begins to look considerably more attractive.[65]

CORPUS LINGUISTICS: FOX OR HEDGEHOG?

Corpus linguistics turns out to be much like Isaiah Berlin's famous fox, when public-meaning originalism actually needs a hedgehog.[66] Like Berlin's fox, the corpus knows many small things, and it can provide researchers with highly valuable insights into numerous aspects of eighteenth-century American life, including regional language variations; evolving patterns of spelling, punctuation, and grammar; evidence of linguistic drift; and the many other observations that can flow from giving scholars an opportunity to

[65] This calculation assumes that these are four independent steps, each of which has an 85 percent probability of being done correctly. Based on various assumptions about the likelihood of error at each step, the extent to which upstream errors could either be fatal or potentially corrected at downstream steps, and so on, the odds of a correct outcome could be higher or lower than 52 percent in any individual instance. The point of the "odds of success" exercise is to show how even a quite modest error rate at each step can have a very significant effect on our confidence that this particular method for determining original meaning will lead to the right answer.

[66] See Isaiah Berlin, *The Hedgehog and the Fox: An Essay on Tolstoy's View of History* (London: Weidenfeld & Nicolson, 1953).

interrogate a vast collection of writings. It is an outstanding linguistic and historical resource, but the search for a single objective meaning is made ever more complicated by learning the many things a fox-like tool discovers in a huge collection of data. The problem with applying corpus linguistics to constitutional interpretation is that public meaning-seeking originalists are looking for a linguistic hedgehog that knows one big thing, namely, the one-and-only-one public meaning of a word or phrase in the American Founding Era. Hedgehogs are much harder to find in the inevitably complex language patterns of a new nation, especially one that was widely dispersed and composed of immigrants who arrived in North America speaking a variety of languages with an even broader range of regional dialects.

Originalism's search for the objective public meaning of constitutional terms based on late eighteenth-century language conventions seemed to be easier in the predigital era. The use of Founding-Era dictionaries gave the appearance of offering interpreters a simpler guide to language usage. Yet the dictionary definitions were not designed to be an objective record of word use by the public. Instead, dictionary writers such as Samuel Johnson[67] and Noah Webster[68] saw a variegated semantic environment and considered it their mission to use their own best judgments to prescribe proper definitions,[69] which scholars and judges have subsequently considered to be correct simply because they were found in the published dictionaries of the time.[70] With hindsight and the benefit of corpus linguistics databases, we can now see the degree to which the dictionaries' hedgehog-like role helped support the notion that there was, in fact, a single conventional meaning of important constitutional terms when that was not necessarily the case.

The basic problem with the use of corpus linguistics to determine meaning thus lies in the difficulty of trying to repurpose a highly useful tool for scholarly studies of language to become something else altogether – essentially a do-it-yourself constitutional dictionary, ideally one containing just the right constitutional meaning, despite evidence of multiple uses. To create that

67 Samuel Johnson, *A Dictionary of the English Language: In Which the Words Are Deduced from Their Originals, and Illustrated in Their Different Significations by Examples from the Best Writers*, 6th ed. (London, 1785).

68 Noah Webster, *An American Dictionary of the English Language* (New York, 1828).

69 Ellen P. Aprill, "The Law of the Word: Dictionary Shopping in the Supreme Court," *Arizona State Law Journal* 30 (1998): 284; Gregory E. Maggs, "A Concise Guide to Using Dictionaries from the Founding Era to Determine the Original Meaning of the Constitution," *George Washington Law Review* 82 (2014): 370–73.

70 Maggs, "Concise Guide," 358–9, 385–6, 389–90; Samuel A. Thumma and Jeffrey L. Kirchmeier, "The Lexicon Has Become a Fortress: The United States Supreme Court's Use of Dictionaries," *Buffalo Law Review* 47 (1999): 227–302.

dictionary of original public meaning, that is, to identify the definitional *unum e pluribus*, interpreters have to figure out what method, beyond their own preferences (which was Johnson's and Webster's primary method),[71] should guide them in deciding which sharp edges to round off in the inevitable cases where the digital data discloses a variety of uses. Doing so requires a clearly articulated, practically feasible, and theoretically defensible approach to linguistic data analytics that does not yet exist.

CONCLUSION

Ultimately, these practical and theoretical issues point to a central problem with much of contemporary originalism's focus on objective public meaning: the assumption that there must be a single identifiable conventional semantic meaning for every word or phrase, and that meaning can be conclusively identified without asking what the Framers were actually trying to convey. As COFEA becomes larger and increasingly representative of usage by a broader public, and as more and more corpus linguistics constitutional research is done, it will become even clearer that many important words had multiple meanings, thus emphasizing the need for a way to determine which conventional meaning is the right one. There is an alternative to going back to eighteenth-century dictionaries, the flaws of which have become more apparent since they have been attacked by corpus linguistics-focused legal scholars,[72] or to counting uses in corpora and then applying some version of the frequency thesis. The constitutional text resulted from a process of reasoned arguments and political compromises: each provision was the solution to a problem or the creation of an opportunity, not just an assemblage of words with a one-and-only-one conventional meaning. To understand the text, courts need to seek the lawmaker's will, not only as expressed in the text, but also as evidenced in the Framers' reasoning, debates, drafts, and compromises. That is exactly what Justice Paterson did to resolve the apparent ambiguity concerning the word "excise" in the *Hylton* case.[73] To be sure, evidence from

[71] Maggs, "Concise Guide," 370–73.

[72] See, among others, Lee and Phillips, "Data-Driven Originalism," 284–90; Barclay et al., "Original Meaning," 527–59; and Stephen C. Mouritsen, "The Dictionary Is Not a Fortress: Definitional Fallacies and a Corpus-Based Approach to Plain Meaning," *Brigham Young University Law Review*, 5 (November 2010): 1915–80.

[73] *Hylton*, 3 US at 176. For originalists seeking to follow an "original methods" approach, *Hylton* demonstrates that seeking "the intention of the Framers," in Paterson's words, is one such method. No similar Founding-Era authority exists for the frequency thesis. On original methods, see, for example, Lee J. Strang, *Originalism's Promise: A Natural Law Account of the American Constitution* (Cambridge: Cambridge University Press, 2019); and

that drafting and debating record would need to be especially powerful to lead courts to assign an original meaning that differed from *all* of the documented examples of word usage at the time. But, when multiple uses were in circulation, the actual choices made by the Framers offer far better guidance than the numbers resulting from applying the frequency thesis to a corpus linguistics search based on a series of questionable assumptions and subjective definitional judgments. The next chapter will show how an analysis of the records of the Framers' discussions and debates can resolve the semantic summing issues relating both to the excise tax clause and the Establishment Clause.

John O. McGinnis and Michael B. Rappaport, *Originalism and the Good Constitution* (Cambridge, MA: Harvard University Press, 2013).

7

The Framers' Intentions Can Solve the Semantic Summing Problem

The goal of this chapter is to show how, in practice, a search for the Framers' intentions – that is, the end–means policy choices they made – can be done in light of the nature of the documentary record, and how it can resolve otherwise difficult interpretive tasks for which public-meaning approaches are inadequate. The competing semantic possibilities for the meaning of the two provisions discussed in Chapter 5, the tax clauses and the Establishment Clause, make it very clear that, in some very important modern Supreme Court cases, the justices cannot reasonably determine the original meaning of the constitutional text without paying careful attention to what the Framers said and did during the process of proposing, debating, and drafting the provisions.[1] By enlisting the aid of the Framers' constitutional debates, it is possible to reach a sound conclusion about which of the competing understandings of the language stands for the original meaning in light of all of the available evidence in the documentary record. There is also evidence of what the Framers of each provision were seeking to accomplish when they proposed the language, and further evidence that the Framers' understandings were known to the ratifiers and the public, and thus point to the meaning that was likely to have been understood by the public as well as the Framers.

The multiple candidates for the original public meaning represent the universe of choices the Framers might have made, and the evidence from the speeches and debates show which one of those choices is correct. Defined

[1] For a fascinating glimpse into the multiple public meanings appearing when the constitutional text is translated for non-English-speaking voters (potentially including ratifiers), see Christina Mulligan, Michael Douma, Hans Lind, and Brian Quinn, "Founding-Era Translations of the U.S. Constitution," *Constitutional Commentary* 31 (2016): 1–53. "The translations … provide examples of situations where there were multiple 'original public meanings' – where members of the public developed different interpretations of the same text." Mulligan et al., "Founding-Era Translations," 2.

in this way, the search for the Framers' "intent" or end–means choice is not an argument that courts should follow the Framers instead of the original public meaning. Rather, it allows interpreters to identify which of the multiple viable semantic possibilities actually represents the Framers' constitutional choice. Beyond the provisions discussed here, further investigation will disclose just how many other constitutional provisions are similarly situated, as suggested by the preceding chapter on corpus linguistics.

It may be worth noting that the conclusions as to the original meanings for which I will argue in this chapter do not necessarily align with the policy choices I would make if I were given the chance to make them. My concerns about the Affordable Care Act's potentially negative effect on medical research are unrelated to my conclusion that the shared responsibility payment, also known as the individual mandate, represents a constitutionally permitted tax without the need for apportionment under Article I.[2] And my interpretation of the Establishment Clause would lead to fewer restrictions on the government's involvement with religion than would probably be wise.[3] The point of this book, however, is not to promote the healthcare, church–state, or other substantive policies that I prefer, but to reflect on how judges and scholars should consider the meaning of the Constitution.

THE TAX CLAUSES

With the semantic evidence pointing in opposite directions about the meaning of "excise," Justice Paterson, in the *Hylton* case, turned instead to the goal that was "obviously the intention" of the Framers, which is that only "a capitation tax and a tax on land" were expected to be included in the concept of the direct taxes, which were the ones requiring apportionment.[4] He explained the choice in terms of ends and means as follows: "The provision was made in favor of the southern states. They possessed a large number of slaves; [and] had extensive tracts of territory, thinly settled, and not very

[2] Donald L. Drakeman, "The Humanities and the Future of the Life Sciences," chap. 2 in *Why We Need the Humanities: Life Science, Law and the Common Good* (Basingstoke: Palgrave Macmillan, 2016). As Chief Justice Roberts says in *National Federation of Independent Business v. Sebelius*: "Because the Constitution permits such a tax, it is not our role to forbid it, or to pass upon its wisdom or fairness." *Nat'l Fed'n of Indep. Bus. v. Sebelius*, 567 US 519 (2012). For a positive view of the Act, see Andrew Koppelman, *The Tough Luck Constitution and the Assault on Health Care Reform* (New York: Oxford University Press, 2013).

[3] Donald L. Drakeman, *Church, State and Original Intent* (New York: Cambridge University Press, 2010), p. 343 n25.

[4] *Hylton v. United States*, 3 US 171, 176–7 (1796).

productive."[5] They were worried that "Congress ... might tax slaves ... and land in every part of the Union after the same rate or measure," which would be unfair to those living in the Southern states. The fear of such an "imposition ... was the reason of introducing the clause in the Constitution" linking representation and direct taxes.[6]

Justice Paterson emphasized that this provision, as was the case with the Constitution as a whole, was the result of hard-fought negotiations. The "Constitution has been considered as an accommodating system; it was the effect of mutual sacrifices and concessions; it was the work of compromise."[7] The justice, who had been a delegate from New Jersey to the Constitutional Convention and had firsthand knowledge of the proceedings, thought this particular compromise was "radically wrong."[8] As a result, although the Court would respect the deal made by the Framers, a compromise that was focused on the taxation of slaves "ought not to be extended by construction."[9] (In this case, Justice Paterson appears to be following then-current British and European jurisprudence, which held that some laws would be deemed "odious," because they were unjust or "at odds with principles founded upon the law of nature."[10] In those cases, the law was "not to be extended beyond its own terms."[11] Meanwhile, laws consistent with "natural and divine laws ... received an expansive interpretation."[12])

Justice Paterson's recollection of the constitutional compromise is supported by our records from the Convention. James Madison's notes, for example, show the extent to which taxation and representation were frequently linked. Initially, Gouverneur Morris suggested "that taxation shall be in proportion to representation,"[13] whereas Pierce Butler of South Carolina sought representation based on "the full number of inhabitants, including all the blacks."[14] In response, Morris said that Butler's concern "would be removed by restraining the rule to *direct* taxation. With regard to indirect taxes on *exports* and imports, and on consumption, the rule would be

[5] *Hylton*, 3 US at 177.
[6] *Hylton*, 3 US at 177.
[7] *Hylton*, 3 US at 177–8.
[8] *Hylton*, 3 US at 178.
[9] *Hylton*, 3 US at 178.
[10] R. H. Helmholz, *Natural Law in Court: A History of Legal Theory in Practice* (Cambridge, MA: Harvard University Press, 2015), p. 108.
[11] Helmholz, *Natural Law in Court*, p. 108. Coincidentally, the time was roughly the same as the time the American Constitution was adopted.
[12] Helmholz, p. 109.
[13] Quoted in *The Papers of James Madison: Purchased by Order of Congress; Being His Correspondence and Reports of Debates* [...], ed. Henry D. Gilpin (New York, 1841), vol. 2, p. 1079.
[14] *Papers of James Madison*, vol. 2, pp. 1079–80.

inapplicable."[15] Then, Morris amended his proposal to say, "provided always that direct taxation ought to be proportioned to representation."[16] William Davie of North Carolina complained that this approach was "meant by some gentlemen to deprive the Southern States of any share of representation for their blacks. He was sure that North Carolina would never confederate on any terms that did not rate them at least as three-fifths. If the Eastern States meant, therefore, to exclude them altogether, the business was at an end."[17] Oliver Ellsworth, from one of those "Eastern States," proposed a compromise: "That the rule of contribution by direct taxation ... shall be the number of white inhabitants, and three-fifths of every other description in the several States."[18]

The issue of slavery would continue to generate considerable controversy. Morris, returning to the topic of the "nefarious institution" of slavery, asked: "[W]hat is the proposed compensation to the Northern States, for a sacrifice of every principle of right, of every impulse of humanity?"[19] The Northern States would be obligated "to march their militia for the defence of the Southern States," while Congress had "indefinite power to tax them by excises, and duties on imports," which are likely to "fall heavier on [Northern States] than on the Southern inhabitants."[20] Ultimately, the tax provisions were adopted by the Convention in the form considered by the Court in *Hylton*, with excises required to be uniform and direct taxes linked to apportionment. As Justice Paterson observed, the provisions represented a hard-fought constitutional bargain, with slavery looming over the debates.

The Virginians were spared the concern over excise taxes on slaves by the Court's decision, while the British excise tax on servants that so exercised Hylton's attorney surfaced again in another controversial case: *Steward Machine Company v. Davis*.[21] That New Deal era case upheld the constitutionality of the annual wage tax on employers under the Social Security Act of 1935. As Justice Benjamin Cardozo wrote, a tax "not different in substance from the one now challenged" was adopted in "1777, before our Constitutional Convention," when the British "Parliament laid upon employers an annual 'duty' of 21 shillings for 'every male Servant' employed in stated forms of

[15] *Papers of James Madison*, vol. 2, p. 1080 (original emphasis). He noted further that "he was persuaded that the imports and consumption were pretty nearly equal throughout the Union." *Papers of James Madison*, vol. 2, p. 1080.

[16] Quoted in *Papers of James Madison*, vol. 2, p. 1081.

[17] *Papers of James Madison*, vol. 2, p. 1081.

[18] Quoted in *Papers of James Madison*, vol. 2, p. 1082.

[19] *Papers of James Madison*, vol. 3, pp. 1263–4.

[20] *Papers of James Madison*, vol. 3, p. 1264.

[21] *Steward Mach. Co. v. Davis*, 301 US 548 (1937).

work."[22] In this case, preconstitutional usage in Britain would stand for the original meaning.

More recently, the justices considered the constitutionality of the "shared responsibility payment," or individual mandate, element of the Affordable Care Act, which was characterized by the Court as a "tax on going without health insurance."[23] The plaintiffs argued that "if the individual mandate imposes a tax, it is a direct tax, and it is unconstitutional because Congress made no effort to apportion it among the States."[24] Citing the *Hylton* case several times, Chief Justice Roberts' opinion of the Court indicated that all of the justices in the *Hylton* case "either directly asserted or strongly suggested that only two forms of taxation were direct: capitations and land taxes."[25] Once again, the Framers' bargain – which was to provide broad taxing powers to the federal government subject to the specified, slavery-related limits – was upheld by the Supreme Court in spite of the lack of settled definitions – then or now – for some of the key terms.

Even though the Supreme Court has generally followed the interpretation of the tax clauses in *Hylton*, that case could be seen as exceptional in that one of the justices had personal knowledge of the Convention debates. Further research, however, shows that the ratifiers should have been on notice of a potentially broad definition of excise. In the Northern states, excises were regularly employed on things such as carriages, as Fisher Ames said in Congress. Elsewhere, Antifederalist delegate Luther Martin's widely reprinted summary of the Convention's activities showed how far an excise could reach: "By the power to lay excises ... the Congress may impose duties on every article of use or consumption, on the food that we eat, on the liquors that we drink, on the clothes that we wear, the glass which enlightens our houses, or the hearths necessary for our warmth and comfort."[26] This summary encompasses not only taxes on the sale of goods (for example, food and liquors), "but also the possession of certain household items ('the glass which enlightens our houses, or the hearths necessary for our warmth and comfort')."[27]

[22] *Steward Mach. Co.*, 301 US at 579–80, citing Revenue Act, 1777, 17 Geo. 3, c. 39.

[23] *Nat'l Fed'n of Indep. Bus.*, 567 US.

[24] *Nat'l Fed'n of Indep. Bus.*, 567 US.

[25] *Nat'l Fed'n of Indep. Bus.*, 567 US.

[26] Luther Martin, "Letter on the Federal Convention of 1787," in *The Debates in the Several State Conventions, on the Adoption of the Federal Constitution, as Recommended by the General Convention at Philadelphia, in 1787* [...], ed. Jonathan Elliot, 2nd ed. (Philadelphia, 1836), vol. 1, p. 368.

[27] Joel Alicea and Donald L. Drakeman, "The Limits of New Originalism," *University of Pennsylvania Journal of Constitutional Law* 15, 4 (April 2013): 1198.

Publications such as Martin's help address the question of whether the Convention delegates' understandings fairly represent the original public meaning since there were no contemporaneous newspaper reports, and Madison's notes were not available until years later. Nevertheless, the fact that many delegates to the Constitutional Convention also participated in ratification debates in the states indicates that ratifiers often had the opportunity to hear from eyewitnesses to the proceedings where the Framers, as a group and often after hard bargaining, had designed the constitutional provisions to accomplish particular goals. Moreover, Martin's extremely lengthy "General Information Delivered to the Legislature of the State of Maryland Relative to the Proceedings of the General Convention Lately Hold at Philadelphia" was reprinted numerous times during the ratification debates, and it "revealed no small portion of the ... proceedings of the Philadelphia Convention – including the drafting history (in some detail) of various clauses."[28] If our sources for the Framers' discussions conflict on a particular issue with other sources reflecting how the ratifiers may have understood the end–means decision represented by the text, the justices will be faced with a documentary summing problem on multiple levels, and, in those cases, interpreters will be confronted with a genuine case of ambiguity. If a consistent message as to the Framers' intentions appears in the records relating to the Framers, and if that information was also available to the ratifiers, then it is reasonable to conclude that the ratifiers and the Framers shared the same subjective understanding of the meaning of the provision.

In summary, in the 1796 *Hylton* case, Justice Paterson, one of the delegates to the Constitutional Convention, said clearly that the Framers designed the tax clauses in Article I, Section 8 to convey broad taxing power, essentially as long as it was not employed as a tool to make slavery economically less attractive for the Southern states, which was the point of the Framers' compromise involving apportionment for direct taxes.[29] The case addressed the question of whether the new federal government would respect the deal that had been worked out. The brief submitted on behalf of Hylton, a Virginian, made very clear what the underlying issue of this case was:

[28] Herbert J. Storing, ed., *The Complete Anti-Federalist*, vol. 2, *Objections of Non-Signers of the Constitution and Major Series of Essays at the Outset* (Chicago: University of Chicago Press, 1981), pp. 19–82. See also Vasan Kesavan and Michael Stokes Paulsen, "The Interpretive Force of the Constitution's Secret Drafting History," *Georgetown Law Journal* 91, 6 (August 2003): 1152; and Merrill Jensen et al., eds., *The Documentary History of the Ratification of the Constitution*, vol. 15, *Commentaries on the Constitution, Public and Private, 18 December 1787 to 31 January 1788* (Madison: State Historical Society of Wisconsin, 1976), pp. 146–50.

[29] See *Hylton v. United States*, 3 US 171 (1796).

> Unhappily for the southern states, they possess a species of property, which is peculiarly exposed, and upon which, if this law stands, the whole burden of government may be exclusively laid. The English precedent will justify the measure, for servants constitute an article in the catalogue of their excises, and an American majority exists, who might inflict, without feeling the imposition.[30]

The prominent Virginia attorney, John Taylor, matched the threat that the excise tax clause could be employed to drive slavery, or slaveholders, out of existence with a counterthreat: "[I]f oppressed, states will combine – the grand divisions of northern and southern will retaliate, as majorities or [minorities] fluctuate – and a retaliation between nations, invariably ends in a catastrophe,"[31] which is a pretty good prediction of what happened half a century later.

With this background, it is possible to reflect on how the Supreme Court dealt with an "updated" version of this interpretive issue: whether the Affordable Care Act's individual mandate was constitutional. In applying the four-part updating inquiry described in Chapter 4 to this issue, we can see that the specific use of the term "excise" was flexible at the time of enactment, and that the Framers expected the tax clauses to be read liberally in contexts other than slavery. That is, the original end–means choice involved giving the federal government a significant amount of taxing flexibility, as long as "Direct Taxes" would be apportioned. In light of twenty-first-century circumstances, has a "fresh set of facts" emerged regarding taxation for the Supreme Court to decide that the meaning of the these clauses, which, early on, permitted taxes on ownership as well as on transactions, could be expanded further to include failing to enter into a buy/sell transaction, that is, the penalty for failing to purchase insurance?[32] Reasonable advocates can likely find good arguments on both sides as to whether such a tax (or, arguably, merely a penalty) represents just another species of the genus of taxes, described in Article 1, Section 8. Citing *Hylton*, Chief Justice Roberts concluded that it qualified as a tax, even though it was not explicitly called one, and, more importantly, was not a direct tax requiring apportionment, saying, as to the definition of direct tax, "the Court [in *Hylton*] was unanimous, and those Justices who wrote opinions either directly asserted or strongly suggested that only two forms of taxation were direct: capitations and land taxes."[33] That is, as

30 John Taylor, *An Argument Respecting the Constitutionality of the Carriage Tax* (Richmond, 1795), p. 20 (emphasis omitted).

31 Taylor, *An Argument*, p. 16.

32 See *Nat'l Fed'n of Indep. Bus. v. Sebelius*, 567 US 519 (2012).

33 *Nat'l Fed'n of Indep. Bus.*, 567 US.

the *Hylton* Court had said, the term "direct tax" should be interpreted narrowly, whereas Article 1, Section 8 should be interpreted liberally.

WHAT THE ESTABLISHMENT CLAUSE WAS DESIGNED TO ACCOMPLISH

The Establishment Clause also provides an ideal setting in which to explore the semantic summing problem because, as with the tax clauses, the original public meaning of the text can fully support essentially opposite interpretations. Only by looking at the public record of the Framers' debates can we choose among the various candidates for the actual meaning of the text at the time it was framed and ratified. As it turns out, that evidence shows that the Establishment Clause was not added to the Constitution to take either side in broad based church–state debates, which – as we saw in the case of the Virginia and Massachusetts religion taxes in Chapter 5 – were at least as contentious then as they are today. It was actually adopted solely to answer a fairly straightforward, narrow question about whether Congress had the power to create a national church along the lines of the Church of England.

I have analyzed the background and drafting of the Establishment Clause in great detail elsewhere.[34] For present purposes, it should be enough to summarize the evidence as follows.[35] There were very few comments on the subject of religious establishments during the debates over ratifying the original (unamended) version of the Constitution, and the same basic themes appeared in various states where they did occur. Someone would express a concern that there could, in the future, be a national establishment of one church to the detriment of the others. In response, proponents of ratification pointed out that Congress has no power over religion, and that America's religious diversity would prevent the establishment of a national religion. The ratifying conventions in three states – Virginia, North Carolina, and New York – eventually proposed amendments in almost identical language: "no particular religious sect or society ought to be favored or established by law in preference to others," largely because Virginia's proposed amendment was adopted nearly verbatim by the other two. New Hampshire proposed,

34 Drakeman, *Church, State, and Original Intent*, chaps. 5 and 7.

35 The following 1,200 words of text and notes are taken, with some modest revisions, from Donald L. Drakeman, "Which Original Meaning of the Establishment Clause Is the Right One?," in *The Cambridge Companion to the First Amendment and Religious Liberty*, eds. Michael D. Breidenbach and Owen Anderson (Cambridge: Cambridge University Press, 2020), pp. 365–95.

"Congress shall make no laws touching religion."[36] In all of these cases, the non-establishment amendment was part of a long list of proposed amendments, many of which involved issues that had been far more prominent in the ratification debates.[37]

In running for Congress, James Madison had promised his Baptist constituents that he would address their concerns about church–state issues.[38] Therefore, when he assembled a Bill of Rights for consideration by the Congress, he included both a clause recognizing the rights of conscience and a non-establishment clause that clearly identified its goal: "nor shall any national religion be established." In introducing the first version of the Establishment Clause to the First Federal Congress, he was reported as saying: "Whether the words are necessary or not, he did not mean to say, but they had been required by some of the State Conventions, who seemed to [think that Congress might have the power] to establish [a religion]."[39] An Antifederalist did not like the use of the word "national," which was then removed, and the proposal was slightly revised to read, "No religion shall be established by law."[40]

The House discussions were very brief, especially compared to the petition-filled controversies that had taken place a few years earlier over religious taxes in Virginia and Massachusetts. Daniel Carroll from Maryland, one of two Roman Catholics in the House, made the only supportive comment. He said: "[M]any sects have concurred ... that they are not well secured under the present constitution." He would not "contend ... about the phraseology" since he just wanted to satisfy the community's wishes. No one else in the legislature spoke in favor of the clause. Roger Sherman said it was unnecessary because "Congress had no authority ... to make religious establishments." Elbridge Gerry wanted to revise it to say, "no religious doctrine shall be established by law," and, in response, Madison emphasized that the amendment meant "that

[36] Neil H. Cogan, ed., *The Complete Bill of Rights: The Drafts, Debates, Sources, and Origins* (New York: Oxford University Press, 1997), pp. 12–13.

[37] "Of the 210 separate amendments recommended either officially or unofficially by the states, covering almost one hundred substantive items, only six of the states had dealt with the subject of religion; four of these included non-establishment clauses, and one state, Maryland, specifically rejected such a provision." Drakeman, *Church, State, and Original Intent*, p. 197, citing Bernard Schwartz, *The Bill of Rights: A Documentary History* (New York: Chelsea House, 1971), vol. 2, p. 983.

[38] Richard Labunski, *James Madison and the Struggle for the Bill of Rights* (New York: Oxford University Press, 2006), chap. 7.

[39] Joseph Gales, ed., *The Debates and Proceedings in the Congress of the United States, with an Appendix* [...], vol. 1, *Comprising (with Volume II) the Period from March 3, 1789 to March 3, 1791, Inclusive* (Washington, DC, 1834), p. 730.

[40] Gales, *Debates and Proceedings*, vol. 1, pp. 729–30.

congress should not establish a religion and enforce the legal observation of it by law."

Connecticut's Samuel Huntington agreed with Madison's meaning but worried that the federal courts might read it in a way that would prevent them from enforcing financial pledges for the support of local churches. At this point, Madison offered to reinsert "national" to clarify that only a "national religion" was being discussed. New Hampshire's Samuel Livermore offered his state's "no touching" provision, saying that "the sense of both provisions was the same," but he, too, was concerned that Madison's language could be subject to "misconstruction." Livermore's language passed thirty-one to twenty votes. A few days later, however, it was replaced by language from Fisher Ames of Massachusetts, which became the House's final version. It read: "Congress shall make no law establishing religion."[41] All of the comments revolved around the theme originally proposed by Madison: no national religion.

The Senate, for which we do not have a record of the debates, responded with: "Congress shall make no law establishing articles of faith or a mode of worship," which corresponds with the definition of establishment later discussed by the courts in New Hampshire and Connecticut: a formal, Church of England-type of national church.[42] The Conference Committee came up with the final version: "Congress shall make no law respecting an establishment of religion," which more closely resembled the House's version ("no law establishing religion") than the Senate's. Beyond these accounts of the congressional debates over the establishment clause, which appeared in several newspapers, we have virtually no contemporaneous commentary.[43] There were no petitions, speeches, or letters to the newspapers. The few private letters from members of Congress and other influential Federalists described the proposed Bill of Rights in phrases like a "tub to the whale" and "frothy and full of wind" – noncontroversial language that could be used to address the Antifederalists' demand for amendments.[44]

[41] Cogan, *Complete Bill of Rights*, pp. 59–62.

[42] Thomas J. Curry, *The First Freedoms: Church and State in America to the Passage of the First Amendment* (New York: Oxford University Press, 1986), p. 116.

[43] The Congressional Record was not an official federal publication. The notetaker present at the debates published the materials in the Record, which was fairly widely available by subscription. Marion Tinling, "Thomas Lloyd's Reports of the First Federal Congress," *William and Mary Quarterly* 18, 4 (October 1961): 519–45. See also James H. Hutson, "The Creation of the Constitution: The Integrity of the Documentary Record," *Texas Law Review* 65, 1 (November 1986): 1–39.

[44] Kenneth R. Bowling, "'A Tub to the Whale': The Founding Fathers and Adoption of the Federal Bill of Rights," *Journal of the Early Republic* 8, 3 (Autumn 1988): 233, 241.

In interpreting the clause, it is important to consider that the final language of the clause was able to satisfy a conference committee composed not only of Roger Sherman and Oliver Ellsworth, staunch supporters of Connecticut's religious taxes, but also James Madison, the leader of the anti-assessment forces in Virginia.[45] There can be no question that these men – and the states they represented – disagreed sharply on the general principle of whether governments should foster religion, and they may also have even disagreed on the definition of the phrase "establishment of religion," at least as to the question of whether it would apply to religious taxes. But, based on the drafting history, it seems clear that all of the participants understood that the clause meant what Madison repeated several times – that "congress should not establish a religion, and enforce the legal observation of it by law," as the British Parliament had established the Church of England.

The records of the Framer's debates most clearly support one of the semantic options identified in Chapter 5. The only issue clearly discussed and decided was a prohibition on what Madison called a "national religion." There is no evidence that the Framers of the Establishment Clause thought that they were taking one side or the other in the broader question of how religion and government should relate to each other, a question that remains unresolved today, which is why the Supreme Court gets so many cases under the religion clauses.

The drafting history also shows that the Establishment Clause was not a "principle" but a "rule" in Jack Balkin's typology. Much of our First Amendment jurisprudence has assumed that it was a principle, that is, something whose meaning, according to Balkin, needs to be continually reconsidered as "we ... apply [it] to our own circumstances in our own time."[46] Interpreters have, therefore, used evidence from the Framers or the history of church and state in colonial America to bolster particular modern formulations of a strict separationist or a nonpreferentialist principle. Yet, the evidence of the debates leading to the proposed Establishment Clause, combined with the drafting history, indicates that the clause did not represent a church–state policy choice beyond answering the specific question of whether the necessary and proper clause conveyed on Congress the power to set up a national church. It turns out that the Establishment Clause was a rule along the lines of the Third Amendment, which specified that "no soldier shall in time of

[45] See, for example, William Casto, "Oliver Ellsworth's Calvinism: A Biographical Essay on Religion and Political Psychology in the Early Republic," *Journal of Church and State* 36, 3 (Summer 1994): 507–26; and Mark David Hall, *Roger Sherman and the Creation of the American Republic* (New York: Oxford University Press, 2013).

[46] Jack M. Balkin, *Living Originalism* (Cambridge, MA: Harvard University Press, 2011), p. 7.

peace be quartered in any house, without the consent of the Owner," and was, therefore, the answer to a specific question and not the creation of a general principle of peacetime civilian/military interactions. In short, asking the interpretive question, "For what principle does the Establishment Clause stand?" is question begging. It assumes that such a principle existed in the first place. Only by studying the nature of the Framers' decision and the rationale for it can judges determine when a provision was originally meant to state a principle.

From an evidentiary point of view, it is certainly important to ask if the views of the handful of members of Congress who spoke on the Establishment Clause issue fairly represented the understanding of the ratifiers and other members of the public. On this issue, the fact that our records of the debates in the First Congress were compiled from newspaper reports should provide considerable comfort. That is, our understanding of the Framers' intentions is based on what any interested people would have seen in the publicly available reports. Absent evidence to the contrary, the newspaper record should be a fair representation of the public's understanding of the policy choice embedded in a clause. Accordingly, since there is virtually no other evidence one way or the other about the ratifiers' understanding of the Establishment Clause, the Framers' debates in the First Congress remain the best evidence of the original policy decision – no national church – manifested by that portion of the First Amendment.[47]

The Framers' end–means choice in the adoption of the Establishment Clause provides a basis for judges seeking to apply the Clause to contemporary cases. Take, for example, a recent challenge to the National Day of Prayer under the Establishment Clause, in which a federal district judge declared the practice unconstitutional.[48] A reasonable search for the original end–means choice could not be completed simply by citing the now familiar "wall of separation" phrase, which is taken from a letter written by Thomas Jefferson a decade after the Bill of Rights was ratified,[49] or, for those less inclined towards separationism, by quoting Joseph Story's comment that the general "sentiment in America" at the time of the Constitution "was, that Christianity

[47] See Drakeman, *Church, State, and Original Intent.*

[48] See *Freedom from Religion Found. v. Obama*, 641 F.3d 803 (7th Cir. 2011), which upheld the constitutionality of the National Day of Prayer after it had been held unconstitutional by the federal district court in *Freedom from Religion Found. v. Obama*, 705 F. Supp. 2d 1039 (W.D. Wis. 2010).

[49] Daniel L. Dreisbach, *Thomas Jefferson and the Wall of Separation between Church and State* (New York: New York University Press, 2002), p. 181.

ought to receive encouragement from the State,"[50] which was published in his commentaries in 1833. Instead of doing this kind of constitutional proof-texting,[51] the justices would need to understand the decision made by the Framers when they adopted the clause. That decision can clearly be seen in the debates in the First Congress where the language was framed. The members of Congress addressed the key issue that had been raised in the ratification debates: the concern that Congress might have the power to create a national established church along the lines of the Church of England. As Madison said on the floor of the House: "[P]eople feared one sect might obtain a pre-eminence, or two combine together, and establish a religion to which they would compel others to conform."[52]

The Congress that framed the Establishment Clause did not see its being inconsistent with a national day of prayer, as can be seen in their resolution, issued on the same day, requesting the President to declare a "National Day of Prayer and Thanksgiving" in recognition of the proposed Bill of Rights.[53] Even if that resolution calling for a national day of prayer and thanksgiving is not direct evidence of the reasons or compromises leading to the Establishment Clause, it represents an example of how the clause was initially interpreted by those who were knowledgeable about that process, as per Coke's *contemporanea expositio* maxim.

If preventing such an institutionalized national church was the original decision, and creating a national day of prayer neither fit into the prevailing definitions of an establishment of religion nor was understood by the Framers as being contrary to their end–means choice at the time of enactment, what "fresh set of facts" might cause a twenty-first-century judge to consider changing that constitutional outcome? To be sure, the nation is more religiously pluralistic now than it was then, but one of the principal reasons for not having a national church was the impressive degree of religious (and nonreligious)

[50] Joseph Story, *Commentaries on the Constitution of the United States: With a Preliminary Review of the Constitutional History* [. . .] (Boston, 1851), vol. 2, p. 593.

[51] "Proof-texting" is typically the biblical equivalent of the friend-at-a-cocktail-party method of citing the Framers. The *Oxford English Dictionary* defines it as "the use of a particular Biblical (or other scriptural) passage to prove a particular doctrine or opinion; (in extended use) the use of any text to prove a specific point." *Oxford Dictionaries Online*, s.v. "proof-texting," accessed September 16, 2018, https://en.oxforddictionaries.com/definition/us/proof-texting. The Wiktionary definition comes closer to the usage with which I grew up: "The practice of using decontextualized quotations from a document (often, but not always, a book of the Bible) to establish a proposition rhetorically through an appeal to authority." *Wiktionary*, s.v. "prooftext," accessed September 16, 2018, https://en.m.wiktionary.org/wiki/prooftext.

[52] Cogan, *Complete Bill of Rights*, p. 60.

[53] Gales, *Debates and Proceedings*, vol. 1, p. 914.

diversity that existed in the early national period. Similarly, both support for, and opposition to, public religiously in the form of a national day of prayer is consistent from then until now. In fact, Jefferson wrote his "wall of separation" letter to explain his preference for not declaring national days of prayer, despite the precedent set by his predecessors – and, as it turns out, despite the fact that almost every president since then has done so as well. That early opposition continues, but it does not seem to have become particularly strong: "A 2010 Gallup Poll, for example, concluded that only 5 percent opposed the practice of a national day of prayer, with 57 percent in favor and 38 percent saying that it 'doesn't matter'."[54]

Nevertheless, a federal district judge held the National Day of Prayer to be unconstitutional in a 2010 case. The court's rationale was explicitly based on a book by Christopher Eisgruber and Lawrence Sager, *Religious Freedom and the Constitution*, in which the authors interpret the Establishment Clause in light of an "equal status" principle: "[I]t is a sign of America's progress in the domain of religious freedom that most Americans prefer to defend their views on grounds that assume or are at least consistent with the equal status of all believers and non-believers, rather than on the ground that some subset of believers should enjoy a preferred constitutional status."[55]

In assessing government activity under this standard, Eisgruber and Sager adopt the concept of "social meaning." Such meanings, in the context of the First Amendment, "flow ... from the cultural characteristics of religions in America – their comprehensiveness; their tendency to treat people as either 'in' or 'out'; their use of ... rituals to signal who is 'in'; and, finally, the profound stakes they attach to the status of 'in' or 'out'."[56] On the strength of these insights, federal district Judge Barbara Crabb concluded that the National Day of Prayer was unconstitutional because "of the unique danger that religious conduct by the government poses for creating 'in' groups and 'out' groups."[57] On appeal, the panel of federal circuit court judges reversed the decision, saying: "It is difficult to see how any reader of the 2010 proclamation would feel excluded or unwelcome."[58]

[54] Drakeman, *Why We Need the Humanities*, p. 102.

[55] Christopher L. Eisgruber and Lawrence G. Sager, *Religious Freedom and the Constitution* (Cambridge, MA: Harvard University Press, 2007), p. 21. I have previously discussed this case, and its reliance on the scholarship of legal philosophers, as an example of the real world impact of the humanities. Drakeman, *Why We Need the Humanities*, pp. 97–102.

[56] Eisgruber and Sager, *Religious Freedom and the Constitution*, p. 164. For a counterargument based on "the incoherence of the idea of social meaning," see Richard Ekins, "Equal Protection and Social Meaning," *American Journal of Jurisprudence* 57, 1 (2012): 35.

[57] *Freedom from Religion Found.*, 705 F. Supp. 2d at 1049.

[58] *Freedom from Religion Found.*, 641 F.3d at 807.

It is hard to find a "fresh set of facts" in this case. The practice remains substantially unchanged since 1789, and, even under the social meaning analysis, the poll data does not necessarily support the conclusion that Americans today agree that there must be an equal status of believers and nonbelievers, at least in the context of a National Day of Prayer. If a different result is now constitutionally appropriate, what needs to change is the end–means choice represented by the Establishment Clause. That choice was a simple decision to forbid a national church, and it was not designed to institute a fundamental principle relating to "in" and "out" groups that would govern all future church–state interactions. It was certainly not motivated by a shared belief that ecclesiastical establishments were good or bad, a topic on which the public and the states had widely varying opinions. The one thing on which all could agree, however, was that any formal, institutional religious establishment like the Church of England would not take place at the national level. To reach Judge Crabb's decision, it would be necessary to change the meaning of the clause to express a new anti-establishment principle.

Whereas an updating interpretation made sense in *Brown*, it did not in the day of prayer case. The nature of the Equal Protection Clause was broader than the narrow Establishment Clause, and the material facts relating to *Brown* had changed, which had not occurred with respect to the national day of prayer. Analyzed in the fashion proposed in this book, the decision whether to update is not as simple as pointing to the Framers "original expected applications" of constitutional provisions versus modern expectations (or at least the expectations of modern judges). The goal of the historical research is to determine what end–means decisions were being made in the adoption of particular provisions, including decisions about the whether the Framers believed that the constitutional provisions stated broad principles (free speech and equal protection of laws are common examples) or narrow rules (for instance, the Establishment Clause and the Third Amendment), to employ Balkin's terminology.[59] Thus, although looking at how the Framers applied the provisions in the same context (for example, the first national day of prayer, the Washington DC-segregated schools), can be a valuable aspect of the research into original meaning, the strength of the Framer-expected outcomes depends on the breadth of the decision that was constitutionalized, and the signals in the language and legislative history relating to how liberally or narrowly the Framers intended it to be interpreted. It is entirely consistent, therefore, not to update the constitutional meaning in a case involving the National

[59] See Balkin, *Living Originalism*.

Day of Prayer, but to do so in the case of segregated schooling under the Equal Protection Clause.

Some commentators and judges have argued that updating is always improper, or, at least, must be restricted as much as possible. At the other end of the spectrum are those who believe that whatever the Framers thought they were doing over 200 years ago is simply irrelevant to a judge's role in contemporary constitutional decision making. The alternative to either end of this spectrum is to understand the nature of the Framers' end–means choice made in adopting the text. In other words, the Court should not a priori decide whether the Framers' expected applications should control the meaning of the text or not; instead, the justices need to consider whether the text and history signal that they should (more likely the case in a rule) or should not (as is probably true for texts clearly stating a broad principle). The degree to which interpreters should be limited to the applications expected by the Framers is a question to be asked of the text and the documentary record, not to be set in advance by interpretive theory.

LEGISLATIVE HISTORY OR CONSTRUCTION?

Lawrence Solum, who has focused considerable attention on the nature and importance of semantic meaning, has suggested that the concept of construction may help address the semantic summing problem.[60] He makes a distinction between interpretation, which is "the linguistic meaning or semantic content of the legal text,"[61] and construction, which "is the process that gives a text legal effect (either [b]y translating the linguistic meaning into legal doctrine or by applying or implementing the text)."[62] The critical difference between the two is that, whereas construction can involve a range of elements of judicial judgment, "the linguistic meaning of a text is a fact about the world."[63] Searches for those facts may lead to ambiguity, that is, the multiple potential meanings arising from the semantic summing problem, but, according to Solum, "ambiguities in legal texts can (usually) be resolved by interpretation."[64] ("[V]agueness," however, "always requires construction."[65]) Judges should typically be able to resolve ambiguities by

60 Lawrence B. Solum, "The Interpretation–Construction Distinction," *Constitutional Commentary* 27, 1 (2010): 95–118.
61 Solum, "Interpretation–Construction Distinction," 96.
62 Solum, 96.
63 Solum, 99.
64 Solum, 98.
65 Solum, 98.

looking at "the publicly available context," which will allow the interpreter "to select among the possible senses of the words and phrases of the text."[66] Solum notes that "it is theoretically possible that there are some ambiguities that cannot be resolved by interpretation," especially where "a text was deliberately written in ambiguous language, perhaps because the drafters could not agree on some point and decided to paper over their disagreement with ambiguous language that would kick the can down the road for resolution by subsequent construction."[67]

In the context of Solum's approach to the interpretation/construction distinction (and it is worth noting that other scholars sometimes define these terms differently[68]), I will argue that it is essential to include historical evidence about the nature of the Framers' end–means choice for the initial analysis leading to an interpretation, and not just use the legislative history to explore how the Framers used the language. If, as Solum suggests, interpreters should be open to the concept that the text "was deliberately written in ambiguous language," and thus represents a "kick the can" policy by the Framers, then they should also be willing to consider that the Framers used language that appears ambiguous to us, at least on its face, but, in fact, was expected to convey a particular decision that resulted from negotiations over ends and means, even in those cases where we may initially think that the language can speak for itself. Clear evidence of such an end–means choice in the documentary record, especially if that evidence, or the associated decision and rationale, was likely to have been publicly available at the time of ratification, will eliminate what appears to be an otherwise irreducible ambiguity.

A text's facial characteristics can be deceptive, at least to twenty-first-century interpreters. The tax clauses show that, without including evidence from the Framers' debates, our first assessment of the textual meaning may not enable us to appreciate the extent to which ambiguity exists or even whether we are looking at a rule or a principle.[69] That is, looking for the original *subjective* meaning only at the point at which we detect ambiguity or vagueness in the *objective* meaning assumes that our detecting abilities –

[66] Solum, 102.

[67] Solum, 107.

[68] See, for example, John O. McGinnis and Michael B. Rappaport, "Original Methods Originalism: A New Theory of Interpretation and the Case against Construction," *Northwestern University Law Review* 103, 2 (2009): 751–802; Keith E. Whittington, *Constitutional Construction: Divided Powers and Constitutional Meaning* (Cambridge, MA: Harvard University Press, 1999); and Randy E. Barnett, *Restoring the Lost Constitution: The Presumption of Liberty* (Princeton, NJ: Princeton University Press, 2004).

[69] As to rules and principles, see Balkin, *Living Originalism*.

more than 200 years later and limited only to our understanding of the text and its public context – are adequate to the task. In the case of the tax clauses, what appears to be a rule-like provision actually represents a broad policy; meanwhile, in looking at the text of the Establishment Clause, interpreters have frequently found a broad principle in a provision that was expressly designed to create only a narrow and specific rule.

CONCLUSION

This chapter set out to show how interpreters can employ the documentary record of the Framers' debates and decisions to resolve ambiguity caused by the "semantic summing problem." Evidence of multiple potential semantic meanings does not necessarily lead to an irresolvable ambiguity. Instead, for at least two provisions that have had very substantial effects on American jurisprudence and political life in the last century, a search for the Framers' end–means choice provides a clear method not only for eliminating semantic ambiguity but also for determining if and how a provision should be updated in light of changing times. Such a focus on identifying the Framers' ultimate end–means choices will also minimize or eliminate the friend-at-a-cocktail party problem that has made some theorists wary of looking to the Framers. James Madison may be responsible for some of America's best-known rhetoric about church–state affairs, thanks to his efforts in Virginia in the 1770s, but what is relevant to the original meaning of the Establishment Clause in the late 1780s are the specific (and considerably different) comments he and others made on the floor of Congress.

My goal, up to this point, has been to show that a search for the Framers' intentions (or, historically, the will of the lawmaker) is the core of what it means to interpret a legally authoritative text, whether judges are generally inclined towards original or updated interpretations. These various chapters have pointed to the historical precedent for defining interpretation in this manner, and have shown that it is not only feasible, in light of the documentary record, but can be the only way to resolve highly controversial cases. The next chapter will turn to how a focus on the Framers is likely to be seen by those who will, or will not, give the Supreme Court's decisions sociological legitimacy, and will inform the justices' understanding of what it means to act with fidelity to their judicial roles.

8

Interpretation and Sociological Legitimacy

Previous chapters have focused primarily on factual issues bearing on theories of constitutional interpretation. These matters include what "interpretation" means; the extent to which a search for the will of lawmaker has long been the central inquiry for judges interpreting legally authoritative texts; the degree to which identifying only the semantic meaning, without consideration of the Framers' subjective understandings, can often fail to provide adequate evidence of the nature of the lawmaker's end–means decision; and how judges have traditionally adapted old laws to new circumstances in a manner consistent with that original decision. This chapter will turn more in the direction of perceptions as it explores how both elite and popular opinion can influence justices' perspectives on interpretive issues. These perception issues fall generally into the Court's need for what Richard Fallon has called "sociological legitimacy," along with the individual justices' views of their "fidelity to role," as described by Lawrence Lessig.

The specific issues underlying the perceptions addressed in this chapter are aspects of what are sometimes considered "conventional wisdom," and they turn out not to be true. The first is the notion that any interpretive approach based on the Framers' understandings is so far out of step with the contemporary thinking in the international community of judges and scholars that it represents little more than a peculiarly American form of "ancestor worship." The second is the belief that calling on the Framers' understandings is principally a tool for advancing conservative social and political views. As a result, these perception issues should not inhibit justices and scholars from returning the Framers' intentions to the core of constitutional theory.

SOCIOLOGICAL LEGITIMACY

Richard Fallon introduces the concept of sociological legitimacy by recounting the story of the adoption of the Constitution, which did not meet the formal legal requirements for revising or replacing the Articles of Confederation. The Framers had far exceeded their designated authority in proposing an entirely new Constitution, and the ratification process failed to comply with the terms for amending the Articles. Nevertheless, the Constitution is the law of the land. Fallon uses this example to illustrate the degree to which "sociological legitimacy" is a critical element of American law and jurisprudence, as are legal and moral legitimacy.[1] "When enough people embraced the Constitution," he writes, "its 'sociological legitimacy' gave it legal legitimacy."[2]

Fallon says that he is "loosely following" Max Weber in defining sociological legitimacy as being "associate[d] ... with beliefs that the law and formal legal authorities ... deserve respect or obedience and with a further disposition to obey the law for reasons beside self-interest."[3] It is based "wholly on facts about what people think, not ... how people ought to think."[4] Much of the work of constitutional theorists relates to legal and moral authority, but "we should care about sociological legitimacy insofar as we care about whether [people] – including Supreme Court Justices, other public officials, and ultimately the public – will be disposed to respect and obey the ... decisions of the Supreme Court."[5]

Fallon's insights into the nature of sociological legitimacy are supported by a rich political science literature that "demonstrates that the Court is concerned about preserving its legitimacy, which involves being sensitive to how the Court is perceived by the public and members of the bar."[6] Tom Clark concludes that the critical message emanating from a great deal of that research is "[t]hat concern for institutional legitimacy, and specifically for reliance on public support to compel compliance with its decisions, can affect judicial decision making."[7] As one justice told Clark in an interview, the perception of the Court's legitimacy is "predicated on whether the public understands that we are a court and act a legitimate way."[8]

1 Richard H. Fallon Jr., *Law and Legitimacy in the Supreme Court* (Cambridge, MA: Harvard University Press, 2018), p. 86.
2 Fallon, *Law and Legitimacy*, p. 86.
3 Fallon, pp. 22–3. On the varying degree of influence of Supreme Court decisions, see Matthew E. K. Hall, *The Nature of Supreme Court Power* (New York: Cambridge University Press, 2011).
4 Fallon, p. 23.
5 Fallon, p. 23, citing Tom R. Tyler, *Why People Obey the Law* (Princeton, NJ: Princeton University Press, 2006).
6 Tom S. Clark, *The Limits of Judicial Independence* (Cambridge: Cambridge University Press, 2011), p. 16.
7 Clark, *Limits*, p. 16.
8 Clark, p. 18.

The Court is periodically reminded of the need to be perceived as acting in a legitimate way by the other branches of government. In one of President Franklin Roosevelt's fireside chats, for example, he spoke strongly about the Court's decisions striking down parts of the New Deal, saying: "The Court ... has improperly set itself up as a third House of the Congress – a super-legislature ... reading into the Constitution words and implications which are not there, and which were never intended to be there."[9] These kinds of concerns about the judiciary overstepping its proper bounds have been raised not only by FDR and his fellow progressives, but also by conservatives, although usually on different issues. For example, Congressman John Schmitz of California described the *Roe v. Wade* abortion case as "judicial tyranny,"[10] and Senator Barry Goldwater, in the wake of the *Brown v. Board of Education* school desegregation case, wrote: "I have great respect for the Supreme Court as an institution, but I cannot believe that I display that respect by submitting abjectly to abuses of power by the Court, and by condoning its unconstitutional trespass into the legislative sphere of government."[11] Taking an even more extreme view, as Keith Whittington recounts, "Governor Orval Faubus ... called out the National Guard in 1957 to prevent the desegregation of the Little Rock schools," ultimately arguing that "the Supreme Court decision is not the law of the land."[12] (In *Cooper v. Aaron*, a unanimous Court disagreed with Governor Faubus, and took the opportunity to remind Arkansas of "some basic ... propositions which are settled doctrine.")[13]

Similarly, when the Court declared unconstitutional the longstanding practice of official prayers and Bible reading in the public schools, Alabama Governor George Wallace proposed personally to go into the schools to lead the prayers that the Court had just struck down, saying: "I don't care what they say in Washington, we are going to keep right on praying and reading the Bible

[9] Franklin D. Roosevelt, "Fireside Chat: On the Reorganization of the Judiciary," March 9, 1937, The American Presidency Project, www.presidency.ucsb.edu/documents/fireside-chat-17. See generally FDR's fireside chat on March 9, 1937, after the Supreme Court struck down two pieces of the New Deal legislation in *A. L. A. Schechter Poultry Corp. v. United States*, 295 US 495 (1935) and *United States v. Butler*, 297 US 1 (1936).

[10] Daniel K. Williams, *Defenders of the Unborn: The Pro-Life Movement before* Roe v. Wade (New York: Oxford University Press, 2016), p. 196.

[11] Barry Goldwater, *The Conscience of a Conservative* (1960; repr., Princeton, NJ: Princeton University Press, 2007), p. 30.

[12] Keith E. Whittington, *Political Foundations of Judicial Supremacy: The Presidency, the Supreme Court, and Constitutional Leadership in U.S. History* (Princeton, NJ: Princeton University Press, 2007), p. 11.

[13] Whittington, *Political Foundations*, p. 2.

in the public schools."[14] On other occasions, as in the New Deal, there have been proposals to increase the number of justices in a way that would give the president an opportunity to appoint more accommodating jurists.[15] Additionally, over the years, Congress has adopted a variety of "jurisdiction stripping" laws designed to keep disputes away from judges altogether. Between 1877 and 2008, for example, there were 308 different proposals in Congress for some form of what Tom Clark has called "court-curbing."[16]

As Keith Whittington points out, legislators will also take positions to appeal to voters, and indirectly to the justices, signaling via "position-taking" that the legislators are sympathetic to public opinion in the face of an unpopular Supreme Court decision.[17] Clark quotes one legislator's comparison of "narrowly tailored legislation, which might pass and actually reverse a judicial policy, and broad legislation that rarely ever passes."[18] In the words of a member of Congress: "One is a scalpel; the other a B-2 bomber. A scalpel is usually more effective, but the B-2 bomber gets all the attention."[19] The B-2 bombers are the proposals that are more likely to find their way into party platforms, political speeches, and the media. They attract attention for the legislator, while alerting the public of the need to elect politicians who will not only vote for good policies, but also propose (in the case of presidents) or confirm (in the case of senators) federal judges who will "do the right thing," however that may be defined. As Democratic Senator Maria Cantwell said in

[14] Quoted in Jonathan Zimmerman, *Whose America? Culture Wars in the Public Schools* (Cambridge, MA: Harvard University Press, 2002), p. 161.

[15] "Had he succeeded, the Court would never have been the same. Recognition of the legitimacy of diluting the votes of obstructive Justices would have severely weakened the Court's ability to enforce the Constitution against other branches." David P. Currie, *The Constitution in the Supreme Court: The Second Century, 1888–1986* (Chicago: University of Chicago Press, 1990), p. 235. For a background to this "court-packing" concept, see William E. Leuchtenburg, "The Origins of Franklin D. Roosevelt's 'Court-Packing' Plan," *The Supreme Court Review* 1966 (1966): 397; and Matthew J. Franck, introduction to *The Doctrine of Judicial Review: Its Legal and Historical Basis and Other Essays*, by Edward S. Corwin (New Brunswick, NJ: Transaction Publishers, 2014), which reprints Professor Corwin's 1914 book. Professor Franck notes that the original concept – "an act of Congress providing that judges under the age of 70 should always comprise a majority of the Court and giving the President power to make additional appointments" to satisfy that condition – was developed by Harvard professor Arthur Holcombe, who sent it to Corwin, who then forwarded it to the attorney general. Franck, introduction to Corwin, *Doctrine of Judicial Review*, p. xiii. It was announced in 1937 but never implemented.

[16] Clark, *Limits*, p. 37.

[17] See, in particular, Whittington's discussion of the votes in Congress about flag burning following the Supreme Court's decision in *Texas v. Johnson*, 491 US 397 (1989). Whittington, *Political Foundations*, pp. 139–41.

[18] Clark, *Limits*, p. 37.

[19] Quoted in Clark, *Limits*, p. 37.

connection with an expected confirmation battle over a replacement for Justice Anthony Kennedy, "My colleagues on both sides of the aisle know that this vote could be one of the key votes of their entire career."[20] Republican President Donald Trump had a similar view: "As president – I mean obviously outside of war and peace – the biggest decision you can make is the selection of a Supreme Court justice."[21]

JUDICIAL REASONING AND SOCIOLOGICAL LEGITIMACY[22]

In the effort to achieve and maintain sociological legitimacy, both in general and in particular cases, the justices of the Supreme Court have the first-mover advantage: the chance to craft persuasive opinions that they believe will be seen – both substantively and methodologically – as legitimate exercises of judicial power, even when people disagree with the outcomes. Those judicial opinions are frequently excerpted in the media and made instantaneously available on the internet.

Interestingly, the now-common opinions of the Court were neither called for in the Constitution nor clearly destined to assume their current form. They were developed, at least in part, to obtain sociological legitimacy for Chief Justice Marshall's efforts to enhance the Supreme Court's power. Today, it is hard to imagine the possibility of a weak and largely unimportant Court, but we should remember that Federalist coauthor and early Chief Justice of the Supreme Court, John Jay, declined to be reappointed in 1801, "telling President Adams that he lacked faith that the Court could acquire enough 'energy, weight and dignity' to play an important role in the nation's affairs."[23]

[20] Quoted in Heather Long, "Maine Sen. Susan Collins Won't Support Any Supreme Court Nominee Looking to Overturn *Roe v. Wade*," *Salt Lake Tribune*, July, 1, 2018, www.sltrib.com/news/nation-world/2018/07/01/maine-sen-susan-collins/.

[21] Quoted in Nicholas Fandos and Emily Cochrane, "Susan Collins, Pivotal Moderate, Says 'Hostility' to Roe Would Sway Her Vote," *New York Times*, July 1, 2018, www.nytimes.com/2018/07/01/us/politics/susan-collins-supreme-court-nominee-abortion.html.

[22] This section is an adaptation of Donald L. Drakeman, "What's the Point of Originalism?" *Harvard Journal of Law and Public Policy* 37, 3 (2014): 1123–50.

[23] Gerald N. Rosenberg, *The Hollow Hope: Can Courts Bring about Social Change?*, 2nd ed. (Chicago: University of Chicago Press, 2008), p. 15 n12. Sandra Frances VanBurkleo describes the early Court as dealing with "the relatively tedious, incremental creation of a tradition in domestic law." Sandra Frances VanBurkleo, "'Honour, Justice, and Interest': John Jay's Republican Politics and Statesmanship on the Federal Bench," in *Seriatim: The Supreme Court before John Marshall*, ed. Scott Douglas Gerber (New York: New York University Press, 1998), p. 51. As David Currie explains: "The relative paucity of early federal legislation, the absence of a general grant of original federal jurisdiction over cases arising under federal law, and the fact that the Court's jurisdiction was largely appellate contributed to a low starting

The missing "weight and dignity" would come soon. Under Marshall, the Court "sought and achieved a moral force as great as that obtained by the presidency and the Congress."[24] One of his primary tools was the now common practice of the Court issuing formal written opinions. There is nothing in the Constitution that explicitly obliges the justices to give reasons for their decisions, and, in the early years, they rarely did. The early Court, which was composed of an impressive collection of Framers and ratifiers, only occasionally issued formal written opinions (or any opinion at all).[25] In fact, when we now read what looks like the opinions of the justices from the first decade or so of the Court's decisions, we are generally seeing notes taken down by a lawyer such as Alexander Dallas or William Cranch, whose business was to publish and sell copies of the notes to other lawyers.[26] In many cases, there were no official statements of the Court's reasoning, and, where we do have seriatim opinions, they represent each justice's comments on the case – usually brief ones, as far as we can tell.[27] Only when Marshall became Chief Justice and, in particular, as he successfully built the Court into a significantly more powerful political entity, did the Court begin issuing formal opinions.

Marshall recognized that the critical practical restriction on the Court's power is that the justices must persuade people that they are *properly* interpreting the Constitution. He was acutely sensitive to this need for the Court to offer good, publicly accessible reasons for its decisions. As his Federalist-dominated Court made a series of controversial decisions during Thomas

caseload." David P. Currie, *The Constitution in the Supreme Court: The First Hundred Years, 1789–1888* (Chicago: University of Chicago Press, 1985), p. 3.

24 Leonard Baker, *John Marshall: A Life in Law* (New York: Macmillan, 1974), p. 414.

25 Currie, *The First Hundred Years*, p. 55; Julius Goebel Jr., *The Oliver Wendell Holmes Devise: History of the Supreme Court of the United States* (Cambridge: Cambridge University Press, 2010), p. 665. Currie writes: "This practice of seriatim opinions would persist until the appointment of Marshall, who put an abrupt end to it." Currie, *The First Hundred Years*, p. 14 n61. Marshall ended seriatim opinions in order to augment the "power and prestige" of the Court. Henry J. Abraham, *The Judicial Process: An Introductory Analysis of the Courts of the United States, England, and France*, 7th ed. (Oxford: Oxford University Press, 1998), p. 199.

26 The Court did not have a salaried, official court reporter until 1817. Morris L. Cohen and Sharon Hamby O'Connor, *A Guide to the Early Reports of the Supreme Court of the United States* (Littleton, CO: F. B. Rothman, 1995), p. 2. See also Gerald T. Dunne, "Early Court Reporters," *Yearbook 1976 Supreme Court Historical Society* (1976): 61–2; and Craig Joyce, "The Rise of the Supreme Court Reporter: An Institutional Perspective on Marshall Court Ascendancy," *Michigan Law Review* 83, 5 (April 1985): 1293–4.

27 Scholars estimate that "Dallas may have failed to report as many as a third of the decisions during the period of his reports," which was 1790–1800. Cohen and O'Connor, *Guide to the Early Reports*, pp. 4, 6. For a discussion of the early Justices and their opinions, see generally Gerber, *Seriatim*. These opinions often appeared in the reporters' volumes years after they were handed down. See Cohen and O'Connor, *Guide to the Early Reports*, pp. 13, 18–19.

Jefferson's administration, he instituted the now-common mechanism by which the Court continually defends its exercise of power by not only saying what the law is, but also by explaining, in a formal written opinion, why the law is the way that it is. The opinion writer, usually Marshall himself in the early years, would set out the reasons supporting the Court's constitutional interpretation, and Marshall worked to discourage the other justices from any sign of dissent.[28] Under Marshall's leadership, as the Court made a grab for more power and prominence in the young nation, the opinion became a tool for self-justification – the Court's way of explaining, or at least claiming, that its growing influence derived from a legitimate and faithful interpretation of the Constitution. Such written opinions would show that the justices were not motivated by political or partisan interests but by good reasons that could be explained to the public.[29]

Both Marshall's goal of enhancing the Court's prestige, and his use of the single opinion of the Court to do so, were controversial. Jefferson, calling it a "most condemnable practice," wrote: "An opinion is huddled up in conclave, perhaps by a majority of one, delivered as if unanimous, and with the silent acquiescence of lazy or timid associates, by a crafty chief judge, who sophisticates the law to his mind, by the turn of his own reasoning."[30]

[28] ZoBell points out that "seldom were dissents published in more than fifteen or twenty per cent of the cases decided in any one term before the early 1900's." Karl M. ZoBell, "Division of Opinion in the Supreme Court: A History of Judicial Disintegration," *Cornell Law Quarterly* 44 (1959): 196. There were certainly dissenters, including Associate Justice Johnson, who confided in Jefferson that dissension was suppressed and that Marshall even wrote opinions "contrary to his [Marshall's] own Judgment and Vote." Quoted in ZoBell, "Division of Opinion," 193 n41. Against the view that Marshall singlehandedly dictated all Court opinions, Charles Hobson contends that Marshall would "defer, when necessary, to the superior learning of others. ... If the Court most often spoke through the chief justice, the opinion was the product of collaborative deliberation, carried out in a spirit of mutual concession and accommodation." Charles F. Hobson, "The Marshall Court, 1801–1835: Law, Politics, and the Emergence of the Federal Judiciary," in *The United States Supreme Court: The Pursuit of Justice*, ed. Christopher Tomlins (Boston: Houghton-Mifflin, 2005), p. 57. Due to the close collegiality among the Justices, "Marshall's pathbreaking opinions" were not "exclusively solo performances. Then as now, constitutional decisions were the outcome of the deliberative process, and as such, more or less composite products." Felix Frankfurter, "John Marshall and the Judicial Function," in *James Bradley Thayer, Oliver Wendell Holmes, and Felix Frankfurter on John Marshall* (Chicago: University of Chicago Press, 1967), p. 142.

[29] Charles Hobson notes that the Marshall Court's ability to combine constitutional interpretation and written opinions allowed the Chief Justice to present the decisions as a standard legal decision "and thereby persuade the American people to accept such pronouncements not as politics but as so much *law*." Hobson, "Marshall Court," p. 71 (original emphasis).

[30] Thomas Jefferson, "To Thomas Ritchie," December 25, 1820, in *The Works of Thomas Jefferson*, ed. Paul Leicester Ford, vol. 12, *Correspondence and Papers 1816–1826* (New York: G. P. Putnam's Sons, 1905), pp. 177–8. Jefferson wrote a year later: "Another most

Controversial or not, Marshall stuck to his guns. As Karl ZoBell notes: "During the first four years after the advent of Marshall, twenty-six decisions were handed down by the Court. The Chief Justice delivered the opinion of the Court in all of these save two, and in those, the senior Justice present delivered the opinion in the absence of Marshall."[31]

In summary, the justices need to convince the other branches of government and the public that their decisions are legitimate and need to be obeyed. Chief Justice Marshall devised the concept of an opinion of the court to accomplish that goal by providing an opportunity to explain the reasons for the decision. The justices are – and will continually be – sensitive to which kinds of reasons are persuasive, and which may be perceived by the Court's various audiences as inappropriate or ineffective.

FIDELITY TO ROLE

Lawrence Lessig has introduced a concept that exists alongside of the Court's need for sociological legitimacy. It is part of his definition of "interpretive fidelity," which has two components: "The first is the question of *fidelity to meaning*. It asks: How does a judge preserve the meaning of the Constitution's text within the current interpretive context?" The second part is the one on which this chapter will focus. Lessig writes: "[I]n answering that first question, the judge is confronted with a second: How does she do this, given the constraints of her role? . . . Put most crudely, that fact forces the judge to ask: 'How much of a nut do I want to be seen to be?'"[32]

Those concerns about how the individual justices are perceived can be rooted in both elite and popular opinion. As Lawrence Baum and Neal Devins have argued: "[T]he Justices have concerns other than maximizing the achievement of their preferred legal policies, and prominent among those concerns is their interest in the regard of other people who are important to them. When the Justices deviate from their preferred legal policies, it may be because of strategic considerations, some of which relate to public opinion. However, it is more often the case that Justices are influenced by the views of other elites who are important to them for

condemnable practice of the Supreme Court to be corrected is that of cooking up a decision in caucus and delivering it by one of their members as the opinion of the court, without the possibility of our knowing how many, who, and for what reasons each member concurred." Quoted in Baker, *John Marshall*, p. 415.

[31] ZoBell, "Division of Opinion," 194.

[32] Lawrence Lessig, *Fidelity and Constraint: How the Supreme Court Has Read the American Constitution* (New York: Oxford University Press, 2019), p. 16.

personal rather than strategic reasons," some of which relate to public opinion.[33] Law professors, for example, are important audiences for the Supreme Court's opinions – "I write my opinions for the law schools," Justice Antonin Scalia once declared[34] – and, to an unquantifiable extent, the broader national and international legal communities. At the same time, the justices' concerns about fidelity to role can be influenced by other public officials and the public itself.

ELITE INTERNATIONAL OPINION ABOUT THE FRAMERS' ROLE IN INTERPRETATION

A number of scholars have suggested that the rest of the modern world has dispensed with any vestigial elements of originalism, and, therefore, a Framer-focused search for the Constitution's original meaning can look merely like a quirky case of twenty-first-century American "ancestor worship."[35] Despite the numerous arguments for a Framer-focused interpretation based on both interpretive history and constitutional theory, such a comparative insight could influence justices to shy away from following an approach that law professors say has been abandoned by their peers in many other countries. In Lessig's terms, it may make them feel as if people whose opinions they respect will perceive them as some sort of "nut." In reality, however, the search for original meaning – and the Framers' intentions – remains an important element in the interpretative arsenal around the world.

Nevertheless, the seemingly conventional wisdom enjoys considerable support in the scholarly literature. James Fleming, remembering his graduate studies decades ago with Princeton's Walter Murphy, "the greatest political science comparative constitutional law scholar of his generation," learned that, even then, "originalism [was] peculiar to the United States. And that it is rejected elsewhere."[36] While Fleming acknowledges that there may be a few counterexamples – he mentions some "convoluted" reasoning of the Turkish

33 Lawrence Baum and Neal Devins, "Why the Supreme Court Cares about Elites, Not the American People," *Georgetown Law Journal* 98, 6 (August 2010): 1517. For an analysis of how various personality traits influence judicial behavior, which may include justices' "understanding of a judge's proper role," see Matthew E. K. Hall, *What Justices Want: Goals and Personality on the U.S. Supreme Court* (New York: Cambridge University Press, 2018), p. 9.

34 Justice Scalia said this at an event at Princeton University in 2012 that I attended.

35 Frank B. Cross, *The Failed Promise of Originalism* (Stanford, CA: Stanford University Press, 2013), p. 3.

36 James E. Fleming, *Fidelity to Our Imperfect Constitution: For Moral Readings and Against Originalisms* (New York: Oxford University Press, 2015), p. 65.

Constitutional Court[37] – Fleming sees Murphy's observation as representing "the conventional wisdom."[38] Similarly, Jack Balkin notes, "Originalism is mostly unknown outside of the United States."[39] He cites the work of comparativists such as Michel Rosenfeld, who writes that "[i]n Europe, recourse to originalism is virtually nonexistent,"[40] and Kim Scheppele, who argues that in "'advanced constitutional systems' ... courts do not generally inquire into original meanings or original intentions."[41]

This country's idiosyncratic tendency "to lionize historical figures" may simply be embarrassing for American judges and constitutional scholars.[42] Could it be that, because of what various authors cite as "cultural contingency" or "uniquely American anxieties," the international legal community thinks that we do not actually have one those "advanced constitutional systems"?[43] In such a transnational context, the arguments set forth in preceding chapters may not be sufficient to convince nonoriginalist theorists that they have heard good enough reasons to give credence to what Scheppele calls the "backward" nature of the American search for original meaning.[44]

This issue needs to be addressed beyond simply saying that we do things differently over here. That being said, since we are considering how the US Supreme Court should interpret the US Constitution, it is important, in

[37] Fleming, *Fidelity to Our Imperfect Constitution*, p. 205 n61, citing Ozan O. Varol, "The Origins and Limits of Originalism: A Comparative Study," *Vanderbilt Journal of Transnational Law* 44, 5 (2011): 1247–8.

[38] Fleming, p. 65.

[39] Jack Balkin, "Why Are Americans Originalist?," in *Law, Society and Community: Socio-Legal Essays in Honour of Roger Cotterrell*, eds. Richard Nobles and David Schiff (Farnham: Ashgate Publishing, 2014), p. 309.

[40] Balkin, "Why Are Americans Originalist?," 309, citing Michel Rosenfeld, "Constitutional Adjudication in Europe and the United States: Paradoxes and Contrasts," *International Journal of Constitutional Law* 2, 4 (October 2004): 656 n83.

[41] Balkin, 309, citing Kim Lane Scheppele, "Jack Balkin Is an American," *Yale Journal of Law and the Humanities* 25, 1 (Winter 2013): 24. Scheppele writes that even Balkin's flexible "text and principle" approach to interpretation in *Living Originalism* "would be a non-starter in the constitutional culture that has become the most influential in the world, the one anchored by the post-World War II German constitution." Scheppele, "Jack Balkin Is an American," 23.

[42] Jamal Greene, "On the Origins of Originalism," *Texas Law Review* 88, 1 (November 2009): 6.

[43] Yvonne Tew, "Originalism at Home and Abroad," *Columbia Journal of Transnational Law* 52, 3 (2014): 836; Lael K. Weis, "What Comparativism Tells Us about Originalism," *International Journal of Constitutional Law* 11, 4 (October 2013): 842; Scheppele, "Jack Balkin Is an American," 24. See also Cross, *Failed Promise of Originalism*, p. 13; Greene, "Origins of Originalism"; Varol, "Origins and Limits of Originalism," 1246; David Fontana, "Response: Comparative Originalism," *Texas Law Review* 88 (2010): 189–99.

[44] Scheppele, "Jack Balkin Is an American," 24, noting that the purposive interpretations followed elsewhere "require ... that we look forward to the imagined future of a polity rather than backward to its historical starting point, as originalism asks of us."

widening our focus to the international sector, not to lose sight of the facts that each country, including our own, has its own constitution (written or unwritten), its own political structures, and a particular approach to the role of the judiciary in national governance. As noted in earlier chapters, the US Supreme Court holds an unusually large amount of final policymaking (or policy-denying) power compared to courts in the countries in which legislatures can override judicial interpretations. We do, in fact, do some things differently over here. At the same time, the reports of the global death of original meaning – save in the "peculiar" setting of the United States – have been exaggerated. As Australian Jeffrey Goldsworthy has recently written: "The idea that originalism is a uniquely modern and American approach to constitutional interpretation is false."[45]

Originalism appears to be thriving in a number of countries outside Europe. Some constitutional comparativists have pointed to the revolutionary origins of a constitution as a likely predictor of judicial interest in the ideas and ideals of the framers who created them. David Fontana makes a distinction between "'revolutionary' constitutions and 'reorganizational' constitutions," noting that in cases where "a constitution is revolutionary, the countries tend to be more focused on the founding moment and so tend to focus more on what might be called an interpretive originalism."[46] Fontana observes that "the post-colonial constitutions of Africa and Latin America, for instance, foster many originalist arguments."[47] In Zimbabwe, for example, the High Court of Harare applied an essentially originalist analysis in a 1998 case "to reject a claim that laws criminalizing sexual acts between males were unconstitutional under the prohibition on sex discrimination."[48] Noting that "because the law predated the Constitution and because Zimbabwe's Constitution . . . did not explicitly prohibit sexual orientation discrimination," the Court concluded that the "framers did not intend to invalidate sodomy laws."[49]

The countries with revolutionary constitutions thus present a potentially more relevant setting for constitutional comparisons than Canada and Australia, the countries on which Jamal Greene focuses in order to showcase the uniqueness of American originalism.[50] Greene points out that, despite

45 Jeffrey Goldsworthy, "Originalism in Australia" *DPCE Online* 31, 3 (October 2017): 607, www.dpceonline.it/index.php/dpceonline/article/view/432.
46 Fontana, "Response," 196.
47 Fontana, "Response," 197–8.
48 Nan D. Hunter, "Discrimination on the Basis of Sexual Orientation," in *Global Perspectives on Constitutional Law*, eds. Vikram David Amar and Mark V. Tushnet (New York: Oxford University Press, 2009), p. 129 n13.
49 Hunter, "Discrimination," 129 n13.
50 Greene, "Origins of Originalism," 4–5.

clear parallels among the United States, Canada, and Australia – including their British colonial past, "stable, liberal, federal democracies," "independent judiciaries," "well-established traditions of judicial review," "written constitutions of long standing," and a common law heritage – the United States' interpretative environment is much different than in these Commonwealth countries.[51] Originalism, he writes, is "little celebrated outside the United States," and, in fact, the "notion that the meaning is . . . fixed at some point in the past and is authoritative in present cases in pooh-poohed by most leading jurists in Canada, South Africa, India, Israel, and throughout most of Europe."[52] Even in Australia, "the text-bound 'original meaning' version of originalism that has been ascendant" recently is now "on the wane."[53] Greene concludes that "Canadian constitutional interpretation is unapologetically . . . teleological," and "Australian originalism has for many years been aggressively textualist. . . . Australian jurists are also generally comfortable incorporating contemporary norms."[54] As far as Greene is concerned, this amounts to a "global rejection of American-style originalism."[55]

The potency of these arguments is at least partially a function of exactly what is being "pooh-poohed" by the international constitutional community. Greene's definition of the peculiarly American form of originalism involves "consider[ing] the original understanding dispositive," whereas, by his count, "[m]ost constitutional lawyers consider original understanding relevant but not dispositive."[56] Greene's report that the elite international legal community believes in the interpretive relevance of a text's original meaning is considerably stronger than I would have expected, and it means at least that Greene's brief against originalism based on international standards is not an argument against the relevance of the original meaning to modern approaches to interpretation.

Because Greene has singled out Canada and Australia, it would also be valuable to highlight at least two additional points of contrast. Even if most constitutional lawyers "consider original understanding relevant," he points

[51] Greene, 4–5.
[52] Greene, 3.
[53] Greene, 3.
[54] Greene, 5. For more on Australian originalism, see Jeffrey Goldsworthy, "Originalism in Constitutional Interpretation," *Federal Law Review* 25, 1 (1997): 1–50; and Jeffrey Goldsworthy, "The Case for Originalism" in *The Challenge of Originalism: Theories of Constitutional Interpretation*, eds. Grant Huscroft and Bradley W. Miller (Cambridge: Cambridge University Press, 2011). See, generally, Jeffrey Goldsworthy, ed., *Interpreting Constitutions: A Comparative Study* (Oxford: Oxford University Press, 2006).
[55] Greene, 3.
[56] Greene, 9.

out that neither Canadian nor Australian jurisprudence has much to say about its framers.[57] On this score, we need to bear in mind that, since the Australian and Canadian constitutions were originally adopted as part of a British Act of Parliament, there were numerous foreign "framers" involved in the process, and, to Fontana's point, these were "reorganizational" rather than "revolutionary" constitutions.[58] Additionally, these countries have adopted a different balance in the separation of powers in their parliamentary systems than exists in the United States, and some of those differences relate directly to constitutional decision making.

Especially noteworthy is the power of both the Canadian Parliament and the provincial Canadian legislatures to override a Supreme Court decision in a constitutional case. According to a publication of the Canadian Library of Parliament, the well-known "notwithstanding clause," Section 33 of the Canadian Charter of Rights and Freedoms, "permits Parliament or a provincial legislature to adopt legislation to override [the] section ... of the Charter [addressing] such fundamental rights as freedom of expression, freedom of conscience, freedom of association and freedom of assembly[,] and [the] sections ... containing the right to life, liberty and security of the person, freedom from unreasonable search and seizure, freedom from arbitrary arrest or detention ... and the right to equality."[59] Although the override can only last for five years, it can be renewed, presumably indefinitely.[60] No equivalent exists in American constitutional politics, where such an override would require a difficult and lengthy constitutional amendment process. Interestingly, the same Library of Parliament publication includes several pages devoted to a section titled, "Framers' Intentions," with quotations from numerous ministers who were involved in the adoption of the notwithstanding clause.[61]

Canada and Australia also inherited from Britain what was often called the "exclusionary rule," a judge-made rule (occasionally honored in the breach), which prohibited the use of evidence from parliamentary debates in statutory interpretation. Linking the exclusionary rule to a 1769 case, Lord Nicolas Browne-Wilkinson described in *Pepper v. Hart* what had been the "general

57 Greene, 9.

58 Fontana, "Response," 196.

59 David Johansen and Philip Rosen, "The Notwithstanding Clause of the Charter," Background Paper BP-194E (Ottawa, Canada: Library of Parliament, 2005), 2, http://publications.gc.ca/collections/Collection-R/LoPBdP/BP-e/bp194-1e.pdf. For more on Australia, see David Kinley, "Constitutional Brokerage in Australia: Constitutions and the Doctrines of Parliamentary Supremacy and the Rule of Law," *Federal Law Review* 22, 1 (1994): 194–204.

60 Johansen and Rosen, "The Notwithstanding Clause," 2.

61 Johansen and Rosen, 5–10.

rule that references to Parliamentary material as an aid to statutory construction is not permissible."[62] Following the decision to modify that rule in the 1992 *Pepper* case, UK judges would be permitted to employ the previously forbidden Parliamentary materials if three conditions were met: the legislation is "ambiguous or obscure," the statements are made by a minister or other promoter of bill, and the statements are clear.[63] More recently, Lord Robin Cooke has noted the "real help" that courts can obtain from referring to the Parliamentary debates, "even if it is not necessarily decisive help," especially to the extent that the statement shows "that the courts will not be thwarting a clear intention of the legislators."[64] Canada and Australia have followed suit in loosening or eliminating the exclusionary rule, but the rule's traditional role in Commonwealth legal culture and the lack of specific nation-building framers involved in their constitutional formation suggest that cultural contingencies in Canada and Australia may influence prevailing attitudes about how their fairly recent constitutions are interpreted, and why their framers' debates may be cited less frequently than in the United States.[65]

Contrasting interpretive practices in different nations inevitably involves complex comparative issues over which reasonable scholars can and do disagree. Rather than wrestling with the question of which countries most closely resemble the United States in the techniques of constitutional interpretation, the nuances of judicial review, the nature of the separation of powers, and the

62 *Pepper (Inspector of Taxes) v. Hart* [1993] AC 593, 630. He cited *Millar v. Taylor* (1769) 4 Burr. 2303, 2332. For a discussion of their rule's relative lack of influence in America, see Robert G. Natelson, "The Founders' Hermeneutic: The Real Original Understanding of Original Intent," *Ohio State Law Journal* 68, 5 (2007): 1268–73. For this case, see, generally, Michael P. Healy, "Legislative Intent and Statutory Interpretation in England and the United States: An Assessment of the Impact of *Pepper v. Hart*," *Stanford Journal of International Law* 35, 2 (Summer 1999): 231–54; James J. Brudney, "Below the Surface: Comparing Legislative History Usage by the House of Lords and the Supreme Court," *Washington University Law Review* 85, 1 (2007): 1–71; and John James Magyar, "The Evolution of Hansard Use at the Supreme Court of Canada: A Comparative Study in Statutory Interpretation," *Statute Law Review* 33, 3 (October 2012): 363–89.

63 *Pepper*, AC 593 at 630. This case has engendered a certain amount of controversy in the law journals. See, for example, Aileen Kavanagh, "*Pepper v Hart* and Matters of Constitutional Principle," *Law Quarterly Review* 121 (January 2005): 101–2; Johan Steyn, "*Pepper v Hart*; A Re-examination," *Oxford Journal of Legal Studies* 21, 1 (Spring 2001): 59–72; Stefan Vogenauer, "A Retreat from *Pepper v Hart*? A Reply to Lord Steyn," *Oxford Journal of Legal Studies* 25, 4 (Winter 2005): 629–74; and Philip Sales, "*Pepper v Hart*: A Footnote to Professor Vogenauer's Reply to Lord Steyn," *Oxford Journal of Legal Studies* 26, 3 (Autumn 2006): 585–92.

64 *R v. Sec'y of State for the Env't, Transp. & the Regions, ex parte Spath Holme Ltd.* [2001] 2 AC 349.

65 See Neil A. Campbell, "Legal Research and the Exclusionary Rule," *Canadian Law Library Review* 36, 4 (2011): 158–66.

revolutionary versus evolutionary nature of their constitutions, it may be more fruitful to shift the perspective from a snapshot to an extended video. Chapter 3 showed that the popularity of each of the approaches to interpreting authoritative legal texts has waxed and waned for centuries. The history of interpretation in Western legal thought shows that the four approaches to discerning and applying the will of the lawmaker – the objective and subjective meaning at the time of enactment, and the objective and subjective meaning as of the date of interpretation – have been in constant circulation, with one or another of the approaches achieving (official or unofficial) dominance from time to time.

In both the UK and the US, mid-nineteenth-century commentaries declared the primacy of original meanings, but the interpretative rule of thumb was reversed a century later, as updated meanings became the norm. In the United Kingdom, the objective meaning at the time of enactment was, in John Manning's phrase, "hornbook law" by at least the mid-nineteenth century, and Sir Rupert Cross described it essentially the same way in the first edition of his influential text on interpretation in the 1970s.[66] Then, a decade later, a second edition of Cross was published, and it declared essentially that updating, or "always speaking," interpretations were the new hornbook law. That current "constitutional orthodoxy," according to Ian Loveland, "is that statutes should (generally) be presumed to be 'always speaking.'" In support, Loveland cites Francis Bennion's influential work, *Statutory Interpretation*:

> [T]he interpreter is to presume that Parliament intended the original Act to be applied at any future time in such a way as to give effect to the original intention. Accordingly the interpreter is to make allowances for any relevant changes that have occurred, since the Act's passing, in law, social conditions, technology, the meaning of words and other matters.[67]

The pattern is much the same in the United States. In the nineteenth century, Thomas Cooley confidently pointed to the authoritativeness of original meaning, a general rule that was later to be supplanted by the living constitution of the Warren Court. It was, in fact, the US Supreme Court's (and scholars') embrace of the living US Constitution that the British scholar Francis Bennion had used to support his own enthusiasm for updating constructions in statutory interpretation. He noted that as "the U.S. Constitution is regarded as 'a living Constitution,' so an ongoing British

[66] John F. Manning, "Textualism and the Equity of the Statute," *Columbia Law Review* 101, 1 (January 2001): 55; Rupert Cross, *Statutory Interpretation* (London: Butterworths, 1976), p. 47.

[67] Ian Loveland, *Constitutional Law, Administrative Law, and Human Rights: A Critical Introduction*, 7th ed. (Oxford: Oxford University Press, 2015), p. 64, citing Francis Bennion, *Statutory Interpretation*, 3rd ed. (London: Butterworths, 1997), p. 686.

Act is regarded 'a living Act'."[68] Ultimately, Bennion, who was the major source cited by the updated Cross and Loveland hornbooks, based his argument, at least in part, on the United States' interpretive environment at that time.

The pendulum now appears to be swinging the other direction, and advocates for the original meaning of statutes and constitutions have been making headway with both courts and scholars. As discussed in earlier chapters, the originalism movement in the United States has focused a great deal of attention on the need for a return to the constitutional meaning at the time of ratification. Originalism has even become more visible in Canada, even though that country has generally been recognized for its dedication to "living tree" interpretations and lacks a "revolutionary" constitution.[69] Scholars have recently pointed to elements of originalist interpretations (even if not by that name) in Canada's Supreme Court, and there is good reason to believe that there will be additional signs of originalism in opinions by Canadian judges in the future.[70] In 2014, Professors Grant Huscroft and Bradley Miller of Western University were appointed as judges. Together, they coedited a widely cited book on originalism, in which Miller wrote that "originalists have had some insights that can bear much fruit if incorporated into Canadian constitutional doctrine."[71]

The importance of a legal text's original meaning has gained ground in the United Kingdom as well. When Lady Brenda Hale's leading judgment for the

68 Rupert Cross, *Statutory Interpretation*, eds. John Bell and George Engle, 3rd ed. (London: Butterworths, 1995), p. 49, citing §288 of Bennion, *Statutory Interpretation*, p. 617, who says that "it is presumed that Parliament intends the court to apply to an ongoing Act a construction that continuously updates its wording to allow for changes since the Act was initially framed (an updating construction)."

69 Peter W. Hogg, "Canada: From Privy Council to Supreme Court," in Goldsworthy, *Interpreting Constitutions*, pp. 85–7.

70 Léonid Sirota and Benjamin Oliphant, "Originalist Reasoning in Canadian Constitutional Jurisprudence," *University of British Columbia Law Review* 50, 2 (2017): 505–74; its abstract reads: "Amongst the fundamental assumptions underlying the practice of Canadian constitutional interpretation is the belief that originalism . . . plays no meaningful role in discerning the meaning of constitutional provisions. This paper sets out to correct that mistaken narrative." See also Benjamin Oliphant and Léonid Sirota, "Has the Supreme Court of Canada Rejected 'Originalism'?," *Queen's Law Journal* 42, 1 (Fall 2016): 107–64; and J. Gareth Morley, "Dead Hands, Living Trees, Historic Compromises: The Senate Reform and Supreme Court Act References Bring the Originalism Debate to Canada," *Osgoode Hall Law Journal* 53, 3 (Summer 2016): 745–98.

71 Bradley W. Miller, "Origin Myth: The Persons Case, the Living Tree, and the New Originalism," in Huscroft and Miller, *Challenge of Originalism*, p. 145. Miller pointed in particular to Lawrence Solum's articulation of the fixation thesis ("a commitment to fixed meanings," in Miller's words). Miller, "Origin Myth," 146.

UK Supreme Court in a 2011 case purported to update the meaning of "domestic violence" in a housing statute so that it included psychological as well as physical violence, negative commentary appeared rapidly in scholarly journals and in the media.[72] The updating interpretation was criticized by Oxford Professor Richard Ekins as an example of amending the statute "by judicial fiat."[73] London School of Economics Professor Neil Duxbury, after reviewing centuries of cases involving statutory interpretation, concluded that "[t]his is perhaps the closest any English judge has ever come to entertaining the possibility of dynamic statutory interpretation without regard for the real or hypothesized intentions of the enacting legislature."[74] University of Nottingham Professor Chris Bevan also agreed with Ekins' assessment that "the fundamental problem with the [updating] approach [in the case] is its inattention to what it is that Parliament did – what it decided and intended to convey – in 1996 . . . in uttering the statutory text."[75]

To the extent that comparativist scholars look only at the UK Supreme Court judgments, they will continue to see the dominance of updating, purposive approaches to interpretation. The Court unanimously adopted what it described as the updated meaning; as Lord Brown wrote, "one does not . . . like to appear old-fashioned."[76] But, looking instead at the reaction to the decision shows that a number of legal scholars at distinguished universities published commentary that instead advocated the old-fashioned approach of focusing on "what it is that Parliament did."[77] Whether this scholarship will become influential enough to convince the UK Supreme Court to employ a more "backward" focus on the meaning at the time of enactment remains to be seen, but it is clear that, at least in the elite legal community, the orthodox devotion to "always speaking," living constructions is being challenged. This case can, therefore, illustrate both the truth of the conventional wisdom that a dynamic interpretation currently prevails in

72 *Yemshaw v. London Borough of Hounslow* [2011] UKSC 3.

73 Richard Ekins, *The Nature of Legislative Intent* (Oxford: Oxford University Press, 2012), p. 265. See also Richard Ekins, "Updating the Meaning of Violence," *Law Quarterly Review* 129 (2013): 17–21.

74 Neil Duxbury, *Elements of Legislation* (Cambridge: Cambridge University Press, 2013), p. 231.

75 Chris Bevan, "Interpreting Statutory Purpose – Lessons from *Yemshaw v Hounslow London Borough Council*," *Modern Law Review* 76, 4 (July 2013): 750, quoting Ekins, "Updating," 19. Bevan calls the description of the purposes identified in the case an "overly broad and illegitimate interpretation" because of the "non-engagement with government housing and homelessness policy in the mid-1990s and the wider political landscape." Bevan, "Interpreting," 753.

76 *Yemshaw*, UKSC 3 at 22.

77 Bevan, "Interpreting," 750, quoting Ekins, "Updating," 19.

the United Kingdom, and the fact that there is growing support for an opposing view among leading scholars.

Looking back to what Kim Scheppele calls "historical starting point[s]" may not be as prevalent in Europe as it is in the United States today, but it is not as much a thing of the past as comparativist scholars have suggested.[78] Beyond the fact that each country has its own unique political and constitutional setting, many centuries of interpretive history show that searches for the original meaning have definitely not been fully replaced by a view to what she has called the "imagined future of a polity."[79]

ELITE AND PUBLIC OPINION ABOUT THE FRAMERS' ROLE IN INTERPRETATION

Much of this book has dealt with the views of constitutional scholars and other elites about the Framers and original meaning. There is no doubt that the justices take scholars' views seriously.[80] But with respect to the broad-based sociological legitimacy of the Court's decisions it is valuable to explore the public's attitudes about interpretation, especially in light of the notion that a focus on original meaning and the Framers is largely a proxy for conservative political preferences. The *New Yorker*'s Jeffrey Toobin writes, for example: "In practical terms, originalism gives constitutional sanction to conservative politics."[81]

78 Scheppele, "Jack Balkin Is an American," 24.

79 Scheppele, 24.

80 The justices routinely cite academic publications, and Justice Kennedy's opinion in *Lawrence v. Texas*, for example, indicated that the justices take the views of legal scholars seriously, although it is not clear whether he was influenced by the academics themselves or by the historical information they had discovered. Justice Kennedy wrote that "in academic writings, and in many of the scholarly *amicus* briefs filed to assist the Court in this case, there are fundamental criticisms of the historical premises relied upon by the ... opinions" in the case that *Lawrence* overturned. *Lawrence v. Texas*, 539 US 558, 567–68 (2003). Unlike the public, however, legal academics have nearly boundless opportunities to express their views on how to interpret the Constitution, from general theories of constitutional interpretation to detailed analyses of particular provisions. As of late, for example, there has been something of a bull market in originalism. According to Lexis Nexis, the yearly number of law review articles that include "originalism" or some variation thereof in the title has increased sixfold over the last twenty years. To the extent that the justices want to know what the academy thinks about constitutional interpretation, that information is not hard to come by.

81 Jeffrey Toobin, "How Scalia Changed the Supreme Court," *New Yorker*, February 13, 2016, www.newyorker.com/news/news-desk/how-scalia-changed-the-supreme-court. See also Keith E. Whittington, "Is Originalism Too Conservative?," *Harvard Journal of Law and Public Policy* 34, 1 (Winter 2011): 29–30; and Robert Post and Reva Siegel, "Originalism as a Political Practice: The Right's Living Constitution," *Fordham Law Review* 75, 2 (November 2006): 545–74.

In considering public opinion on matters of interpretation, we need to bear in mind that it is based on what people believe, irrespective of whether we think that they are right or wrong, misguided or ill-informed. As Fallon notes: "[S]ociological legitimacy depends wholly on facts about what people think, not an independent moral appraisal of how people ought to think."[82] Accordingly, this is not an argument that jurisprudential issues of interpretive theory should be based on whatever might be popular with the public. Few members are fully informed about the issues, nor have they read the relevant scholarship. But they do interpret things every day, and they have views about judicial interpretation that can influence their votes for public officials and contribute to the broader environment in which the Court seeks sociological legitimacy. As Steven D. Smith points out, "We – not only lawyers but citizens generally – routinely find ourselves engaged in . . . debates [about meaning]."[83]

Before exploring the specific interpretation issues, it is worth noting that the public takes constitutional issues very seriously. Presidential candidate Donald Trump, for example, pledged to appoint originalist jurists at a time when there was an open seat on the Court.[84] Exit polls from the 2016 election showed that 70 percent of voters thought Supreme Court appointments were an important issue, and 21 percent believed that they were the most important factor in the election.[85] The 70 percent citing the importance of Supreme Court appointments was almost exactly divided between Clinton and Trump voters, showing that the perception of the importance of the Court is similar across party lines.

On the issue of the correct way to interpret the Constitution, public opinion surveys have consistently shown that the American public divides roughly evenly when they are asked to pick between originalism and a "living" or "modern" constitutional interpretation.[86] The results tend to split along conservative-liberal lines. But a specially commissioned survey that explored these

82 Fallon, *Law and Legitimacy*, 23. Nevertheless, Fallon points out that "enhanced sociological legitimacy is morally relevant insofar as it seems necessary to sustain a climate of mutual respect among citizens and of recognition by citizens of the government's right to rule, both generally and in particular ways." Fallon, 159.

83 Steven D. Smith, *Law's Quandary* (Cambridge, MA: Harvard University Press, 2004), p. 101.

84 "In His Own Words: The President's Attacks on the Courts," Brennan Center for Justice, New York University School of Law, June 5, 2017, www.brennancenter.org/analysis/his-own-words-presidents-attacks-courts.

85 "Exit Polls," CNN, updated November 23, 2019, www.cnn.com/election/2016/results/exit-polls.

86 Jamal Greene has summarized these polls as follows:

> Today, a substantial portion of the American public reports an affinity for originalism. A 2005 Fox News poll asked the following question of registered voters:

issues in more detail demonstrates remarkably bipartisan interest in giving the Framers a prominent role in the interpretive process, irrespective of whether people favor a fixed or living Constitution.[87] The answers came from approximately 1,000 Americans who were surveyed by YouGov in July 2012.

The original meaning approach came out somewhat ahead (60 percent to 40 percent) when respondents were asked whether the Supreme Court should rule based on what the "Constitution meant when it was originally written," or what it "means in current times." When the respondents who picked "What the Constitution means in current times" were then asked what relevance, if any, the original meaning should have when the Court is interpreting the Constitution, nearly 80 percent of them said that it should be "one of various factors that should be considered," with only 3 percent opting to have the Court ignore it completely. In total, then, over 90 percent of all respondents believe that original meaning should play at least some role in the Supreme Court's decision making.[88]

Respondents were also asked to consider a variety of types of evidence potentially bearing on the original meaning, including dictionaries of that era, and the likely understandings of average voters or the ratifiers, along with what the Framers were trying to accomplish. Although many respondents

> Which of the following comes closest to your view of how the Constitution should be interpreted by the U.S. Supreme Court? Judges should base their rulings on what they believe the Constitution's framers meant when it was originally written. Judges should base their rulings on what they believe the Constitution means in today's world.
>
> Forty-seven percent of respondents chose the "Framers' intent" option, while only thirty-six percent chose contemporary meaning. In a more polemically worded July 2008 poll conducted by Quinnipiac University, forty percent of respondents reported believing that "[i]n making decisions, the Supreme Court should only consider the original intentions of the authors of the Constitution." Fifty-two percent of respondents favored the proposed alternative, that "[i]n making decisions, the Supreme Court should consider changing times and current realities in applying the principles of the Constitution." This number is in line with identically worded Quinnipiac polls in 2007, 2005, and 2003.

Jamal Greene, "Selling Originalism," *Georgetown Law Journal* 97, 3 (March 2009), 695. For a more extensive review of originalism-related surveys, see Jamal Greene, Nathaniel Persily, and Stephen Ansolabehere, "Profiling Originalism," *Columbia Law Review* 111, 2 (March 2011), 362–70.

87 The survey was conducted over the Internet by YouGov as part of a 1003-person YouGov Omnibus survey of the general population conducted July 20–23, 2012. YouGov calculates the margin of error to be ±3.4 percent. See Drakeman, "What's the Point of Originalism?"

88 This data is consistent with the results of a 2009 survey in which 92 percent of the respondents answered "very" or "somewhat" important to the following question: "How important would you say it is for a good Supreme Court judge to . . . uphold the values of those who wrote our constitution two hundred years ago?" Greene et al., "Profiling Originalism," 364–5.

thought that all of the potential sources were relevant, approximately two-thirds identified "What the Constitution's Framers intended it to mean" as the most important source for determining the original meaning. That two-thirds included a majority of responders in each of the self-identified categories of liberal, moderate, and conservative.

In this environment, it should not be surprising to find the Framers invoked in Supreme Court opinions, and that turns out to be the case. Founding-Era history and the Framers themselves appear not only in opinions from the conservative wing of the Court, but also from the more progressive justices as well. Justice Elena Kagan even made a point of saying at her confirmation hearing, "We are all originalists."[89] To be sure, Justice Kagan and Justice Scalia may not have necessarily defined the rules and regulations of originalism in the same way, but there can be little doubt that the original meaning represents an important foundation for constitutional interpretation and continues to play a strong role in Supreme Court opinions.

In the 2011 First Amendment case *Arizona Christian School v. Winn*, for example, Justice Kagan's dissenting opinion for essentially the liberal wing of the Court (Justices Ruth Bader Ginsberg, Stephen Breyer, and Sonia Sotomayor joined her opinion), cited Samuel Johnson's *Dictionary of the English Language* and James Madison's "Memorial and Remonstrance Against Religious Assessments," along with numerous articles and books about the Founding Era.[90] Justice Anthony Kennedy's majority opinion also pointed to the views expressed by Madison, whom he called "the leading architect of the [First Amendment's] religion clauses."[91] The same phrase about First Amendment architecture, along with additional discussions of Madison's church–state views, subsequently appeared in a 2012 unanimous opinion for the Court written by Chief Justice John Roberts in *Hosanna-Tabor Evangelical Lutheran Church v. EEOC*.[92] Altogether, federal and state courts have cited James Madison over 100 times in religion cases since the dawn of modern Establishment Clause jurisprudence with the *Everson v. Board of Education* case in 1947.[93] As Phillip Muñoz has pointed out: "Even Justice William Brennan, no champion of 'originalism,' claimed that in the context of

89 Quoted in "Kagan: 'We Are All Originalists.'" *The BLT: The Blog of LegalTimes*, June 29, 2010, http://legaltimes.typepad.com/blt/2010/06/kagan-we-are-all-originalists.html.

90 *Arizona Christian Sch. Tuition Org. v. Winn*, 563 US 125 (2011).

91 *Winn*, 563 US at 141, quoting *Flast v. Cohen*, 392 US 83, 103 (1968).

92 *Hosanna-Tabor Evangelical Lutheran Church & Sch. v. EEOC*, 565 US 171 (2012).

93 See Donald L. Drakeman, "James Madison and the First Amendment Establishment of Religion Clause," in *Religion and Political Culture in Jefferson's Virginia*, eds. Garrett Ward Sheldon and Daniel L. Dreisbach (Lanham, MD: Rowman & Littlefield, 2000), p. 219.

prayer in public schools, 'the line we must draw between the permissible and the impermissible is one which accords with history and faithfully reflects the understanding of the Founding Fathers'."[94]

The religion clauses are not the only places where the Court has focused on original meaning and has cited specific Framers. In a discussion of Section 1 of the Fourteenth Amendment in *McDonald v. Chicago* (2010), for example, both Justice Samuel Alito's majority opinion and Justice Clarence Thomas' concurring opinion contained analyses of specific statements made during floor debates by members of the 39th Congress. Additionally, to settle a jurisdictional question, Justice David Souter's opinion for the Court in the less well-known case of *JPMorgan Chase v. Traffic Stream Infrastructures* (2002) looked to the statements of James Wilson at the Pennsylvania ratification convention and of James Madison and Alexander Hamilton in *The Federalist*.[95] The same triumvirate appeared in Justice Breyer's majority opinion in *U.S. v. Hatter* (2001), a case about judicial compensation, in which the justice cited James Wilson's lectures on law and one of his speeches at the Pennsylvania ratifying convention, along with sections of *The Federalist*.[96]

In the Elections Clause case, *Arizona State Legislature v. Arizona Independent Redistricting Commission* (2015), Justice Ginsberg's majority opinion examined "the historical record" to identify the "dominant purpose" of the clause, as explained by James Madison during the Constitutional Convention, prompting a vigorous rebuttal from the Chief Justice, whose dissenting opinion countered with comments from a range of Framers, including a convention speech by George Mason. These are just a sampling of references to the Framers in recent years. Even Justice Scalia, who was well-known for leading the effort to replace Old Originalism's focus on the Framers with New Originalism's textualism, could not always resist turning to the Framers. Michael Ramsey has identified "eight Scalia opinions citing the Convention debates in support of a substantial argument."[97]

The Supreme Court began consulting the Framers at its first opportunity, just a few years after ratification, and has continued to do so in a wide range of twenty-first-century cases.[98] The Court's references to the Framers have

[94] Vincent Phillip *Muñoz*, "The Original Meaning of the Establishment Clause and the Impossibility of its Incorporation," *University of Pennsylvania Journal of Constitutional Law* 8, 4 (August 2006): 585 n3.

[95] *JPMorgan Chase Bank v. Traffic Stream (BVI) Infrastructure Ltd.*, 536 US 88, 95–6 (2002).

[96] *United States v. Hatter*, 532 US 557, 567–9 (2001).

[97] Michael D. Ramsey, "Beyond the Text: Justice Scalia's Originalism in Practice," *Notre Dame Law Review* 92, 5 (2017): 1965.

[98] See, for example, *Hylton v. United States*, 3 US 171 (1796), as discussed in Chapter 5.

remained remarkably consistent. Gordon Lloyd has calculated that about 30 percent of the approximately 100 cases in the Marshall Court referred at least once to the Framers.[99] Of these thirty-three cases, a dozen cite the Constitutional Convention, five point to records from the state ratifying conventions, and eight refer to the First Congress, along with a few references to a variety of other Founding Era documents. Likewise, about thirty percent of the opinions from twentieth-century Burger and Rehnquist Courts cite the Framers.[100] The justices have a long and distinguished record of consulting the Framers in the process of interpretation, not only to identify the Constitution's meaning, but to preserve its sociological legitimacy with "We the People."

CONCLUSION

In spite of my concerns that the Framers have been pushed to the periphery (or beyond) of academic constitutional theory, the Framers have retained a prominent role in constitutional interpretation on an impressively bipartisan basis in the views of Supreme Court justices, elected officials, and the public. It turns out that such a considerable level of interest in original meaning is not out of sync with leading scholars and judges around the world, despite a considerable body of scholarship to the contrary. As a result, justices who desire to enhance the Court's sociological legitimacy, as well as to maintain their own fidelity to their traditional roles, should not be deterred from focusing on the Framers' intentions in matters of interpretation. By the same token, and for additional reasons discussed in the next chapter, they should be wary of making judgments in constitutional cases that are inconsistent with those intentions.

[99] Gordon Lloyd, "*Marshall v. Madison*: The Supreme Court and Original Intent, 1803–35," *Criminal Justice Ethics* 32, 1 (April 2013): 24.

[100] Ramsey, "Beyond the Text," 24–5. For a similar analysis showing that "members of the First Congress invoked originalist arguments a number of times," but pointing out that on any particular issue, "these arguments were positioned among many other arguments and were not necessarily the dispositive ones," see Louis J. Sirico Jr., "Original Intent in the First Congress," *Missouri Law Review* 71, 3 (Summer 2006): 691.

9

Noninterpretive Decisions

Prior chapters have demonstrated that the concept of "interpretation" has had fixed boundaries for centuries. The various approaches – objective, subjective, fixed, or dynamic – all relate to a process of identifying the lawmaker's will, or, in our case, the Framers' intentions. There are also longstanding debates over where to find the best evidence of the Framers' end–means choice, when updated interpretations are appropriate, the proper role of judicial precedent, and the like. Nearly all of our current debates over constitutional interpretation have happened before, including those involving complex insights from linguistics, philosophy, and history that feel very modern to us. My goal has been to remind the participants in today's debates that the will of the lawmaker has been the fixed core around which those debates have revolved. Before concluding, however, it is important to return to the genuinely new argument about interpretation that appeared in the twentieth century: the idea that Supreme Court justices should make their own judgment of the best national policy and write their opinions in whatever judicial language will give the impression that the decision represents an interpretation of the Constitution.

THE SUPREME COURT AS A "SUPER-LEGISLATURE"

The idea that the judicial branch is really just a "super-legislature"[1] that should rule on interpretive questions based on whatever decisions will lead to the best result, or will make "our constitutional order best,"[2] has been gaining ground with a number of leading scholars. In the past, this claim that "the justices are

[1] Brian Leiter, "Constitutional Law, Moral Judgment, and the Supreme Court as Super-Legislature," *Hastings Law Journal* 66, 6 (2015): 1601–16.

[2] Cass R. Sunstein, "There Is Nothing that Interpretation Just Is," *Constitutional Commentary* 30, 2 (2015): 200 n39.

just making it up" has been reserved for decisions with which we strongly disagree, whether it is *Bush v. Gore* on one side of the political spectrum, or *Obergefell v. Hodges* on the other. But, over the last generation or two, a number of prominent constitutional theorists have argued that the Court clearly does make policy judgments,[3] that it should do so,[4] and that traditional interpretive arguments can be effectively employed by the justices to provide legitimacy for those policy judgments. That is, once justices have identified the right outcome in a case based on what they think should be the optimal national policy, they can then justify that conclusion by appealing to whichever constitutional language or related principles can support the result. "[P]olicy making is a standard and legitimate function of modern courts, as standard and well-accepted as fact-finding or the interpretation of authoritative texts,"[5] write Malcolm Feeley and Edward Rubin. Meanwhile interpretation is, according to Cass Sunstein, a "capacious rubric,"[6] capable of supporting a range of potential outcomes. The argument in this chapter is that it is not capacious enough to encompass de novo policymaking by the Supreme Court.

A results-driven approach to constitutional decision making falls outside the definition of interpretation that has prevailed for centuries, as discussed in the proceeding chapters, because it does not involve the application to a particular case of the lawmaker's end–means policy judgment as expressed in the constitutional text (irrespective of whether that interpretation relates to the meaning as of the date of enactment or as updated). Instead, a results-driven approach puts the Court in the primary policymaking role. In these cases, the goal of the justices is to focus on identifying the best result for the country, after which they can either announce the policy rationale behind the decision, or work back to a plausible rationale for justifying that result by making a retrofitted argument about the meaning of the Constitution.

3 See, for example, Leiter, "Constitutional Law," 1615: "Lawmakers cannot anticipate all problems that will arise, but in a civilized society, we need courts to provide authoritative resolutions of disputes that are left unsettled by the existing sources of law. Courts play that role, and the 'higher' the court, the more likely it is that court will be asked to exercise circumscribed moral and political judgment, akin to what we expect from honest legislators."

4 See, for example, Malcolm M. Feeley and Edward L. Rubin, *Judicial Policy Making and the Modern State: How the Courts Reformed America's Prisons* (New York: Cambridge University Press, 1999).

5 Edward L. Rubin and Malcolm M. Feeley, "Judicial Policy Making and Litigation against the Government," *University of Pennsylvania Journal of Constitutional Law* 5, 3 (2003): 617–18, invoking Owen Fiss's argument that the federal courts, in fact, have an obligation to make policy. See Owen M. Fiss, "Foreword: The Forms of Justice," *Harvard Law Review* 93, 1 (1979): 1–58.

6 Sunstein, "There Is Nothing," 207.

This proposed judicial policymaking power can potentially be very broad, but it may not be unlimited. As Brian Leiter points out: "[F]irst, the Court can only pass on issues that are brought before it; and second, the Court is constrained, to some extent, by its past decisions and by constitutional and legislative texts."[7] Nevertheless, since "those constraints *underdetermine* the Court's decisions in most cases, . . . the Court essentially makes its final choice among the legally viable options based on the moral and political values of the Justices."[8] Similarly, Sunstein says: "Among the reasonable alternatives, any particular approach to the Constitution *must* be defended on the ground that it makes the relevant constitutional order better rather than worse."[9] This chapter will address two questions about policymaking by the Supreme Court in constitutional cases. First, should we encourage justices to engage in noninterpretive policymaking in cases arising under the Constitution? Second, if they do, should they say they are doing so, or should they write opinions as if, in Justice Kagan's words, "it's the law all the way down"?[10]

The idea of the court as a super-legislator is part of a burgeoning body of transnational scholarship encouraging judges to base decisions primarily on their outcomes rather than on the traditional processes of interpretation.[11] These scholars are less interested in the age-old arguments about how the courts should interpret legal texts, and more on the role of the courts, especially the Supreme Court of the United States and other apex courts, in setting national policy. These theorists see constitutions, charters, laws, and regulations as an invitation for judges to weigh the likely outcomes of various

7 Leiter, "Constitutional Law," 1601.

8 Leiter, 1601 (original emphasis).

9 Sunstein, "There Is Nothing," 212 (emphasis added).

10 Quoted in Paul Kane, "Kagan Sidesteps Empathy Question, Says 'It's Law All the Way Down,'" *Washington Post*, June 29, 2010, www.washingtonpost.com/wp-dyn/content/article/2010/06/29/AR2010062903935.html.

11 Eveline T. Feteris, "The Rational Reconstruction of Argumentation Referring to Consequences and Purposes in the Application of Legal Rules: A Pragma-Dialectical Perspective," *Argumentation* 19, 4 (November 2005): 459–70; Flavia Carbonell, "Reasoning by Consequences: Applying Different Argumentation Structures to the Analysis of Consequentialist Reasoning in Judicial Decisions," *Cogency* 3, 2 (Summer 2011): 81–104; Péter Cserne, "Consequence-Based Arguments in Legal Reasoning: A Jurisprudential Preface to *Law and Economics*," in *Efficiency, Sustainability, and Justice to Future Generations*, ed. Klaus Mathis (New York: Springer, 2011); and Klaus Mathis, "Consequentialism in Law," in Mathis, *Efficiency, Sustainability, and Justice*. These discussions frequently invoke Neil MacCormick, *Legal Reasoning and Legal Theory* (Oxford: Oxford University Press, 1978). See also Maksymilian Del Mar, "The Forward-Looking Requirement of Formal Justice: Neil MacCormick on Consequential Reasoning," *Jurisprudence* 6, 3 (2015): 432 n10, which argues that scholars "tend to refer to consequentialist arguments in a much broader sense than MacCormick does, especially in his later work."

possible decisions, and then choose the one that, on balance, makes the world a better place.[12]

Surprisingly few of the theoretical discussions have explored how these results-driven decisions relate to judges' traditional role as interpreters of authoritative legal texts. When the issue has occasionally appeared, the principal inquiry has been whether the court's reasoning should be "open" or "covert."[13] A number of European legal scholars have argued for disclosing the court's actual reasoning as "a requirement of methodological honesty and transparency."[14] For example, Klaus Mathis "calls for the judge . . . not to hide behind imaginary 'fundamental principles' . . . of the legal order . . . but . . . should, just like the legislator, consciously justify [the decision] in autonomous terms," not only for the sake of "methodological honesty but also as the only way that a judicial ruling can become accessible to discussion and acceptance."[15]

Meanwhile, a number of other scholars, especially in the United States, have embraced a covert mode in which judges reach decisions for whatever policy-related reasons they find persuasive, but the court's publicly disclosed rationale is written instead in the conventional language of interpretation. Mark Tushnet has written, for example, that if he were a judge, he would consider "which result is . . . likely to advance the cause of socialism," and then, having picked the desired result, he "would write an opinion in some currently favoured version of Grand Theory [of the Constitution]."[16] Similarly, when Christopher Eisgruber described the use of history in judicial opinions, he lauded its purely instrumental value in persuading people who would otherwise have the wrong understanding of the demands of justice: "When the judge's decision flies in the face of national electoral majorities, the task of reconciling [the judges' conception of] justice and . . . public

[12] See Robert Cooter, "Constitutional Consequentialism: Bargain Democracy versus Median Democracy," *Theoretical Inquiries in Law* 3, 1 (2002): 1–20; Raimo Siltala, *Law, Truth, and Reason: A Treatise on Legal Argumentation* (New York: Springer, 2011); Adrian Vermeule, *The Constitution of Risk* (New York: Cambridge University Press, 2014); George Letsas, "Rescuing Proportionality," in *Philosophical Foundations of Human Rights*, eds. Rowan Cruft, S. Matthew Liao, and Massimo Renzo (Oxford: Oxford University Press, 2015); and Bart van der Sloot, "The Practical and Theoretical Problems with 'Balancing': Delfi, Coty and the Redundancy of the Human Rights Framework," *Maastricht Journal of European and Comparative Law* 23, 3 (2016): 439–59.

[13] Ulfrid Neumann, "Juristische Argumentationstheorie," in *Handbuch Rechtsphilosophie*, eds. Eric Hilgendorf and Jan C. Joerden (Stuttgart, Germany: J. B. Metzler, 2017).

[14] Mathis, "Consequentialism in Law," 20; see also Mathis, 15 nn71–2.

[15] Mathis, 18.

[16] Mark Tushnet, "The Dilemmas of Liberal Constitutionalism," *Ohio State Law Journal* 42, 1 (1981): 424.

opinion will be especially challenging. Here historical argument may play a special role. By appealing to history," which judges, commentators, and the public have long seen as a valid approach to interpretation, "judges may attach a popular pedigree to unpopular decisions."[17]

Sunstein has argued that the usually conflicting views of leading theorists and jurists – he cites Ronald Dworkin, Justice Antonin Scalia, John Hart Ely, and others – are all legitimate contenders in the realm of interpretative theory, but they largely miss the point. Because these conflicting views are all legitimate modes of interpretation – and, therefore, none has a valid claim to exclusivity – judges can be flexible and pick whichever one plausibly justifies the best judicial decision. In "not ruling out"[18] any of the traditional interpretative approaches, Sunstein does not invoke the full degree of postmodernism implied by his title, "There Is Nothing that Interpretation Just Is," which would require him to make what he calls the "preposterous" claim that the meaning of a legal text is "entirely up for grabs."[19] Instead, he admits that empowering judges "to do whatever they want" would jeopardize the rule of law.[20] Yet, "among the permissible alternatives," he argues, "identification of the proper approach to constitutional interpretation requires attention to whether it would make our constitutional order better or worse."[21]

Before discussing these issues in more detail, it is important to note that this chapter will not recapitulate the familiar themes of the debate over whether courts should ever consider the consequences of their rulings, as opposed to sticking solely to matters of legal principle.[22] That debate will undoubtedly continue, despite the difficulties as a practical matter of denying Hart's factual observation that lawyers often believe that "it is perfectly proper and indeed at times necessary for judges to take account of the impact of their decisions on the general community welfare."[23] Moreover, it would be naïve to imagine, for

[17] Christopher L. Eisgruber, *Constitutional Self-Government* (Cambridge, MA: Harvard University Press, 2001), pp. 126–7.

[18] Sunstein, "There Is Nothing," 194.

[19] Sunstein, 212.

[20] Joseph Raz, "The Rule of Law and Its Virtue," chap. 11 in *The Authority of Law: Essays on Law and Morality*, 2nd ed. (Oxford: Oxford University Press, 2009).

[21] Sunstein, "There Is Nothing," 207.

[22] Ronald Dworkin, *Taking Rights Seriously* (London: Bloomsbury, 1997); John Bell, *Policy Arguments in Judicial Decisions* (Oxford: Oxford University Press, 1983); and H. L. A. Hart, "American Jurisprudence through English Eyes: The Nightmare and the Noble Dream," chap. 4 in *Essays in Jurisprudence and Philosophy* (Oxford: Clarendon Press, 1983).

[23] Hart, "American Jurisprudence," 141 n16. Also, as Neil MacCormick has pointed out, "the interrelated elements of consequentialist argument, argument from coherence, and argument from consistency are everywhere visible in the Law Reports." MacCormick, *Legal Reasoning*, p. 250 n3.

example, that the US Supreme Court paid no attention to the fact that a presidential election hung in the balance with their statutory and constitutional interpretation in *Bush v. Gore*,[24] or that it was making a controversial choice as to a matter of great public interest in *Obergefell*.

In practice, if not in all theories of adjudication, lawyers, judges, and scholars have long recognized that courts will, in at least some cases, turn an eye towards the consequences of their decisions. The point of this chapter is neither to deny that possibility nor to advance a novel theory of why judges should never give in to the temptation to do so. The issue being addressed instead revolves around the fact that lawmakers and the public tend to believe that when judges say they are making a decision based on their interpretation of an authoritative text they are, in fact, doing so, albeit with an occasional consideration of the consequences. By contrast, the growing scholarly momentum promoting policy-based decisions could lead to a fundamental reversal of the polarity of judicial decision making. Decisions could shift from focusing on the process of interpretation, with outcome-oriented concerns supplementing interpretive ones, to a new approach in which judges will *primarily* make decisions based on which outcome they believe will lead to the best overall national policy.

Only relatively recently in the history of interpretation have there been efforts by scholars to broaden the term's definition to include plausible readings of legal texts that serve the arguably higher purpose of generating a desirable predetermined result. Ian Maclean points out that some "modern commentators have claimed that . . . the criterion of truth may be abandoned altogether in favour of plausibility and successful . . . argument." The claim that such an approach would count as a legitimate exercise in legal interpretation, he observes, "would not have been conceded by . . . Renaissance jurists,"[25] nor is it visible throughout American history until quite recently.

In their proposals for outcomes-based decisions, legal theorists encourage courts to use their own judgments about what would be good policies as the basis for the judicial decision-making process. In such cases, the law will change as a result of the judicial decision rather than by an act of a lawmaking body. The interpretation of legal texts in such an environment will no longer focus primarily on what the lawmaker did at the time of enactment, or even what it *would* do now, but, instead, on what the country *should* do now, even if the lawmaker

[24] *Bush v. Gore*, 531 US 98 (2000).

[25] Ian Maclean, *Interpretation and Meaning in the Renaissance: The Case of Law* (Cambridge: Cambridge University Press, 1992), pp. 75–6. As Mathis points out, Martina Deckert also "sees no place for consequentialist interpretation in the classic canon of methods." Klaus Mathis, "Consequentialism in Law," 16 n85. See Martina R. Deckert, *Folgenorientierung in der Rechtsanwendung* (Munich: C. H. Beck, 1995).

previously did, and would continue to do, something else altogether. That is, for literally hundreds – and probably thousands – of years, the process of judicially interpreting authoritative legal texts has encompassed a well-known cluster of competing approaches, all centered on the will of the lawmaker. Only recently have scholars suggested that we should expand that definition to include any decision that the justices believe will lead to the optimal policy result if it can be defended publicly with an after-the-fact construction of a plausible interpretive argument. The notion that the "ends justify the meanings" may be appealing to those who approve of the outcomes of the cases, but it is not what interpretation has been for virtually all of recorded legal history. In light of that extensive background, it is important to consider whether judicial policymaking could, in practice, generate good answers to difficult questions of public policy.

In considering these theoretical issues, we need to bear in mind that the arguments at the base of judicial policymaking are not merely a reiteration of legislative purpose-enhancing theories of interpretation.[26] Those approaches ask the courts to look to signals in the lawmaker's text or intention as to what constitutes good and bad outcomes, and they encourage judges to interpret the language in the manner that is most consistent with those purposes. A significant strain in the judicial policymaking literature calls instead for judges to reject (or to be open to rejecting) the lawmaker's choices for ones they prefer. That is, courts will replace the goals or purposes chosen by the lawmaker with ones they believe will lead to better results for the country. Steven D. Smith has pointed out that it is possible to construct a political community "in which elected officials enact texts ... but judges are then free to reauthor those texts to carry out their own intentions via the process of interpretation," although he "cannot think of anyone who admits to favoring such a position."[27] These proposals for outcome-determined interpretations appear to be just what Smith describes, and the covert version would allow judges to take advantage of the sociological legitimacy conveyed by using the traditional language of interpretation without being constrained by the actual process of interpretation.

RESULTS-DRIVEN DECISIONS

One significant consequence of judges engaged in pragmatic and consequentialist decision making is that courts – small bodies of judges usually trained as

[26] Aharon Barak, *Purposive Interpretation in Law* (Princeton, NJ: Princeton University Press, 2005).

[27] Steven D. Smith, *Law's Quandary* (Cambridge, MA: Harvard University Press, 2004), p. 131.

lawyers – will either join or replace lawmaking bodies such as legislatures as the dominant policy makers for contested social and political issues. It assumes that courts are (or at least can often be) better judges of the optimal policy goals than legislatures, an assumption that includes an ability to accurately predict the consequences of their decisions – that is, they must reliably be able to assess whether the goals they have in mind will actually occur. As Eveline Feteris has pointed out, the policy choice of a particular judicial decision has both a normative aspect – Y is a good consequence – and an empirical element, that is, decision X by the court will, in fact, produce the desired Y outcome.[28] Taking on a primary policymaking role thus poses a substantially higher burden on judges than simply identifying a good policy. As is the case for legislatures, judges selecting policies need to pick the ones that will lead to the best outcomes in the real world.[29] Predictive skills are thus an essential element of choosing a policy. In light of all we know today about the science of policy formation and prediction, courts are not as well constituted to make these judgments as larger and more diverse lawmaking bodies.

When legal scholars at great research universities consider contested issues of public policy, it is fairly easy for them to assume that wise and effective policies will best be identified by small groups of extremely well-educated people who can consult the most informed experts in the relevant fields – in short, people like themselves – rather than in the messy and conflict-ridden legislative process.[30] Yet, as Adrian Vermeule and Paul Yowell have pointed out, contemporary organizational theory emphasizes the critical element of diversity in formulating effective public policies, a characteristic often found lacking in small groups of judges, such as the Supreme Court, or, for that matter, university professors and professional experts.[31] Citing Aristotle's "wisdom of the multitude," Yowell observes that a "legislature typically has hundreds of members with experience in various professions and types of

[28] Feteris, "Rational Reconstruction," 462.

[29] For a discussion of the failure of proponents of judicial consequentialism to provide judges with adequate guidance about how to make such decisions, see Carbonell, "Reasoning by Consequences," 97–102.

[30] Jeremy Waldron, "Judicial Review and Judicial Supremacy," NYU School of Law, Public Law Research Paper, No. 14–57 (October 2014), https://ssrn.com/abstract=2510550.

[31] Vermeule argues for the "epistemic superiority of legislatures to courts under a broad range of conditions, especially in matters of constitutional law," for three principal reasons: "The first . . . is sheer numerosity . . . . Second, legislatures are more representative than courts, and representation produces knowledge . . . . Third, and crucially, a typical modern legislature is more diverse than a typical modern judiciary." Adrian Vermeule, *Law and the Limits of Reason* (Oxford: Oxford University Press, 2009), 10–11. See Paul Yowell, *Constitutional Rights and Constitutional Design: Moral and Empirical Reasoning in Judicial Review* (Oxford: Hart Publishing, 2018).

government service, and they have a variety of educational backgrounds and personal knowledge of the regions they represent," thus providing the legislature with a body of "collective knowledge" based on a "degree of diversity of background and expertise" that is "not possessed by a . . . court."[32]

Scott Page has recently offered mathematical proofs for the proposition that "collective ability equals individual ability plus diversity," and that "diversity trumps ability."[33] Page's work advances the theoretical basis for the "wisdom of crowds" literature that focuses on how large groups are better than small groups at solving problems, especially social and political policy issues, precisely because of the larger group's diversity. One critical reason is the need for what Page calls "toolbox diversity." For many areas of public policy, the insights and approaches found in any one discipline may simply be insufficient. Instead, it is essential to share "perspectives, heuristics, interpretations, and predictive models across the disciplines."[34] Judges' legal education is very deep, but its narrowness will not necessarily create a better base from which to create policies than legislators, who may better reflect the diversity found in the public.[35] Judges can, of course, supplement their own expertise with expert advice from other disciplines, but so can the legislature, and it is not clear that judges have the training and capacity to evaluate that advice as well as legislatures.[36] Accordingly, there is no reason to be confident that the Supreme Court will necessarily be better than Congress or state legislatures at choosing outcomes, or even at being more thoughtful consumers of the expertise offered by other disciplines. At the same time, the legislatures themselves, which often consist of hundreds of members, are not only far more diverse than small judicial panels, but they have the capacity and often the funding to commission expert analyses where needed, whereas the Court must generally rely on the limited, and not necessarily objective, materials submitted by the parties to the case.

Even if the justices were able to identify optimal policies, they would still need to achieve those policy goals in our complex and conflicted societies.

[32] Yowell, *Constitutional Rights*, pp. 98–9. See Jeremy Waldron, *The Dignity of Legislation* (Cambridge: Cambridge University Press, 1999).

[33] Scott E. Page, *The Difference: How the Power of Diversity Creates Better Groups, Firms, Schools, and Societies* (Princeton, NJ: Princeton University Press, 2007), p. 121.

[34] Page, *The Difference*, pp. 348–9.

[35] Lee Epstein, Jack Knight, and Andrew D. Martin, "The Norm of Prior Judicial Experience and Its Consequences for Career Diversity on the U.S. Supreme Court," *California Law Review* 91, 4 (July 2003): 903.

[36] Yowell says, following an examination of numerous instances of courts employing social science data: "I have argued that courts lack institutional capacities to acquire and assess empirical research and that in many cases courts make mistakes in understanding statistical analysis and social science methodology." Yowell, *Constitutional Rights*, p. 88.

The Court's limited range of enforcement tools, and its inability to adapt easily to changing circumstances, will make it even harder for judicial policymaking to bring about the desired good than it would be for the legislature to achieve the same goal. In fact, other branches of government may actively impede compliance with the courts' directives. The executive and legislative branches of government can employ an extensive array of tools to seize the policy initiative from the courts, from jurisdiction-stripping legislation to court-packing plans.[37]

Supreme Court justices lack not only a direct ability to implement their decisions, but also good tools with which to predict how others will do so. An essential element of judicial policymaking is being able to see into the future clearly enough to select the right pathway that leads to the desired good outcome. Decision scientists have learned a great deal about what kinds of groups make the best predictions, and courts have few, if any, of the relevant qualities. Philip Tetlock has invoked Isaiah Berlin's famous fox and hedgehog analogy to observe that if "we want realistic odds on what will happen next," it is better to ask "Berlin's prototypical fox," which "know[s] many little things, draw[s] from an eclectic arrange of traditions, and accept[s] ambiguity and contradiction" than a hedgehog, which "toil[s] devotedly within one tradition, and reach[s] for formulaic solutions to ill-defined problems."[38] (It is worth noting that Tetlock believes that the best we can expect are merely "realistic" odds "coupled to a willingness to admit mistakes," a trait for which courts are not well-known.) Judges, of course, look quite like hedgehogs in this case, and "formulaic-solutions to ill-defined problems" is a reasonable description of much of the judicial decision-making process. Experts tend to be hedgehogs, as well, and Tetlock notes that when "we pit experts against minimalist performance benchmarks – dilettantes, dart-throwing chimps, and assorted extrapolation algorithms – we find few signs that expertise translates into greater ability to make [good] forecasts."[39] And so, the Court is likely, on balance, to be a less capable judge of consequences than legislatures, and turning to experts will be of little or no additional value.

Predicting the future is hard, even for lawyers and judges used to talking about "foreseeable" events. Despite growing enthusiasm for "decision-support systems and artificial intelligence,"[40] those fields have not mastered the

[37] Tom S. Clark, *The Limits of Judicial Independence* (Cambridge: Cambridge University Press, 2011).

[38] Philip E. Tetlock, *Expert Political Judgment: How Good Is It? How Can We Know?* (Princeton, NJ: Princeton University Press, 2005), p. 1.

[39] Tetlock, *Expert Political Judgment*, p. 19.

[40] Cserne, "Consequence-Based Arguments," pp. 31–54.

prediction of human behavior. They may function adequately in some areas, but it is hard, either in the abstract or in practice, to imagine how artificial intelligence models will fully account for the many moving parts involved in resolving highly controversial issues of public policy and fundamental rights.

Especially in the realm of these fundamental rights cases, yet another challenge to judicial policymaking is the fact that the decisions themselves may be the roots of their own undoing. That is, if the courts opt for one side of a highly contested issue, the political backlash could lead not only to the opposite results of those intended by the court, but, potentially, to a broader effort to diminish the power of the court to establish other good policies in the future. Take, for example, the legal and political movements that have arisen to counter what their supporters believe is an inappropriate degree of judicial policymaking by courts.[41] The conservative legal movement of the past several decades has sought to constrain judges by advocating originalism in constitutional interpretation and textualism in statutory interpretation. It has emphasized the need to appoint Supreme Court justices in this intellectual mold, and an impressive number of those who granted a surprising victory to President Donald Trump said that they did so because the Supreme Court appointment was the most important issue in the election.[42] In short, one of the predictable consequences of judicial consequentialism in politically divisive cases is the rise of significant political opposition based not only on the outcomes of the cases, but also in response to the idea that judges should play such a powerful role in policy setting. Accordingly, any predictions made by the courts in assessing the consequences of their decisions will need to take into account the possibility that their selection of optimal solutions to social and political problems could be short-lived and that the political counter-reaction to the Court taking on a strong policymaking role may be powerful enough to bring about the opposite result.

For example, the Supreme Court has issued a number of controversial decisions that have favored individual rights over some communities' preferences. Prior to *Roe v. Wade*, individual states had different policies on the issue of abortion, based on the preferences of those communities.[43] As a question of the proper interpretation of the Constitution, these issues are certainly challenging, and there have been vigorous arguments between those wedded to historical meanings, which likely favor the community choices, or updated

[41] Steven M. Teles, *The Rise of the Conservative Legal Movement: The Battle for Control of the Law* (Princeton, NJ: Princeton University Press, 2008).

[42] "Exit Polls," CNN, updated November 23, 2019, www.cnn.com/election/2016/results/exit-polls.

[43] *Roe v. Wade*, 410 US 113 (1973).

meanings, which may support the finding of a fundamental individual right that would outweigh local legislative preferences.

Let us assume, for the sake of argument, that the justices' preferred consequences would be for women to have the right to choose. That is how the Court decided the case, but will that be, in fact, the consequence of the decision? It certainly has been for some people, in some places, for an initial period of time. But the conservative legal movement has focused heavily on reversing *Roe v. Wade*. If the Court becomes dominated by conservatives, it is possible that a future consequence of the *Roe* decision could be the judicial declaration of a constitutional right to life from the time of conception. Such a decision would not only eliminate the right to choose to terminate a pregnancy, but it would also prevent a return to the status quo ante, which enabled each of the fifty states to decide whether to permit or prohibit abortions. That is, the state-by-state approach, which resulted in permissive laws in some locales, and very restrictive ones elsewhere, could be replaced with a new national standard of prohibition, which would mean that the actual long-term consequence of the *Roe v. Wade* decision would be to eliminate the right to choose rather than to protect and expand it.

The goal of this discussion is not to revisit the merits of this decision. It is to point out that long-term consequences can be very different from short-term ones, and that a dedicated judicial policymaker would need to consider and accurately calibrate all of them. Since decision science tells us that small bodies of like-minded, similarly trained people are especially bad at doing that sort of thing, the actual consequences of judicial policymaking are likely to be completely unpredictable, as the public and the other branches of government struggle to guess how the justices themselves will guess about the future.[44]

The importance of considering these downstream effects arises from the fact that judicial policymaking sounds so easy and straightforward. The Supreme Court should pick the best outcome, and not let inconvenient historical attachments to specific notions of interpretation interfere with doing whatever is best. If the justices are concerned that the public will fail to accept open declarations of judicial policymaking, the covert approach can be employed to give the appearance that the process of judging has remained unaltered. It will have changed, of course, with the ends driving the meanings, not occasionally,

[44] MacCormick acknowledges that judges are "badly placed" to assess the "long-term social consequences" of legal rules, and distinguishes "hypothetical cases" that are "reasonably foreseeable" and engaging in "probabilistics" or predictive analyses. See Del Mar, "The Forward-Looking Requirement," 449–50 n3. It is hard to see how an outcome could be foreseeable without predicting and, therefore, considering which outcomes are most probable.

not with consequences appearing as just one of many considerations, but as potentially the dominant force in Supreme Court decision making. Even so, achieving what appear to be the right outcomes may seem worth a significant shift in the Supreme Court's job description. But if the job is changing, then it seems sensible to change how the justices describe their reasoning as well. What reason – apart from seeking sociological, political, and legal legitimacy on false grounds – is there for the Court to say that a noninterpretive decision involves an interpretation of the Constitution?

TRANSPARENCY IN JUDICIAL DECISION MAKING

As much of this book has argued, and as Ekins and Goldsworthy have observed: "For at least six centuries, common law courts have maintained that the primary object of … interpretation 'is to determine what intention is conveyed either expressly or by implication by the language used,' or in other words, 'to give effect to the intention of the [lawmaker] as that intention is to be gathered from the language employed having regard to the context in connection with which it is employed'." They point out that this focus on the lawmaker's decisions "has often been described as 'the only rule,' 'the paramount rule,' 'the cardinal rule' or 'the fundamental rule of interpretation, to which all others are subordinate'."[45] Many commentators have opined as to what these rules mean, and have described what they believe to be the proper limits on judges serving either as "faithful agents," or perhaps as "independent cooperative actors"[46] with the other branches. Even independent actors need to be cooperative, however, and there is a common thread throughout: judicial decisions interpreting written laws should be based on an understanding of the lawmaker's acts. Although the lawmaker's policy choices may ultimately be affected by judges' decisions, the process of judging involves understanding and considering seriously what the lawmaker did. Whether judicial interpretations have been narrow or extensive, or oriented primarily towards historical accuracy or towards the contemporary reading of the text, these interpretations have been fundamentally focused on the lawmaker's choices rather than the judges' policy preferences.[47]

[45] Richard Ekins and Jeffrey Goldsworthy, "The Reality and Indispensability of Legislative Intentions," *Sydney Law Review* 36, 1 (2014): 39–68.

[46] Kent Greenawalt, "Judges as Faithful Agents or Independent, Cooperative Actors?," chap. 2 in *Statutory and Common Law Interpretation* (Oxford: Oxford University Press, 2013).

[47] Dworkin, for example, in describing the moral reading of the Constitution, notes that "constitutional interpretation must begin in what the framers said." Ronald Dworkin, *Freedom's Law: The Moral Reading of the American Constitution* (1996; repr., Oxford: Oxford University Press, 2005), p. 10.

If judges, especially justices of the Supreme Court, adopt a new and different approach to making decisions in constitutional cases, they need to say so. Numerous scholars have argued that this shift to judicial policymaking needs to be out in the open based on the importance of transparency. These arguments by Mathis, Kramer, Carbonell, and others are echoed by Kent Greenawalt, who observes that for judges to be "deceptive," that is, "they know that they are deciding on a consequentialist basis but they conceal that fact," would lead to a "distressing lack of transparency."[48] Transparently committing to noninterpretive policymaking lets judges open any necessary political debates, but it does so at the expense of inviting criticism on the grounds that they have exceeded their proper judicial function. Their defense to that criticism needs to be on the basis that the common good will best be served by the Supreme Court taking on a more powerful policymaking role than it has claimed in the past. That a number of contemporary American scholars may see this overt approach as a losing political position, or at least a formidable task, would seem to be the major reason for appealing to grand theories (Tushnet), history (Eisgruber), or any plausible approach that gets the outcome right to camouflage the actual grounds for the decisions.

There is a substantial practical drawback to the covert approach, however. If claiming to engage in a bona fide act of interpretation is really just a convenient cover story for a better policy, then it would be best if nothing impeded the Court's ability to make the best decision. It will not be easy for the Supreme Court to choose the decision that will, in reality, lead to the best outcome, and that task will be made even more difficult by having to select from the limited pool of potential policies that can plausibly be described as the result of the process of interpretation. While decision science points to the benefits of diversity and knowing many small things, the covert approach further confines justices who are already lacking in those attributes. As a result, the effort to seek sociological legitimacy by appearing to respect the traditional limits of judicial authority will make the Court's already difficult task immeasurably harder.

Another problem arising from using interpretive language to describe noninterpretive judicial policymaking is the potential for devaluing the concept of truth in the branch of government that is frequently called on to distinguish truth from falsehood. Philosopher Harry Frankfurt's famous book *On Bullshit* offers important insights into the risks of covert policymaking. He makes a distinction between lying and its considerably more pernicious relative, bullshitting. The critical question is how much we value the truth. "The

[48] Greenawalt, *Statutory and Common Law Interpretation*, p. 264.

liar," he writes, "is inescapably concerned with truth-values. In order to invent a lie at all, he must think he knows what is true." In contrast, "the bullshitter hides [the fact] that the truth-values of his statements are of no central interest to him." The bullshitter "does not care whether the things he says describe reality correctly. He just picks them out, or makes them up, to suit his purpose."[49] Similarly, when a judicial act of policymaking is described incorrectly as the result of an interpretation, the process of interpretation stops being about truth, and instead is all about consequences, with the language of interpretation just "picked out" or "made up" to suit the outcome. That shift could have profound consequences for the legal system.

Among the various arms of government, the judiciary is where we most often expect judgments specifically relating to truth. The law is replete with references to the value of truth telling, from witnesses sworn to tell the truth to arguments about the true meaning of a text or its true intentions. The Supreme Court has described trials as a "search for truth,"[50] and, in international human rights law, truth has even become a potential remedy.[51] Covert policymaking asks Supreme Court justices to cheapen the value of truth by being indifferent to whether the way they describe their decisions is a true representation of either the meaning of the law or the reason they reached that particular decision. Perhaps it is; perhaps not. It does not matter as long as it gives the appearance of plausibly justifying the decision. The resulting problem is the one articulated by Frankfurt, who points out that "excessive indulgence" in "making assertions without paying attention to anything except what it suits one to say, [means that] a person's normal habit of attending to the ways things are may become attenuated or lost."[52] Our indifference to whether we are being truthful can thus cause us to lose our ability to know what is true, or even how to evaluate whether something is true or false. Such a loss of respect for the value of truthfulness in our highest court – and potentially for

49 Harry G. Frankfurt, *On Bullshit* (Princeton, NJ: Princeton University Press, 2005), pp. 51–2, 55–6.

50 *Nix v. Whiteside*, 475 US 157, 171 (1986).

51 See the summary in Thomas M. Antkowiak, "Truth as Right and Remedy in International Human Rights Experience," *Michigan Journal of International Law* 23, 4 (Summer 2002): 977–1013.

52 Frankfurt, *On Bullshit*, p. 60. Additionally, arguments for judicial candor generally build on the underlying value of truth. See David L. Shapiro, "In Defense of Judicial Candor," *Harvard Law Review* 100, 4 (February 1987): 731–50; and Micah Schwartzman, "Judicial Sincerity," *Virginia Law Review* 94, 4 (2008): 987–1027. See also Richard H. Fallon Jr., *Law and Legitimacy in the Supreme Court* (Cambridge, MA: Harvard University Press, 2018), p. 11: "Good faith . . . require[s] that the Justices – like the rest of us – sincerely believe what they say when engaging in constitutional argument."

the understanding of what truth entails – could be a very damaging consequence of covert policymaking.

ARBITRARINESS AND THE RULE OF LAW

The rule of law has many aspects and forms.[53] Without needing to delve deeply into those complex jurisprudential issues, one observation is important to note in connection with the issues discussed in this chapter. The common theme among all descriptions of the rule of law is that the administration of the law should not be arbitrary, which is the primary threat of covert judicial policymaking. Consequentialist courts will subvert this characteristic of the rule of law. Without signaling any change in how courts have interpreted the laws for much of recorded history, judges will begin regularly trying to predict short- and long-term outcomes, perhaps strategically deciding individual cases in a manner less related to their merits than to how the court can move the law in a different direction than the one chosen by the lawmaker.[54] Because judges are rarely representative of the diversity or the preferences of the public at large, it will be difficult for them to make optimal policy decisions, or for the other branches and the public to be able to predict what the court will do. Layered on top of these substantial issues will be the fact that the Court may seek to disguise the justices' thinking by issuing public rationales that are selected merely because they offer a potentially plausible basis for reaching the same decision in a completely different way.

Transparently described judicial policymaking in controversial political arenas challenges traditional notions of the meaning of interpretation and the limits of judicial power, but at least the public and the political branches of

[53] Jeremy Waldron, "The Rule of Law," in *Stanford Encyclopedia of Philosophy*, article published June 22, 2016, last modified July 1, 2016, https://plato.stanford.edu/entries/rule-of-law/.

[54] The negative consequences of judicial policymaking highlighted here do not exhaust the potentially powerful arguments against having judges interpret laws and constitutions based on an overall calculation of future societal good. When the Supreme Court reaches decisions in litigated cases, for example, there is the possibility that the interests of the parties could be ignored or diminished in the court's effort to create a desired policy outcome. Damages could be assessed, or criminal convictions upheld or dismissed, not because of the parties' actions in light of existing legal norms, but in an attempt to achieve a perceived greater good. I have largely omitted these classic arguments against judicial policymaking not because they are necessarily invalid but because advocates for such an expanded judicial role have undoubtedly already discounted them. Judges disturbed by the possibility that the otherwise valid claims of some individuals will be sacrificed to the interests of society as a whole are unlikely to be attracted to consequentialist policymaking in the first place. My goal in this chapter is to show that judicial policymaking (especially if done covertly) is a bad idea even for those who would be willing to make the necessary trade-offs in individual cases.

government will see it coming, and can subject it to open debate and, if appropriate, political opposition. A lack of transparency seeks to hide those challenges behind a facade of plausibility that will decrease the likelihood of a good outcome, potentially devalue the notion of truth, and introduce a worrying degree of arbitrariness into Supreme Court constitutional decision making.[55]

THEORIES OF INTERPRETATION VS. THEORIES OF JUDICIAL POWER

Various theorists have urged justices to be good pragmatic reasoners so as to make our constitutional order the best it can be,[56] while Vermeule et al. have cited powerful evidence from the social scientific literature demonstrating that the Supreme Court is less capable of making good choices than the political branches.[57] Arguing that "legislatures enjoy comparative epistemic advantages over courts even, or especially, in matters constitutional,"[58] Vermeule reaches what he describes as "Thayerian conclusions,"[59] including "judicial deference to legislative development of constitutional law through statutes."[60] Along somewhat parallel lines, Richard Fallon, in his analysis of the Court's moral, political, and sociological legitimacy, calls for at least "a modest recalibration" of the Court's willingness to get in the middle of highly controversial social and political issues, and argues that "the Court's relative lack of restraint – or refusal to give greater deference to the reasonable judgments of more democratically accountable institutions – raises significant issues about fairness in the allocation of political power within our political system."[61] In short, "the

55 For a broader rule-of-law argument against judges "exploit[ing] the inherent indeterminacy of law to produce results they desire," see Brian Z. Tamanaha, *Law as a Means to an End: Threat to the Rule of Law* (Cambridge: Cambridge University Press, 2006), p. 250.

56 Sunstein, "There Is Nothing."

57 Vermeule, *Law and the Limits*.

58 Sunstein, "There Is Nothing," 193–212.

59 Vermeule, *Law and the Limits*, p. 16. See, for example, James B. Thayer, "The Origin and Scope of the American Doctrine of Constitutional Law," *Harvard Law Review* 7, 3 (October 1893): 129–56.

60 Vermeule, *Law and the Limits*, p. 14. As "precursors," Vermeule also cites Jeremy Bentham and Jeremy Waldron. See J. H. Burns and H. L. A. Hart, eds., *The Collected Works of Jeremy Bentham: A Comment on the Commentaries and a Fragment on Government* (1977; repr., Oxford: Oxford University Press, 2008); and Jeremy Waldron, *Law and Disagreement* (Oxford: Oxford University Press, 1999). Bentham, an English philosopher who called himself a "Philo-Yankee," would be pleased: "He sent his *Fragment on Government* to Franklin in 1780, and later offered his services to President Madison, and the various state governors, as their codifier of laws and constitutional architect." D. P. Crook, "The United States in Bentham's Thought," *Australian Journal of Politics and History* 10, 2 (August 1964): 196.

61 Fallon, *Law and Legitimacy*, p. 167.

Justices exert more authority to limit democratic decision making than they should."[62] Judge Richard Posner asks the right question: "[W]hat prevents the descent of the judiciary into an abyss of unchanneled discretionary justice that would render law so uncertain and unpredictable that it would no longer be law but instead would be the exercise of raw political power by politicians called judges?"[63]

Answering that question would require a complete account of a theory of judicial decision making and the separation of powers, which is well beyond the scope of this book. For present purposes, the important issue is that these debates over judicial power create a risk that the concept of interpretation will be skewed out of recognition, with attendant risks to the value of truth and the rule of law. If legal theorists believe that the Supreme Court should be the ultimate decision maker for controversial issues of social and political policy, and they cling to the idea that when the Court does so, it must be "interpreting" the Constitution, then they have little choice but to advance a capacious theory of constitutional interpretation that includes not actually interpreting the Constitution.

A far better approach is transparency. If the Court is going to be a policymaker, it should act and sound like one. Instead of employing language about original or aspirational readings of the Constitution, the opinions would read more like legislative committee reports. The reasons specified in the opinions would be the pragmatic, political, consequentialist, or other analyses that convinced a majority of the justices that they have identified the best policy decision for serving the common good. Not only will those policy reports enable the public to understand the rationales for the decisions, but the very different style and substance of the reports will clearly differentiate these opinions from ones issued in the course of the Court's normal duties as the interpreter of the Constitution. In the policy cases, it would no longer be relevant that the "Fourteenth Amendment does not enact Mr. Herbert Spencer's Social Statics."[64]

CONCLUSION

The Court's role as interpreter is clear, and the theory and practice of interpretation are based on a rich history of legal tradition and commentary. This

62 Fallon, p. 167.

63 Richard A. Posner, *How Judges Think* (Cambridge, MA: Harvard University Press, 2010), p. 372.

64 *Lochner v. New York*, 198 US 45, 75 (1905) (Holmes, J., dissenting). Moreover, since the policy decisions would not be constitutional decisions, they could be overturned by an ordinary act of Congress.

book has been an effort to explain and revive that tradition. In doing so, it has demonstrated that interpretation involves applying the will of the lawmaker, not the will of the Court, to the case at hand. For thousands of years, the public and its elected representatives have looked to the courts to provide answers to difficult and important issues involving interpretation, something for which judges are well-trained and well-placed to do. When that traditional process metamorphizes into pure political policymaking, the justices need to defend it as such, and not put at risk the Court's essential role as the authoritative interpreter of legal texts.

10

Conclusion

Of all the great works of English literature, the one most commonly cited in judicial opinions came not from the pen of Shakespeare or Milton, but from Oxford mathematician Charles Lutwidge Dodgson, better known as Lewis Carroll. In a succinct colloquy, he memorably summed up the challenges – and opportunities – involved in the process of interpretation. "'When I use a word,' Humpty Dumpty said in rather a scornful tone, 'it means just what I choose it to mean – neither more nor less'."[1] To this "making it up as he goes along" explanation of meaning, Alice gives what sounds like a sensible response: "'The question is,' said Alice, 'whether you *can* make words mean so many different things'."[2] Humpty Dumpty's response should warm the hearts of the most flexible of modern interpreters: "'The question is,' said Humpty Dumpty, 'which is to be master – that's all'." Humpty Dumpty has been so relevant to discussions of interpretation that it took a 165-page law review article just to summarize the judicial references to this short dialogue in a children's book.[3]

[1] Lewis Carroll, *Through the Looking Glass and What Alice Found There* (Philadelphia, 1897), p. 123. *Alice's Adventures in Wonderland* was cited by courts over 170 times in just the ten years between 2006 and its 150th anniversary in 2015, 124 of which were federal court cases. Sean Doherty, "Alice-in-Wonderland's Adventures in Case Law," *Legal Current*, November 2, 2015, www.legalcurrent.com/alice-in-wonderlands-adventures-in-case-law. Meanwhile, a separate survey of federal cases over 100 years finds fairly modest numbers of references to "literary" authors: "George Orwell (61 citations); William Shakespeare (35); Franz Kafka (34); John Milton (20); Homer, Chaucer, and Oscar Wilde (14 each)." M. Todd Henderson, "Citing Fiction," *The Green Bag* 11, 2 (2008): 178.

[2] Carroll, *Through the Looking Glass*, p. 123.

[3] See Parker B. Potter Jr., "If Humpty Dumpty Had Sat on the Bench ... : An Eggheaded Approach to Legal Lexicography," *Whittier Law Review* 30, 3 (2009): 367–532. In a discussion of whether a single correct understanding of the original meaning is identifiable, it is especially apt that this scene from *Alice's Adventures in Wonderland* has been employed in arguments

For centuries, judges and scholars have tried to answer the question of how judges should interpret legal texts. This task is daunting, and inevitably prone to debate, even when courts are seeking to resolve basic disputes over the meaning of statutes, or scholars and students are discussing the application of a hypothetical ban on vehicles in the park.[4] One Humpty Dumpty-quoting Ohio judge struggled with what would appear to be a clearly drafted provision of the municipal codes, as follows:

> Is someone drinking a beer on a deck covered by a roof . . . with only one side wall . . . indoors or outdoors? The simplest solution might be that, since there is no door at all, it would be impossible to be outdoors. But that would raise the question of whether installing a free-standing door would suffice. I fear not. Surely you have to go out a door somewhere to get to this deck – so does that make it outdoors? Maybe the problem is that you don't go in a door, so you can't be indoors on the deck.[5]

Ultimately, the judge concluded that the deck was outdoors on the grounds that "a roof does not make outdoors in."[6]

These are the kinds of issues that have bedeviled judges for thousands of years, and have stimulated scholars to produce countless tomes explicating the history and methods of interpretation throughout the ages (a weighty literature that has just become one book heavier). In reading the chapters discussing that history, it may seem strange, especially for graduates of American law schools, to see the extent to which modern interpretative debates have largely restated longstanding issues. Legal history, especially pre-American legal history, for which the sources are usually in Latin, is rarely featured in our required curricula. Moreover, to the extent that we do teach students about the history that might be relevant to our studies of American law, our focus has often been on the case-by-case creation of the common law. In doing so, we tend to forget that the interpretation of legal texts has been an essential part of the work of judges even in common law countries, and, equally importantly, that the Framers were familiar with the great jurists who wrote about interpretive issues not only in common law

both for and against the proposition that people such as legislators, judges, parties to contracts, and others can make words mean whatever they want them to mean. Potter, 395. See also Parker B. Potter Jr., "Wondering about Alice: Judicial References to *Alice in Wonderland* and *Through the Looking Glass*," *Whittier Law Review* 28, 1 (2006): 177.

4 See H. L. A. Hart, "Positivism and the Separation of Law and Morals," *Harvard Law Review* 71, 4 (February 1958): 607.

5 Potter, "Humpty Dumpty," 372, quoting *Pupco Prop. Mgmt. v. City of Cincinnati*, 868 NE2d 738, 740–42 (Ohio Ct. App. 2007).

6 Potter, "Humpty Dumpty," 373.

England, but also on the European Continent and in Scotland, where the civil law – originally Roman law – prevailed.

In light of the broader sense of the Western legal tradition outlined in Chapter 3, we can stop arguing about whether particular updating methods only appeared fairly recently to promote specific political agendas, and, therefore, were unknown to the Founding generation. Legal scholars around the time of the Constitution can be found arguing for the original meaning of documents in some cases, and for more contemporary readings in others, and patriot leaders would certainly not shy away from offering updated interpretations of the Magna Carta if it helped strengthen their arguments against British rule. Founding-Era lawyers and statesmen, trained by their readings not only of Blackstone and Coke, but also of Grotius, Pufendorf, Hotman, and other continental commentators, understood these debates in their historical context, and they deployed the full arsenal of interpretive methods in legal practice and political debate. We can also set aside the claims that originalism is merely a clever cover story for an underlying commitment to politically conservative outcomes. In fact, Justice Rutledge, author of one of the most enduring and influential examples of originalist analysis in First Amendment law, later admitted that the history was a cover story for his politically liberal views.[7]

We will continue to argue, as did our predecessors, about whether the meaning as of the time of enactment should be the rule, or the exception with "living" interpretations prevailing instead. That debate over what should be twenty-first-century hornbook law on the issue of static versus dynamic interpretations asks us to address very important (and impressively longstanding) issues relating to questions of the separation of powers and popular sovereignty, the dead hand problem, and the like. This book has not been designed to resolve all those debates, but to highlight the fact that the same issues have been matters of debate for a very long time.

[7] *Everson v. Bd. of Educ.*, 330 US 1 (1947). See Chapter 2. For the degree to which Rutledge's views represented the prevailing liberal attitudes of the time, see John T. McGreevy, *Catholicism and American Freedom: A History* (New York: W. W. Norton, 2004); John T. McGreevy, "Thinking on One's Own: Catholicism in the American Intellectual Imagination, 1928–1960," *Journal of American History* 84, 1 (June 1997): 97–131; and Ken I. Kersch, *Constructing Civil Liberties: Discontinuities in the Development of American Constitutional Law* (Cambridge: Cambridge University Press, 2004), p. 314: "The Court's modern doctrine concerning religion ... was invented during a surge of anti-Catholicism in the 1940s. This surge united intellectuals, liberal Protestants, and Reform Jews, all of whom ... worked to construct Roman Catholicism as especially divisive and dangerous – in a Cold War context that put a premium on ecumenicism in the service of Americanism."

The prevailing, or hornbook, view has cycled between original and dynamic (or flexible) approaches to interpretation throughout American history. John Manning points out that English courts at the time of the Revolution could use "reason and equity" to interpret texts flexibly, but, over the course of the next 100 years, a much stricter textualism would become dominant.[8] Thereafter, we can see that, through the course of the twentieth century, dynamic or living approaches would supplant the plain meaning rule in the hornbooks in England and the United States,[9] with Justice Brennan saying in 1985, for example: "Current Justices read the Constitution in the only way that we can: as twentieth-century Americans .... [T]he ultimate question must be: What do the words of the text mean in our time?"[10] More recently, the interpretive winds have blown in the other direction. There has been enough of a resurgence of textualism in the twenty-first century for Justice Kagan to say, "We are all originalists,"[11] and, for Justice Gorsuch to write, "[R]espect for the separation of powers implies originalism in the application of the Constitution and textualism in the interpretation of statutes."[12] Gorsuch continues, "These tools have served as the dominant methods for interpreting legal texts for most of our history."[13] That statement would be somewhat more accurate if he had said "much" rather than "most," but, even as written, he captures the key point: history, by itself, will not identify which interpretive mode best reflects the common core of all of the approaches: the intent of the lawmaker. Instead, it shows a cycling between these ever-present adversaries, which has regularly been resolved, as Gorsuch points out, by reference to the separation of powers.

What interpretive approach should emerge from a proper understanding of the separation of powers is a critically important topic that is well beyond the scope of this work. Nor has this book set out to present a complete theory of judicial decision making, which would require an analysis of all of the familiar modalities and categories of judicial decisions that have been identified by

[8] John F. Manning, "Textualism and the Equity of the Statute," *Columbia Law Review* 101, 1 (January 2001): 35.

[9] See Chapter 3.

[10] William J. Brennan Jr., "The Constitution of the United States: Contemporary Ratification," *South Texas Law Review* 27, 3 (1986): 438. For the United Kingdom, see Rupert Cross, *Statutory Interpretation*, eds. John Bell and George Engle, 2nd ed. (London: Butterworths, 1987), p. 49: "The U.S. Constitution is regarded as 'a living Constitution,' so an ongoing British Act is regarded 'a living Act'."

[11] "Special Coverage of Elena Kagan's Confirmation Hearing," CNN Transcript, June 29, 2010, http://edition.cnn.com/TRANSCRIPTS/1006/29/cnr.01.html.

[12] Neil Gorsuch, *A Republic, if You Can Keep It* (New York: Random House, 2019), p. 10.

[13] Gorsuch, *A Republic*, p. 10.

Philip Bobbitt and others.[14] Important recent books have also added valuable insights into topics ranging from the role of precedent[15] to that of judicial review,[16] and those topics also require far more thoughtful consideration than could be given here. This book's specific focus has been on what it has meant to interpret a legally authoritative text for many generations, and to show how that traditional definition of interpretation maps on to the creation and interpretation of the US Constitution.

With this background in mind, I have proposed that constitutional theory should pay considerably more attention to the one theme that has been a constant through the various cycles of interpretive methods: a search for the will of the lawmaker. This concept of ascertaining the lawmaker's intention as the source of the meaning of the legally effective propositions specified by a written text is well attested by history, yet unusually complicated by the American ratification process and the limitations of the documentary record. These complexities, combined with the challenge of discovering a single intention of a lawmaking body consisting of "many myndes," have encouraged even many originalists to downplay or disregard the Framers. With living constitutionalists seeking to detach constitutional interpretation from its eighteenth-century past, and many originalists turning to a search for the objective public meaning, the Framers' intentions are often missing from constitutional theory, even as the Supreme Court appears to call on them regularly. This book has been an effort to say that theorists' interest in highlighting problems associated with competing theories has too often resulted in throwing the baby out with the bathwater,[17] and that the Court has been right to continue to cite the Framers, even when, in my view, it has done it incorrectly.

I began by suggesting ways in which interpreters can work their way through the theoretical and practical difficulties of ascertaining the Framers intentions, including the basic question of whether the people who framed the Constitution should really count as its Framers. Then, building on Richard Ekins' analysis of legislative intent, I argued that what it means to seek the

[14] See Philip Bobbitt, *Constitutional Interpretation* (Oxford: Blackwell, 1991); Philip Bobbitt, *Constitutional Fate: Theory of the Constitution* (New York: Oxford University Press, 1982); Brandon J. Murrill, *Modes of Constitutional Interpretation* (Washington, DC: Congressional Research Service, 2018); and numerous others.

[15] Randy J. Kozel, *Settled Versus Right: A Theory of Precedent* (Cambridge: Cambridge University Press, 2017).

[16] Keith E. Whittington, *Repugnant Laws: Judicial Review of Acts of Congress from the Founding to the Present* (Lawrence: University Press of Kansas, 2019); and Louis Fisher, *Reconsidering Judicial Finality: Why the Supreme Court Is Not the Last Word on the Constitution* (Lawrence: University Press of Kansas, 2019).

[17] I would like to thank Lee Strang for suggesting this helpful phrase.

intention of the Framers is to identify the end–means decision, together with the rationale for that decision, represented by the constitutional text. To oversimplify, it was what they thought they were doing, and why they did it that way. Even the Framers who voted against a provision would know what problem it was meant to solve, and why the clause was designed to solve it in that particular fashion, even though they would have preferred to solve it another way.

The Framers added the various provisions in the Constitution for reasons, and those reasons provide an essential foundation not only for interpreters to identify the original meaning of the text, but also for them to consider how to interpret an eighteenth-century document in light of unforeseeable twenty-first-century circumstances. That updating method starts with an understanding of the original meaning, and seeks to keep the interpreter's attention focused on the Framers' choice of ends and means, including their understanding of whether it should be interpreted broadly or narrowly. That approach, which is rooted in the common law tradition of Coke and Blackstone, has been most recently explicated and adopted by the Supreme Court of the United Kingdom.

I have also argued that, except for scholarly exercises meant solely to represent theoretical possibilities in an ideal case scenario, constitutional theory needs to engage directly with the relevant facts. The next section of the book was an effort to do so. It addressed examples drawn from two highly controversial clauses – the tax clauses relevant to Social Security and the Affordable Care Act, and the First Amendment's Establishment Clause – to examine the degree to which a search for the objective public meaning of the text can underdetermine its meaning. I then showed how that semantic ambiguity is probably not resolved, and may actually be exacerbated, by the new techniques associated with digital research into corpus linguistics databases. Despite these semantic challenges, it can actually be possible for interpreters to obtain a reasonably clear picture of the Framers' policy judgment – their end–means choice and the reasons for it – represented by the various clauses.

To be successful in that effort, it is essential to return to the documentary record of the Framers' debates, deliberations, and negotiations that has been largely sidelined by what John Manning has described as the widely shared commitment to "intent skepticism."[18] The interpreter's focus should be specifically on the final, negotiated deal struck by the Convention or Congress, not what any one Framer, even famous or influential ones, might have wanted to achieve. The best evidence of that intention of the Framers remains the text, as Blackstone pointed out, but the text, especially as read by judges over 200 years removed from its drafting, may give a different impression to us than it

[18] John F. Manning, "Inside Congress's Mind," *Columbia Law Review* 115, 7 (2015): 1932–3.

gave to the Framers, ratifiers, and the public at the time. The examples of the tax clauses and the Establishment Clause show how that can be the case.

Once justices have accurately identified the original meaning of the provision in light of the Framers' intentions, they may feel that even the updating approach outlined here will not be enough to create outcomes that are compatible with the justices' sense of justice, fairness, or fundamental rights – or perhaps with what looks to them simply to be a sounder public policy. In those cases, conventional interpretive approaches would impede the Supreme Court from achieving what the justices believe is the best possible outcome. In *Looking Glass* terms, the justices may seek to seize mastery over the meanings, at least to the extent of going well beyond what interpretation has meant throughout history.

For strong-willed or ambitious statesmen and jurists, then and now, interpreting and applying the will of the lawmaker could be considerably less interesting than having a direct hand in setting the political course. To set that new political course is not an act of interpretation, however. Since time immemorial, judges have interpreted laws in light of the will of the lawmaker. When the justices no longer seek primarily to understand and apply that original end–means decision, but instead create new policies based on their own determinations of what would be a good outcome, they have taken on a new and different role. I have discussed why small groups of judges, such as the Supreme Court, are not epistemologically well equipped to make good decisions in those contexts, especially compared to larger and more diverse legislative bodies.

Despite these drawbacks, if the Court chooses to wade into controversial policy disputes, it should adopt a commitment to full disclosure and transparency. It is important for the public to have confidence that judges will faithfully interpret the written law as they always have – by seeking to determine and apply the will of the lawmaker. But if the Court is going to be a policymaker, it should act and sound like one rather than employ conventional interpretive language to mask the justices' actual thinking. Then, the other branches of government and the public can address the separation of powers issues, and make a decision about the proper role of the Supreme Court in twenty-first-century America.

THE FRAMERS AND HISTORY

At the outset of the book, I quoted Harvard historian Jill Lepore on the rhetorical value of the Framers.[19] She writes: "When in doubt in American

[19] Jill Lepore, *The Whites of Their Eyes: The Tea Party's Revolution and the Battle over American History* (Princeton, NJ: Princeton University Press, 2011), p. 14.

politics, left, right, or center, deploy the Founding Fathers."[20] Rhetorical value may be very different from actual value, however, and she spends most of the book disparaging the originalist movement that started in the 1970s, calling originalism "lousy history." She writes: "Set loose in the culture, and tangled together with fanaticism, originalism looks like history, but it's not. It's historical fundamentalism, which is to history what astrology is to astronomy, what alchemy is to chemistry, what creationism is to evolution."[21] Whereas fellow historian, Jack Rakove, even while bemoaning the "cruel and unusual use often made of historical materials in contemporary political debate," argues that "[h]istorians, qua historians . . . have no normative stake in any particular mode or rule of constitutional interpretation,"[22] Lepore's book would seem to be an effort to drive a normative stake through the heart of contemporary originalism.

It comes as a surprise, then, over 100 pages later, when Lepore admits that, as she puts it: "Jurists and legislators need to investigate what the Framers meant."[23] Indeed they do. Beyond the arguments in this book, it makes considerable intuitive sense that the authors of our national charter meant something by the language they choose, and that we should do our best to learn what it was. We should also share her concern that some efforts to do so have been motivated and shaped by preexisting political attachments – on both the right and the left. If we are open to the idea that the Framers might not have meant what we would like them to have meant, and that our goal is not a merely plausible argument but one rooted sufficiently in the relevant facts to be genuinely persuasive, then it will be easier to obtain and maintain bipartisan commitment to a common understanding of the meaning of interpretation.

In this approach to thinking about Supreme Court decisions, I have tried to follow that advice, and my goal has not been to promote any particular set of policies or outcomes in specific constitutional cases. (In fact, neither the Establishment Clause nor the tax clause analysis reached the conclusion I would choose if I were the policymaker.) This work has instead been an exercise in trying to figure out what it means for judges to interpret a legally authoritative text – or at least what it has meant for an exceedingly long time – and how those

20 Lepore, *Whites of Their Eyes*, p. 7.

21 Lepore, pp. 112, 118, 123.

22 Jack N. Rakove, "Confessions of an Ambivalent Originalist," *New York University Law Review* 78, 4 (October 2003): 1347, 1350.

23 Lepore, *Whites of Their Eyes*, p. 124. Although Lepore and I certainly agree on this point, we differ as to how to ascertain the intentions of the Framers regarding the religion clauses. See Donald L. Drakeman, *Why We Need the Humanities: Life Science, Law and the Common Good* (Basingstoke: Palgrave Macmillan, 2016), pp. 103–6.

insights relate to the US Constitution. If the lessons of history prove accurate, my proposals for addressing these challenging issues will not settle long contested methodological debates once and for all, but my hope is that they may encourage others who are interested in the same questions to do some new thinking in old directions.

Bibliography

Abraham, Henry J. *The Judicial Process: An Introductory Analysis of the Courts of the United States, England, and France*. 7th ed. Oxford: Oxford University Press, 1998.

Ackerman, Bruce A. "The Storrs Lectures: Discovering the Constitution." *Yale Law Journal* 93, 6 (1984): 1013–72.

Alexander, Larry. "Originalism, the Why and the What." *Fordham Law Review* 82, 2 (November 2013): 539–44.

Alexander, Larry. "Simple-Minded Originalism." Chap. 4 in *The Challenge of Originalism: Theories of Constitutional Interpretation*, eds. Grant Huscroft and Bradley W. Miller. Cambridge: Cambridge University Press, 2011.

Alexander, Larry and Saikrishna Prakash. "Is that English You're Speaking? Why Intention Free Interpretation Is an Impossibility." *San Diego Law Review* 41, 3 (August–September 2004): 967–95.

Alexy, Robert. *Theorie der juristischen Argumentation: Die Theorie des rationalen Diskurses als Theorie der juristischen Begründung*. Frankfurt: Suhrkamp Verlag, 1978.

Alicea, Joel. "Forty Years of Originalism." *Policy Review*, 173 (June/July 2012): 69–79.

Alicea, Joel and Donald L. Drakeman. "The Limits of New Originalism." *University of Pennsylvania Journal of Constitutional Law* 15, 4 (April 2013): 1161–20.

Amar, Akhil Reed. *America's Constitution: A Biography*. New York: Random House, 2005.

Amar, Akhil Reed. *The Bill of Rights: Creation and Reconstruction*. New Haven, CT: Yale University Press, 1998.

Amar, Akhil Reed. "Philadelphia Revisited: Amending the Constitution Outside Article V." *University of Chicago Law Review* 55, 4 (1988): 1043–104.

Antkowiak, Thomas M. "Truth as Right and Remedy in International Human Rights Experience." *Michigan Journal of International Law* 23, 4 (Summer 2002): 977–1013.

Aprill, Ellen P. "The Law of the Word: Dictionary Shopping in the Supreme Court," *Arizona State Law Journal* 30 (1998): 275–336.

Articles Agreed upon by the Archbishops and Bishops of Both Provinces, and the Whole Clergy: In the Convocation Holden at London, in the yeere 1562. For the Avoiding of Diversities of Opinion, and for the stablishing of Consent Touching True Religion. London: Bonham Norton & John Bill, 1629.

Baade, Hans W. "'Original Intent' in Historical Perspective: Some Critical Glosses." *Texas Law Review* 69, 5 (April 1991): 1001–108.
Backus, Isaac. *An Appeal to the Public for Religious Liberty, Against the Oppressions of the Present Day*. Boston, 1773.
Bailey, Michael A. and Forrest Maltzman. *The Constrained Court: Law, Politics, and the Decisions Justices Make*. Princeton, NJ: Princeton University Press, 2011.
Baker, John. "The Legal Force and Effect of Magna Carta." Chap. 6 in *Magna Carta: Muse and Mentor*, ed. Randy J. Holland. Toronto: Thomson Reuters, 2014.
Baker, Leonard. *John Marshall: A Life in Law*. New York: Macmillan, 1974.
Balkin, Jack. "Why Are Americans Originalist?" Chap. 18 in *Law, Society and Community: Socio-Legal Essays in Honour of Roger Cotterrell*, eds. Richard Nobles and David Schiff. Farnham: Ashgate Publishing, 2014.
Balkin, Jack M. *Living Originalism*. Cambridge, MA: Harvard University Press, 2011.
Balkin, Jack M. "What *Brown* Teaches Us about Constitutional Theory." *Virginia Law Review* 90, 6 (October 2004): 1537–78.
Balkin, Jack M. "Preface." In *What* Brown v. Board of Education *Should Have Said: The Nation's Top Legal Experts Rewrite America's Landmark Civil Rights Decision*, ed. Jack M. Balkin. New York: New York University Press, 2002, pp. ix–xii.
Balkin, Jack M. "Rewriting *Brown*: A Guide to the Opinions." *What* Brown v. Board of Education *Should Have Said: The Nation's Top Legal Experts Rewrite America's Landmark Civil Rights Decision*, ed. Jack M. Balkin. New York: New York University Press, 2002, pp. 44–76.
Barak, Aharon. *Purposive Interpretation in Law*. Princeton, NJ: Princeton University Press, 2005.
Barber, Sotirios A. and James E. Fleming. *Constitutional Interpretation: The Basic Questions*. New York: Oxford University Press, 2007.
Barclay, Stephanie H., Brady Earley, and Annika Boone. "Original Meaning and the Establishment Clause: A Corpus Linguistics Analysis." *Arizona Law Review* 61 (2019): 505–60.
Barnett, Randy. "Originalism and *Brown*." *Volokh Conspiracy* (blog), May 12, 2005, www.volokh.com/posts/1115921115.shtml.
Barnett, Randy E. *Restoring the Lost Constitution: The Presumption of Liberty*. Princeton, NJ: Princeton University Press, 2004.
Barnett, Randy E. "New Evidence of the Original Meaning of the Commerce Clause." *Arkansas Law Review* 55, 4 (2003): 847–900.
Barnett, Randy E. "An Originalism for Nonoriginalists." *Loyola Law Review* 45, 4 (Winter 1999): 611–54.
Barnett, Randy E. *The Structure of Liberty: Justice and the Rule of Law*. Oxford: Oxford University Press, 1998.
Barnett, Randy E. and Evan D. Bernick. "The Letter and the Spirit: A Unified Theory of Originalism." *Georgetown Law Journal* 107, 1 (October 2018): 1–56.
Bassham, Gregory and Ian Oakley. "New Textualism: The Potholes Ahead." *Ratio Juris* 28, 1 (March 2015): 127–48.
Baude, William. "Is Originalism Our Law?" *Columbia Law Review* 115, 8 (December 2015): 2349–408.
Baude, Will. "Does Originalism Justify Brown, and Why Do We Care So Much?" *Volokh Conspiracy* (blog), *Washington Post*, January 24, 2014, www.washingtonpost

.com/news/volokh-conspiracy/wp/2014/01/29/does-originalism-justify-brown-and-why-do-we-care-so-much.
Baude, William and Jud Campbell. "Early American Constitutional History: A Source Guide." Unpublished manuscript, October 31, 2018, https://perma.cc/326P-Q9V7.
Baum, Lawrence and Neal Devins. "Why the Supreme Court Cares about Elites, Not the American People." *Georgetown Law Journal* 98, 6 (August 2010): 1515–82.
Beard, Charles A. *The Republic*. New York: Viking Press, 1943.
Bell, John. *Policy Arguments in Judicial Decisions*. Oxford: Oxford University Press, 1983.
Bennion, Francis. *Statutory Interpretation*. 3rd ed. London: Butterworths, 1997.
Berger, Raoul. "'Original Intention' in Historical Perspective." *George Washington Law Review* 54, 2/3 (1985–86): 296–337.
Berger, Raoul. *Government by Judiciary: The Transformation of the Fourteenth Amendment*. Cambridge, MA: Harvard University Press, 1977.
Berlin, Isaiah. *The Hedgehog and the Fox: An Essay on Tolstoy's View of History*. London: Weidenfeld & Nicolson, 1953.
Berman, Harold J. *Law and Revolution: The Formation of the Western Legal Tradition*. Cambridge, MA: Harvard University Press, 1983.
Berman, Mitchell N. "Originalism Is Bunk." *New York University Law Review* 84, 1 (April 2009): 1–96.
Bevan, Chris. "Interpreting Statutory Purpose – Lessons from *Yemshaw v Hounslow London Borough Council*." *Modern Law Review* 76, 4 (July 2013): 742–56.
Beveridge, William, ed. *The Thirty Nine Articles of Religion, Established in the Church of England: With Expository Observations* [...] *Extracted from the Learned and Famous Exposition of* [...] *Bishop Beveridge*. London: M. Lewis, 1757.
Bickel, Alexander M. "The Original Understanding and the Segregation Decision." *Harvard Law Review* 69, 1 (November 1955): 1–65.
Bilder, Mary Sarah. *Madison's Hand: Revising the Constitutional Convention*. Cambridge, MA: Harvard University Press, 2015.
Bingham, Tom. *The Rule of Law*. London: Allen Lane, 2010.
Blackstone, William. *Commentaries on the Laws of England: In Four Books*, ed. George Sharswood. Philadelphia, 1893.
Blackstone, William. *Commentaries on the Laws of England: In Four Books; With an Analysis of the Work*, eds. Edward Christian, Joseph Chitty, Thomas Lee, John Eykyn Hoyenden, and Archer Ryland. 19th ed. New York, 1846.
Bobbitt, Philip. *Constitutional Interpretation*. Oxford: Blackwell, 1991.
Bobbitt, Philip. *Constitutional Fate: Theory of the Constitution*. New York: Oxford University Press, 1982.
Bork, Robert H. "Neutral Principles and Some First Amendment Problems." *Indiana Law Journal* 47, 1 (Fall 1971): 1–35.
Bowling, Kenneth R. "'A Tub to the Whale': The Founding Fathers and Adoption of the Federal Bill of Rights." *Journal of the Early Republic* 8, 3 (Autumn 1988): 223–51.
Boyd, Danah and Kate Crawford. "Critical Questions for Big Data: Provocations for a Cultural, Technological, and Scholarly Phenomenon." *Information, Communication & Society* 15, 5 (June 2012): 662–79.
Boyer, Paul S. "Borrowed Rhetoric: The Massachusetts Excise Controversy of 1754." *William and Mary Quarterly* 21, 3 (July 1964): 328–51.

Braman, Eileen. *Law, Politics, and Perception: How Policy Preferences Influence Legal Reasoning*. Charlottesville: University of Virginia Press, 2009.
Bratman, Michael E. *Faces of Intention: Selected Essays on Intention and Agency*. Cambridge: Cambridge University Press, 1999.
"The Brennan Center Jorde Symposium: The Living Constitution: A Symposium on the Legacy of Justice William J. Brennan, Jr." *California Law Review* 95, 6 (December 2007).
Brennan Jr., William J. "The Constitution of the United States: Contemporary Ratification." *South Texas Law Review* 27, 3 (Fall 1986): 433–46.
Bressman, Lisa Schultz and Abbe R. Gluck. "Statutory Interpretation from the Inside: An Empirical Study of Congressional Drafting, Delegation, and the Canons, Part II." *Stanford Law Review* 66, 4 (April 2014): 725–802.
Brest, Paul. "The Misconceived Quest for Original Understanding." *Boston University Law Review* 60, 2 (March 1980): 204–38.
Brink, David O. "Semantics and Legal Interpretation (Further Thoughts)." *Canadian Journal of Law and Jurisprudence* 2, 2 (July 1989): 181–92.
Broom, Herbert. *A Selection of Legal Maxims: Classified and Illustrated*. London, 1845.
Brudney, James J. "Below the Surface: Comparing Legislative History Usage by the House of Lords and the Supreme Court." *Washington University Law Review* 85, 1 (2007): 1–72.
Buckland, W. W. *A Text-Book of Roman Law*. 3rd ed. Revised by Peter Stein. Cambridge: Cambridge University Press, 2007.
Buckley, Thomas E. *Church and State in Revolutionary Virginia, 1776–1787*. Charlottesville: University Press of Virginia, 1977.
Bullock, Charles J. "Direct and Indirect Taxes in Economic Literature." *Political Science Quarterly* 13, 3 (September 1898): 442–76.
Burgh, J[ames]. *Political Disquisitions; Or, An Enquiry into Public Errors, Defects, and Abuses, Illustrated by, and Established Upon Facts and Remarks, Extracted from a variety of Authors, Ancient and Modern: Calculated to Draw the Timely Attention of Government and People, to a Due Consideration of the Necessity, and the Means, of Reforming those Errors, Defects, and Abuses; of Restoring the Constitution, and Saving the State*. Vol. 1. Philadelphia, 1775.
Burns, J. H. and H. L. A. Hart, eds. *The Collected Works of Jeremy Bentham: A Comment on the Commentaries and a Fragment on Government*. 1977; repr. Oxford: Oxford University Press, 2008.
Burrows, J. F. "The Problem of Time in Statutory Interpretation." *New Zealand Law Journal* (1978).
Burstein, Andrew. *Democracy's Muse: How Thomas Jefferson Became an FDR Liberal, a Reagan Republican, and a Tea Party Fanatic, All the While Being Dead*. Charlottesville: University of Virginia Press, 2015.
BYU Law & Corpus Linguistics. Accessed August 27, 2019, https://lawcorpus.byu.edu.
Calabresi, Steven G., ed. *Originalism: A Quarter-Century of Debate*. Washington, DC: Regnery, 2007.
Calabresi, Steven G. and Stephanie Dotson Zimdahl. "The Supreme Court and Foreign Sources of Law: Two Hundred Years of Practice and the Juvenile Death Penalty Decision." *William and Mary Law Review* 47, 3 (December 2005): 743–909.

Campbell, Neil A. "Legal Research and the Exclusionary Rule." *Canadian Law Library Review* 36, 4 (2011): 158–66.
Carbonell, Flavia. "Reasoning by Consequences: Applying Different Argumentation Structures to the Analysis of Consequentialist Reasoning in Judicial Decisions." *Cogency* 3, 2 (Summer 2011): 81–104.
Carpenter, David. "Magna Carta and Society: Women, Peasants, Jews, the Towns and the Church." Chap. 4 in *Magna Carta*, trans. David Carpenter. London: Penguin, 2015.
Carroll, Lewis. *Through the Looking Glass and What Alice Found There*. Philadelphia, 1897.
Casto, William. "Oliver Ellsworth's Calvinism: A Biographical Essay on Religion and Political Psychology in the Early Republic." *Journal of Church and State* 36, 3 (Summer 1994): 507–26.
"The Church of England a True and Apostolicall Church." Chap. 3 in *Constitutions and Canons Ecclesiasticall: Treated upon by the Bishop of London, President of the Convocation of the Province of Canterbury, and the Rest of the Bishops and Clergie of the Said Province*. London, 1604.
Clark, Kenneth B., Isidor Chein, and Stuart W. Cook. "The Effects of Segregation and the Consequences of Desegregation: A (September 1952) Social Science Statement in the *Brown v. Board of Education of Topeka* Supreme Court Case." *American Psychologist* 59, 6 (September 2004): 495–501.
Clark, Tom S. *The Limits of Judicial Independence*. Cambridge: Cambridge University Press, 2011.
Cogan, Neil H., ed. *The Complete Bill of Rights: The Drafts, Debates, Sources, and Origins*. New York: Oxford University Press, 1997.
Cohen, Morris L. and Sharon Hamby O'Connor. *A Guide to the Early Reports of the Supreme Court of the United States*. Littleton, CO: F. B. Rothman, 1995.
Coke, Edward. *The Fourth Part of the Institutes of the Laws of England: Concerning the Jurisdiction of Courts*. London, 1809.
Coke, Edward. *The Second Part of the Institutes of the Laws of England: Containing the Exposition of Many Ancient and Other Statutes*. London, 1797.
Colby, Thomas B. "The Sacrifice of the New Originalism." *Georgetown Law Journal* 99, 3 (March 2011): 713–78.
Collins Webster's Dictionary, Revised and Updated. London: HarperCollins, 2007.
Collinson, Patrick. *The Religion of Protestants: The Church in English Society, 1559–1625*. Oxford: Clarendon Press, 1982.
Conservative Party. *Protecting Human Rights in the UK: The Conservatives' Proposals for Changing Britain's Human Rights Laws*. London: Alan Mabbutt, 2014, www.conservatives.com/~/media/files/downloadable%20Files/human_rights.pdf.
Cooley, Thomas M. *A Treatise on the Constitutional Limitations which Rest upon the Legislative Power of the States of the American Union*. Boston, 1868.
Cooter, Robert. "Constitutional Consequentialism: Bargain Democracy versus Median Democracy," *Theoretical Inquiries in Law* 3, 1 (2002): 1–20.
Cornell, Saul. "The People's Constitution vs. The Lawyer's Constitution: Popular Constitutionalism and the Original Debate over Originalism." *Yale Journal of Law and the Humanities* 23, 2 (Summer 2011): 295–338.
Cornell, Saul. "Originalism on Trial: The Use and Abuse of History in *District of Columbia v. Heller*." *Ohio State Law Journal* 69, 4 (2008): 625–40.

Cornell, Saul. *The Other Founders: Anti-Federalism and the Dissenting Tradition in America, 1788–1828*. Chapel Hill: University of North Carolina Press, 1999.
Corpora of Historical English (1500s–Early/Mid 1900s). Accessed August 27, 2019, http://davies-linguistics.byu.edu/personal/histengcorp.htm.
Corpus of Founding Era American English (COFEA). Accessed September 13, 2019, https://lcl.byu.edu/projects/cofea/.
Craies, William Feilden. *A Treatise on Statute Law: With Appendices Containing Statutory and Judicial Definitions of Certain Words and Expressions used in Statutes, Popular and Short Titles of Statutes, and the Interpretation Act, 1889*. 2nd ed. London: Stevens & Haynes, 1911.
Crook, D. P. "The United States in Bentham's Thought." *Australian Journal of Politics and History* 10, 2 (August 1964): 196–204.
Cross, Frank B. *The Failed Promise of Originalism*. Stanford, CA: Stanford University Press, 2013.
Cross, Rupert. *Statutory Interpretation*, eds. John Bell and George Engle. 3rd ed. London: Butterworths, 1995.
Cross, Rupert. *Statutory Interpretation*, eds. John Bell and George Engle. 2nd ed. London: Butterworths, 1987.
Cross, Rupert. *Statutory Interpretation*. London: Butterworths, 1976.
Cserne, Péter. "Consequence-Based Arguments in Legal Reasoning: A Jurisprudential Preface to *Law and Economics*." In *Efficiency, Sustainability, and Justice to Future Generations*, ed. Klaus Mathis. New York: Springer, 2011.
Cunningham, Clark D. and Jesse Egbert. "Scientific Methods for Analyzing Original Meaning: Corpus Linguistics and the Emoluments Clauses." Legal Studies Research Paper, No. 2019–02, Georgia State University College of Law, February 2019, https://ssrn.com/abstract=3321438.
Currie, David P. *The Constitution in the Supreme Court: The Second Century, 1888–1986*. Chicago: University of Chicago Press, 1990.
Currie, David P. *The Constitution in the Supreme Court: The First Hundred Years, 1789–1888*. Chicago: University of Chicago Press, 1985.
Curry, Thomas J. *The First Freedoms: Church and State in America to the Passage of the First Amendment*. New York: Oxford University Press, 1986.
Curry, Thomas John. "The First Freedoms: The Development of the Concepts of Religion and Establishment." PhD diss., Claremont Graduate School, 1983.
Davidson, Donald. "Radical Interpretation." *Dialectica* 27, 3/4 (1973): 313–28.
Davies, Thomas Y. "Recovering the Original Fourth Amendment." *Michigan Law Review* 98, 3 (December 1999): 547–750.
Deckert, Martina R. *Folgenorientierung in der Rechtsanwendung*. Munich: C. H. Beck, 1995.
Del Mar, Maksymilian. "The Forward-Looking Requirement of Formal Justice: Neil MacCormick on Consequential Reasoning." *Jurisprudence* 6, 3 (2015): 429–50.
Dorf, Michael C. "The Use of Foreign Law in American Constitutional Interpretation: A Revealing Colloquy between Justices Scalia and Breyer." *FindLaw*, January 19, 2005, https://supreme.findlaw.com/legal-commentary/the-use-of-foreign-law-in-american-constitutional-interpretation.html.
Drakeman, Donald L. "Which Original Meaning of the Establishment Clause Is the Right One?" In *The Cambridge Companion to the First Amendment and Religious*

Liberty, eds. Michael D. Breidenbach and Owen Anderson. Cambridge: Cambridge University Press, 2020, pp. 365–95.
Drakeman, Donald L. "Consequentialism and the Limits of Interpretation: Do the Ends Justify the Meanings?" *Jurisprudence* 9, 2 (2018): 300–318.
Drakeman, Donald L. "Constitutional Counterpoint: Legislative Debates, Statutory Interpretation and the Separation of Powers." *Statute Law Review* 38, 1 (February 2017): 116–24.
Drakeman, Donald L. *Why We Need the Humanities: Life Science, Law and the Common Good*. Basingstoke: Palgrave Macmillan, 2016.
Drakeman, Donald L. "The Antifederalists and Religion." In *Faith and the Founders of the American Republic*, eds. Daniel L. Dreisbach and Mark David Hall. New York: Oxford University Press, 2014, pp. 120–43.
Drakeman, Donald L. "What's the Point of Originalism?" *Harvard Journal of Law and Public Policy* 37, 3 (2014): 1123–50.
Drakeman, Donald L. *Church, State and Original Intent*. New York: Cambridge University Press, 2010.
Drakeman, Donald L. "James Madison and the First Amendment Establishment of Religion Clause." In *Religion and Political Culture in Jefferson's Virginia*, eds. Garrett Ward Sheldon and Daniel L. Dreisbach. Lanham, MD: Rowman & Littlefield, 2000, pp. 219–34.
Dreier, Ralf. "Interpretation." In *Staatslexikon*. 7th ed. Freiburg: Herder, 1987.
Dreisbach, Daniel L. *Thomas Jefferson and the Wall of Separation between Church and State*. New York: New York University Press, 2002.
Dreisbach, Daniel L. and Mark David Hall, eds. *The Sacred Rights of Conscience: Selected Readings on Religious Liberty and Church–State Relations in the American Founding*. Indianapolis, IN: Liberty Fund, 2009.
Duke, George, and Robert P. George, eds. *The Cambridge Companion to Natural Law Jurisprudence*. Cambridge: Cambridge University Press, 2017.
Dunne, Gerald T. "Early Court Reporters," *Yearbook 1976 Supreme Court Historical Society* (1976): 61–72.
Duxbury, Neil. *Elements of Legislation*. Cambridge: Cambridge University Press, 2013.
Dworkin, Ronald. *Freedom's Law: The Moral Reading of the American Constitution*. Oxford: Oxford University Press, 1996; repr. 2005.
Dworkin, Ronald. "Comment." In *A Matter of Interpretation: Federal Courts and the Law*, by Antonin Scalia. Princeton, NJ: Princeton University Press, 1997, pp. 115–28.
Dworkin, Ronald. *Taking Rights Seriously*. London: Bloomsbury, 1997.
Dworkin, Ronald. *Law's Empire*. Cambridge, MA: Harvard University Press, 1986.
Dworkin, Ronald. *A Matter of Principle*. Cambridge, MA: Harvard University Press, 1985.
Easterbrook, Frank H. "Statutes' Domains." *University of Chicago Law Review* 50, 2 (Spring 1983): 481–503.
Ehrett, John S. "Against Corpus Linguistics." *Georgetown Law Journal Online* 108 (Spring 2019): 50–73.
Eisgruber, Christopher L. *Constitutional Self-Government*. Cambridge, MA: Harvard University Press, 2001.
Eisgruber, Christopher L. "The Living Hand of the Past: History and Constitutional Justice." *Fordham Law Review* 65, 4 (March 1997): 1611–26.

Eisgruber, Christopher L. and Lawrence G. Sager. *Religious Freedom and the Constitution*. Cambridge, MA: Harvard University Press, 2007.
Ekins, Richard. “Objects of Interpretation.” *Constitutional Commentary* 32, 1 (2017): 1–26.
Ekins, Richard. “Updating the Meaning of Violence.” *Law Quarterly Review* 129 (2013): 17–20.
Ekins, Richard. “Equal Protection and Social Meaning.” *American Journal of Jurisprudence* 57, 1 (2012): 21–8.
Ekins, Richard. *The Nature of Legislative Intent*. Oxford: Oxford University Press, 2012.
Ekins, Richard and Jeffrey Goldsworthy. “The Reality and Indispensability of Legislative Intentions.” *Sydney Law Review* 36, 1 (2014): 39–68.
Elkins, Zachary, Tom Ginsburg, and James Melton. *The Endurance of National Constitutions*. New York: Cambridge University Press, 2009.
Elliot, Jonathan, ed. *The Debates in the Several State Conventions, on the Adoption of the Federal Constitution, as Recommended by the General Convention at Philadelphia, in 1787, Together with the Journal of the Federal Convention*, [...] *Collected and Revised from Contemporary Publications by Jonathan Elliot*, ed. Jonathan Elliot. 2nd ed. Philadelphia, 1836.
Ellis, Joseph J. *Founding Brothers: The Revolutionary Generation*. New York: Knopf, 2000.
Ely, John Hart. *Democracy and Distrust: A Theory of Judicial Review*. Cambridge, MA: Harvard University Press, 1980.
Endlich, G. A. *A Commentary on the Interpretation of Statutes*. Jersey City, NJ, 1888.
Epstein, Lee, Jack Knight, and Andrew D. Martin. “The Norm of Prior Judicial Experience and Its Consequences for Career Diversity on the U.S. Supreme Court.” *California Law Review* 91, 4 (July 2003): 903–66.
Eskridge Jr., William N. “All about Words: Early Understandings of the ‘Judicial Power’ in Statutory Interpretation, 1776–1806.” *Columbia Law Review* 101, 5 (June 2001): 990–1106.
Eskridge Jr., William N. “The New Textualism.” *UCLA Law Review* 37, 4 (April 1990): 621–92.
Eskridge Jr., William N. and Philip P. Frickey. “Statutory Interpretation as Practical Reasoning.” *Stanford Law Review* 42, 2 (January 1990): 321–84.
“Exit Polls.” CNN. Updated November 23, 2019, www.cnn.com/election/2016/results/exit-polls.
Fallon Jr., Richard H. *Law and Legitimacy in the Supreme Court*. Cambridge, MA: Harvard University Press, 2018.
Feeley, Malcolm M. and Edward L. Rubin. *Judicial Policy Making and the Modern State: How the Courts Reformed America's Prisons*. New York: Cambridge University Press, 1999.
Ferguson, James R. “Reason in Madness: The Political Thought of James Otis.” *William and Mary Quarterly* 36, 2 (April 1979): 194–214.
Feteris, Eveline T. “The Rational Reconstruction of Argumentation Referring to Consequences and Purposes in the Application of Legal Rules: A Pragma-Dialectical Perspective.” *Argumentation* 19, 4 (November 2005): 459–70.
Finnis, John. “Judicial Power: Past, Present and Future.” Lecture presented at Gray's Inn, London, October 20, 2015, https://papers.ssrn.com/sol3/papers.cfm?abstract_id=2710880.

Finnis, John. *Natural Law and Natural Rights*. 2nd ed. New York: Oxford University Press, 2011.
Finnis, John. *Aquinas: Moral, Political, and Legal Theory*. New York: Oxford University Press, 1998.
Finnis, John, Joseph Boyle, and Germain Grisez. *Nuclear Deterrence, Morality and Realism*. New York: Oxford University Press, 1987.
Fish, Stanley. "The Intentionalist Thesis Once More." Chap. 5 in *The Challenge of Originalism: Theories of Constitutional Interpretation*, eds. Grant Huscroft and Bradley W. Miller. Cambridge: Cambridge University Press, 2011.
Fish, Stanley. "Working on the Chain Gang: Interpretation in the Law and in Literary Criticism." *Critical Inquiry* 9, 1 (September 1982): 201–16.
Fisher, Louis. *Reconsidering Judicial Finality: Why the Supreme Court Is Not the Last Word on the Constitution*. Lawrence: University Press of Kansas, 2019.
Fiss, Owen M. "Foreword: The Forms of Justice." *Harvard Law Review* 93, 1 (1979): 1–58.
Flaherty, David H. "An Introduction to Early American Legal History." In *Essays in the History of Early American Law*, ed. David H. Flaherty. Chapel Hill: University of North Carolina Press, 1969, pp. 1–40.
Flaherty, Martin S. "History 'Lite' in Modern American Constitutionalism." *Columbia Law Review* 95, 3 (April 1995): 523–90.
Fleet, Elizabeth. "Madison's 'Detached Memoranda.'" *William and Mary Quarterly* 3, 4 (October 1946): 534–68.
Fleming, James E. *Fidelity to Our Imperfect Constitution: For Moral Readings and Against Originalisms*. New York: Oxford University Press, 2015.
Fontana, David. "Response: Comparative Originalism." *Texas Law Review* 88 (2010): 188–99.
Ford, Paul Leicester, ed. *The Autobiography of Thomas Jefferson, 1743–1790*. Philadelphia: University of Pennsylvania Press, 2005.
Foxe, John. *The New and Complete Book of Martyrs; Or, An Universal History of Martyrdom: being Foxe's Book of Martyrs, Revised and Corrected, with Additions and Great Improvements: Containing an Authentic Account of the Lives, Persecutions and Suffering of the Holy Martyrs* [...]. Vol. 1. New York, 1794.
Franck, Matthew J. Introduction to *The Doctrine of Judicial Review: Its Legal and Historical Basis and Other Essays*, by Edward S. Corwin. New Brunswick, NJ: Transaction Publishers, 2014.
Frankfurt, Harry G. *On Bullshit*. Princeton, NJ: Princeton University Press, 2005.
Frankfurter, Felix. "John Marshall and the Judicial Function." In *James Bradley Thayer, Oliver Wendell Holmes, and Felix Frankfurter on John Marshall*. Chicago: University of Chicago Press, 1967.
Frost, Daniel. "Getting into Mischief: On What It Means to Appeal to the U.S. Constitution." *International Journal for the Semiotics of Law* 28, 2 (2015): 267–87.
Gales, Joseph, ed. *The Debates and Proceedings in the Congress of the United States, with an Appendix, Containing Important State Papers and Public Documents, and All the Laws of a Public Nature; with a Copius Index, compiled from Authentic Materials*. Vols. 1–2, *March 3, 1789, to March 3, 1791*. Washington, DC, 1834.
George, Robert P. "Natural Law, the Constitution, and the Theory and Practice of Judicial Review." *Fordham Law Review* 69, 6 (2001): 2269–84.

George, Robert P. *In Defense of Natural Law*. Oxford: Oxford University Press, 1999.
Gillman, Howard. "The Collapse of Constitutional Originalism and the Rise of the Notion of the 'Living Constitution' in the Course of American State-Building." *Studies in American Political Development* 11, 2 (Fall 1997): 191–247.
Gluck, Abbe R. and Lisa Schultz Bressman. "Statutory Interpretation from the Inside: An Empirical Study of Congressional Drafting, Delegation, and the Canons, Part I." *Stanford Law Review* 65, 5 (May 2013): 901–1025.
Goebel Jr., Julius. *The Oliver Wendell Holmes Devise: History of the Supreme Court of the United States*. Cambridge: Cambridge University Press, 2010.
Goebel Jr., Julius and Joseph H. Smith, eds. *The Law Practice of Alexander Hamilton: Documents and Commentary*. New York: Columbia University Press, 1980.
Goldfarb, Neal. "Corpus Linguistics in Legal Interpretation: When Is It (In)appropriate?" Lecture presented at BYU Law School, Provo, UT, February 6–8, 2019, https://papers.ssrn.com/sol3/papers.cfm?abstract_id=3333512.
Goldford, Dennis J. *The American Constitution and the Debate over Originalism*. New York: Cambridge University Press, 2005.
Goldsworthy, Jeffrey. "Originalism in Australia." *DPCE Online* 31, 3 (October 2017): 607–15, www.dpceonline.it/index.php/dpceonline/article/view/432.
Goldsworthy, Jeffrey. "The Case for Originalism." In *The Challenge of Originalism: Theories of Constitutional Interpretation*, eds. Grant Huscroft and Bradley W. Miller. Cambridge: Cambridge University Press, 2011.
Goldsworthy, Jeffrey, ed. *Interpreting Constitutions: A Comparative Study*. Oxford: Oxford University Press, 2006.
Goldsworthy, Jeffrey. "Originalism in Constitutional Interpretation." *Federal Law Review* 25, 1 (1997): 1–50.
Goldwater, Barry. *The Conscience of a Conservative*. 1960; repr. Princeton, NJ: Princeton University Press, 2007.
Gorsuch, Neil. *A Republic, if You Can Keep It*. New York: Random House, 2019.
Green, Christopher R. "'This Constitution': Constitutional Indexicals as a Basis for Textualist Semi-Originalism." *Notre Dame Law Review* 84, 4 (2009): 1607–74.
Greenawalt, Kent. "Philosophy of Language, Linguistics, and Possible Lessons about Originalism." Chap. 2 in *The Nature of Legal Interpretation: What Jurists Can Learn about Legal Interpretation from Linguistics and Philosophy*, ed. Brain G. Slocum. Chicago: University of Chicago Press, 2017.
Greenawalt, Kent. *Statutory and Common Law Interpretation*. Oxford: Oxford University Press, 2013.
Greene, Jamal. "On the Origins of Originalism." *Texas Law Review* 88, 1 (November 2009): 1–90.
Greene, Jamal. "Selling Originalism." *Georgetown Law Journal* 97, 3 (March 2009): 657–722.
Greene, Jamal, Nathaniel Persily, and Stephen Ansolabehere. "Profiling Originalism." *Columbia Law Review* 111, 2 (March 2011), 356–418.
Grey, Thomas C. "Do We Have an Unwritten Constitution?" *Stanford Law Review* 27, 3 (February 1975): 703–18.
Grice, Paul. *Studies in the Way of Words*. Cambridge, MA: Harvard University Press, 1989.
Grice, H. P. "Logic and Conversation." In *Syntax and Semantics*, eds. Peter Cole and Jerry L. Morgan. Vol. 3, *Speech Acts*. New York: Academic Press, 1975.

Grice, H. P. "Utterer's Meaning and Intentions." *Philosophical Review* 78, 2 (April 1969): 147–77.

Grice, H. P. "Utterer's Meaning, Sentence-Meaning, and Word-Meaning." *Foundations of Language* 4, 3 (August 1968): 225–42.

Griffin, Stephen M. "Rebooting Originalism." *University of Illinois Law Review*, 4 (2008): 1185–223.

Grotius, Hugo. *De jure belli ac pacis libri tres in quibus jus naturae & gentium, item juris publici praecipua explicantur : cum annotatis auctoris, ejusdemque dissertatione de Mari libero, ac libello singulari De aequitate, indulgentia, & facilitate, nec non Joann. Frid. Gronovii v.c. notis in totum opus De jure belli ac pacis*. 1720.

Hale, Brenda Marjorie. "Beanstalk or Living Instrument? How Tall Can the European Convention on Human Rights Grow?" Lecture presented at Gray's Inn, London, June 16, 2011, www.gresham.ac.uk/lecture/transcript/print/beanstalk-or-living-instrument-how-tall-can-the-european-convention-on-human/.

Hall, Mark David. *Roger Sherman and the Creation of the American Republic*. New York: Oxford University Press, 2013.

Hall, Matthew E. K. *What Justices Want: Goals and Personality on the U.S. Supreme Court*. New York: Cambridge University Press, 2018.

Hall, Matthew E. K. *The Nature of Supreme Court Power*. New York: Cambridge University Press, 2011.

Hamburger, Philip. *Law and Judicial Duty*. Cambridge, MA: Harvard University Press, 2008.

Hamburger, Philip A. "Natural Rights, Natural Law, and American Constitutions." *Yale Law Journal* 102, 4 (1993): 907–60.

Hamburger, Philip A. "The Constitution's Accommodation of Social Change." *Michigan Law Review* 88, 2 (November 1989): 239–327.

Hamilton, Alexander. "The Examination Number XV." March 3, 1802 in *The Papers of Alexander Hamilton*, edited by Harold C. Syrett. Vol. 25, *July 1800–April 1802*. New York: Columbia University Press, 1977.

Hamilton, Alexander. *The Federalist Papers*. No. 83. in *The Avalon Project: Documents in Law, History and Diplomacy*, http://avalon.law.yale.edu/18th_century/fed83.asp.

Hamilton, Alexander. "Opinion on the Constitutionality of an Act to Establish a Bank." February 23, 1791 in *The Papers of Alexander Hamilton*, edited by Harold C. Syrett. Vol. 8, *February 1791–July 1791*. New York: Columbia University Press, 1965.

Hart, H. L. A. "American Jurisprudence through English Eyes: The Nightmare and the Noble Dream." Chap. 4 in *Essays in Jurisprudence and Philosophy* (Oxford: Clarendon Press, 1983).

Hart, H. L. A. "Positivism and the Separation of Law and Morals." *Harvard Law Review* 71, 4 (February 1958): 593–629.

Healy, Michael P. "Legislative Intent and Statutory Interpretation in England and the United States: An Assessment of the Impact of *Pepper v. Hart*." *Stanford Journal of International Law* 35, 2 (Summer 1999): 231–54.

Helmholz, R. H. *Natural Law in Court: A History of Legal Theory in Practice*. Cambridge, MA: Harvard University Press, 2015.

Hendrickson, David C. *Peace Pact: The Lost World of the American Founding*. Lawrence: University Press of Kansas, 2003.

Hening, William Waller. *The Statutes at Large: Being a Collection of All the Laws of Virginia, from the First Session of the Legislature in the Year 1619*. Richmond, 1809.
Herenstein, Ethan J. "The Faulty Frequency Hypothesis: Difficulties in Operationalizing Ordinary Meaning through Corpus Linguistics." *Stanford Law Review Online* 70 (December 2017): 112–22.
Hershovitz, Scott, ed. *Exploring Law's Empire: The Jurisprudence of Ronald Dworkin*. Oxford: Oxford University Press, 2006.
Hessick, Carissa Byrne. "Corpus Linguistics and the Criminal Law." *Brigham Young University Law Review*, 6 (2017): 1503–30.
Hobson, Charles F. "The Marshall Court, 1801–1835: Law, Politics, and the Emergence of the Federal Judiciary." In *The United States Supreme Court: The Pursuit of Justice*, ed. Christopher Tomlins. Boston: Houghton-Mifflin, 2005, pp. 47–74.
Hoeveler, J. David. *Creating the American Mind: Intellect and Politics in the Colonial Colleges*. Lanham, MD: Rowman & Littlefield, 2002.
Hoffer, Peter Charles. *Law and People in Colonial America*. Baltimore, MD: Johns Hopkins University Press, 1998.
Hogg, Peter W. "Canada: From Privy Council to Supreme Court." Chap. 2 in *Interpreting Constitutions: A Comparative Study*, ed. Jeffrey Goldsworthy. Oxford: Oxford University Press, 2006.
Holton, Woody. *Unruly Americans and the Origins of the Constitution*. New York: Hill & Wang, 2007.
Hotman, Franciscus. *Antitribonianus Sive Dissertatio de Studio Legum*. 1603.
Howard, A. E. Dick. "Magna Carta's American Journey." Chap. 8 in *Magna Carta: Muse and Mentor*, ed. Randy J. Holland. Toronto: Thomson Reuters, 2014.
Hunter, Nan D. "Discrimination on the Basis of Sexual Orientation." In *Global Perspectives on Constitutional Law*, eds. Vikram David Amar and Mark V. Tushnet. New York: Oxford University Press, 2009, pp. 116–29.
Hurst, D. J. "Palm Trees in the House of Lords: Some Further Thoughts on Boland's Case." *Statute Law Review* 4, 3 (Autumn 1983): 142–65.
Hurst, D. J. "The Problem of the Elderly Statute." *Legal Studies* 3, 1 (March 1983): 21–42.
Hutson, James H. "The Creation of the Constitution: The Integrity of the Documentary Record." *Texas Law Review* 65, 1 (November 1986): 1–39.
"In His Own Words: The President's Attacks on the Courts." Brennan Center for Justice at New York University School of Law. June 5, 2017, www.brennancenter.org/analysis/his-own-words-presidents-attacks-courts.
Jefferson, Thomas. To James Madison, September 6, 1789. In *The Papers of Thomas Jefferson*, ed. Julian P. Boyd. Vol. 15, *27 March 1789 to 30 November 1789*. Princeton, NJ: Princeton University Press, 1958, p. 396.
Jefferson, Thomas. To Thomas Ritchie, December 25, 1820. In *The Works of Thomas Jefferson*, ed. Paul Leicester Ford. Vol. 12, *Correspondence and Papers 1816–1826*. New York: G. P. Putnam's Sons, 1905, pp. 177–8.
Jensen, Merrill, ed. *The Documentary History of the Ratification of the Constitution*. Vol. 1, *Constitutional Documents and Records, 1776–1787*. Madison: State Historical Society of Wisconsin, 1976.
Jensen, Merrill, John P. Kaminski, and Gaspare J. Saladino, eds. *The Documentary History of the Ratification of the Constitution*. Vol. 15, *Commentaries on the*

Constitution, Public and Private, 18 December 1787 to 31 January 1788. Madison: State Historical Society of Wisconsin, 1976.

Johansen, David and Philip Rosen. "The Notwithstanding Clause of the Charter." Background Paper BP-194E. Ottawa, Canada: Library of Parliament, 2005, http://publications.gc.ca/collections/Collection-R/LoPBdP/BP-e/bp194-1e.pdf.

Johnson, Samuel. *A Dictionary of the English Language: In Which the Words Are Deduced from Their Originals, and Illustrated in Their Different Significations by Examples from the Best Writers*, 6th ed. (London, 1785).

Josephus, Flavius. *The Whole, Genuine, and Complete Works of Flavius Josephus ... Translated from the Original in the Greek Language, And diligently Revised and Compared with the Writings of Contemporary Authors, of Different Nations, on the Subject* [...], trans. George Henry Maynard. New York, 1792.

Joyce, Craig. "The Rise of the Supreme Court Reporter: An Institutional Perspective on Marshall Court Ascendancy." *Michigan Law Review* 83, 5 (April 1985): 1291–391.

Kahn, Ronald. "The Constitution Restoration Act, Judicial Independence, and Popular Constitutionalism." *Case Western Reserve Law Review* 56, 4 (Summer 2006): 1083–1118.

Kaplan, Abraham. *The Conduct of Inquiry: Methodology for Behavioral Science*. New York: Routledge, 2017.

Katzmann, Robert A. *Judging Statutes*. New York: Oxford University Press, 2014.

Kavanagh, Aileen. "*Pepper v Hart* and Matters of Constitutional Principle." *Law Quarterly Review* 121 (January 2005): 98–122.

Kavanagh, Aileen. "Original Intention, Enacted Text, and Constitutional Interpretation." *American Journal of Jurisprudence* 47 (2002): 255–98.

Kersch, Ken I. "The Talking Cure: How Constitutional Argument Drives Constitutional Development." *Boston University Law Review* 94, 3 (May 2014): 1083–108.

Kersch, Ken I. *Constructing Civil Liberties: Discontinuities in the Development of American Constitutional Law*. Cambridge: Cambridge University Press, 2004.

Kesavan, Vasan, and Michael Stokes Paulsen. "The Interpretive Force of the Constitution's Secret Drafting History." *Georgetown Law Journal* 91, 6 (August 2003): 1113–214.

Kim, Clare. "Justice Scalia: Constitution Is 'Dead.'" *MSNBC*, January 29, 2013, updated October 2, 2013, www.msnbc.com/the-last-word/justice-scalia-constitution-dead.

Kinley, David. "Constitutional Brokerage in Australia: Constitutions and the Doctrines of Parliamentary Supremacy and the Rule of Law." *Federal Law Review* 22, 1 (1994): 194–204.

Koppelman, Andrew. *The Tough Luck Constitution and the Assault on Health Care Reform*. New York: Oxford University Press, 2013.

Kozel, Randy J. *Settled Versus Right: A Theory of Precedent*. Cambridge: Cambridge University Press, 2017.

Labunski, Richard. *James Madison and the Struggle for the Bill of Rights*. New York: Oxford University Press, 2006.

Lawson, Gary. "On Reading Recipes ... and Constitutions." *Georgetown Law Journal* 85, 6 (June 1997): 1823–36.

Lee, Thomas R. and James C. Phillips. "Data-Driven Originalism." *University of Pennsylvania Law Review* 167, 2 (January 2019): 261–335.

Leiter, Brian. "Constitutional Law, Moral Judgment, and the Supreme Court as Super-Legislature." *Hastings Law Journal* 66, 6 (2015): 1601–17.

Lepore, Jill. *The Whites of Their Eyes: The Tea Party's Revolution and the Battle over American History*. Princeton, NJ: Princeton University Press, 2011.

Lessig, Lawrence. *Fidelity and Constraint: How the Supreme Court Has Read the American Constitution*. New York: Oxford University Press, 2019.

Letsas, George. "Rescuing Proportionality." In *Philosophical Foundations of Human Rights*, eds. Rowan Cruft, S. Matthew Liao, and Massimo Renzo. Oxford: Oxford University Press, 2015, pp. 316–40.

Leuchtenburg, William E. "The Origins of Franklin D. Roosevelt's 'Court-Packing' Plan." *Supreme Court Review* 1966 (1966): 347–400.

Levinson, Sanford. *Constitutional Faith*. Princeton, NJ: Princeton University Press, 1988.

Lloyd, Gordon. "*Marshall v. Madison*: The Supreme Court and Original Intent, 1803–35." *Criminal Justice Ethics* 32, 1 (April 2013): 20–50.

Lofgren, Charles A. "The Original Understanding of Original Intent?" *Constitutional Commentary* 5, 1 (Winter 1988): 77–114.

Loveland, Ian. *Constitutional Law, Administrative Law, and Human Rights: A Critical Introduction*. 7th ed. Oxford: Oxford University Press, 2015.

MacCormick, Neil. *Legal Reasoning and Legal Theory*. Oxford: Oxford University Press, 1978.

Maclean, Ian. *Interpretation and Meaning in the Renaissance: The Case of Law*. Cambridge: Cambridge University Press, 1992.

Maclean, Ian. "Responsibility and the Act of Interpretation: The Case of Law." In *The Political Responsibility of Intellectuals*, eds. Ian Maclean, Alan Montefiore, and Peter Winch. Cambridge: Cambridge University Press, 1990, pp. 161–88.

Madison, James. *The Federalist Papers*. No. 37. in *The Avalon Project: Documents in Law, History and Diplomacy*, http://avalon.law.yale.edu/18th_century/fed37.asp.

Madison, James. *The Federalist Papers*. No. 40 in *The Avalon Project: Documents in Law, History and Diplomacy*, http://avalon.law.yale.edu/18th_century/fed40.asp.

Madison, James. *The Papers of James Madison: Purchased by Order of Congress; Being His Correspondence And Reports of Debates During the Congress of the Confederation and His Reports of Debates in the Federal Convention: Now Published from the Original Manuscripts Deposited in the Department of State*, ed. Henry D. Gilpin. Vol. 2. New York: J. & H.G. Langley, 1841.

Maggs, Gregory E. "A Concise Guide to Using Dictionaries from the Founding Era to Determine the Original Meaning of the Constitution," *George Washington Law Review* 82 (2014): 358–93.

Maggs, Gregory E. "A Concise Guide to the Records of the State Ratifying Conventions as a Source of the Original Meaning of the U.S. Constitution." *University of Illinois Law Review*, 2 (2009): 457–96.

Magyar, John James. "The Evolution of Hansard Use at the Supreme Court of Canada: A Comparative Study in Statutory Interpretation." *Statute Law Review* 33, 3 (October 2012): 363–89.

Maier, Pauline. *Ratification: The People Debate the Constitution, 1787–1788*. New York: Simon & Schuster, 2010.

Manning, John. *Commentaries on the First Book of Blackstone*. Chapel Hill, NC, 1899.
Manning, John F. "Inside Congress' Mind." *Columbia Law Review* 115, 7 (November 2015): 1911–52.
Manning, John F. "The Role of the Philadelphia Convention in Constitutional Adjudication." *George Washington Law Review* 80, 6 (November 2012): 1753–93.
Manning, John F. "Textualism and the Equity of the Statute." *Columbia Law Review* 101, 1 (January 2001): 1–127.
Manning, John F. "Textualism and the Role of *The Federalist* in Constitutional Adjudication." *George Washington Law Review* 66, 5/6 (June–August 1998): 1337–65.
Manning, John F. "Textualism as a Nondelegation Doctrine." *Columbia Law Review* 97, 3 (April 1997): 673–739.
Marmor, Andrei. "Meaning and Belief in Constitutional Interpretation." *Fordham Law Review* 82, 2 (November 2013): 577–96.
Marmor, Andrei. *Social Conventions: From Language to Law*. Princeton, NJ: Princeton University Press, 2009.
Marmor, Andrei. "The Pragmatics of Legal Language." *Ratio Juris* 21, 4 (December 2008): 423–52.
Martin, Francisco Forrest. *The Constitution as Treaty: The International Legal Constructionalist Approach to the U.S. Constitution*. New York: Cambridge University Press, 2007.
Martin, Luther. "The Genuine Information, Delivered to the Legislature of the State of Maryland, Relative to the Proceedings of the General Convention, Lately Held at Philadelphia." In *The Complete Anti-Federalist*, ed. Herbert J. Storing. Vol. 2, *Objections of Non-Signers of the Constitution and Major Series of Essays at the Outset*. Chicago: University of Chicago Press, 1981, pp. 27–82.
Martin, Peter. *The Dictionary Wars: The American Fight over the English Language*. Princeton, NJ: Princeton University Press, 2019.
Mascott, Jennifer L. "Who Are 'Officers of the United States'?" *Stanford Law Review* 70, 2 (February 2018): 443–564.
Mathis, Klaus. "Consequentialism in Law." In *Efficiency, Sustainability, and Justice to Future Generations*, ed. Klaus Mathis. New York: Springer, 2011.
McConnell, Michael W. "Establishment and Disestablishment at the Founding, Part I: Establishment of Religion." *William and Mary Law Review* 44, 5 (2003): 2104–208.
McConnell, Michael W. "Originalism and the Desegregation Decisions." *Virginia Law Review* 81, 4 (May 1995): 947–1140.
McEnery, Tony and Andrew Hardie. *Corpus Linguistics: Method, Theory and Practice*. Cambridge: Cambridge University Press, 2012.
McGinnis, John O. and Michael B. Rappaport. "Unifying Original Intent and Original Public Meaning." *Northwestern University Law Review* 113, 6 (2019): 1371–418.
McGinnis, John O. and Michael B. Rappaport. *Originalism and the Good Constitution*. Cambridge, MA: Harvard University Press, 2013.
McGinnis, John O. and Michael B. Rappaport. "Original Methods Originalism: A New Theory of Interpretation and the Case against Construction." *Northwestern University Law Review* 103, 2 (2009): 751–802.
McGreevy, John T. *Catholicism and American Freedom: A History*. New York: W. W. Norton, 2004.

McGreevy, John T. "Thinking on One's Own: Catholicism in the American Intellectual Imagination, 1928–1960." *Journal of American History* 84, 1 (June 1997): 97–131.

McLoughlin, William G. *New England Dissent, 1630–1833: The Baptists and the Separation of Church and State*. Cambridge, MA: Harvard University Press, 1971.

McManis, Charles R. "The History of First Century American Legal Education: A Revisionist Perspective." *Washington University Law Quarterly* 59, 3 (1981): 597–660.

Meese III, Edwin. "The Supreme Court of the United States: Bulwark of a Limited Constitution," *South Texas Law Review* 27, 3 (Fall 1986): 455–66.

Meese III, Edwin. "Speech of Attorney General Edwin Meese III to the American Bar Association." Speech given at The American Bar Association, July 9, 1985. www.justice.gov/sites/default/files/ag/legacy/2011/08/23/07–09-1985.pdf.

Miller, Bradley W. "Origin Myth: The Persons Case, the Living Tree, and the New Originalism." In *Challenge of Originalism*, eds. Grant Huscroft and Bradley W. Miller. Cambridge: Cambridge University Press, 2011.

Moak, Nathaniel C. *Reports of Cases Decided by the English Courts: With Notes and References to Kindred Cases and Authorities*. Vol. 29. Albany, NY, 1882.

Morgan, Edmund S., ed. *Prologue to Revolution: Sources and Documents on the Stamp Act Crisis, 1764–1766*. Chapel Hill: University of North Carolina Press, 1959.

Morison, Samuel Eliot. *A History of the Constitution of Massachusetts*. Boston: Wright & Potter, 1917.

Morley, J. Gareth. "Dead Hands, Living Trees, Historic Compromises: The Senate Reform and Supreme Court Act References Bring the Originalism Debate to Canada." *Osgoode Hall Law Journal* 53, 3 (Summer 2016): 745–98.

Morse, Jedidiah. *The American Universal Geography, or, A View of the Present State of All the Empires, Kingdoms, States, and Republics in the Known World, and of the United States of America in Particular, In Two Parts* [. . .]. Vol. 1. Boston, 1793.

Mouritsen, Stephen C. "Corpus Linguistics in Legal Interpretation: An Evolving Interpretive Framework." *International Journal of Language and Law* 6 (2017): 67–89.

Mouritsen, Stephen C. "The Dictionary Is Not a Fortress: Definitional Fallacies and a Corpus-Based Approach to Plain Meaning." *Brigham Young University Law Review*, 5 (November 2010): 1915–80.

Mullett, Charles F. "Coke and the American Revolution." *Economica*, 38 (November 1932): 457–71.

Mulligan, Christina, Michael Douma, Hans Lind, and Brian Quinn. "Founding-Era Translations of the U.S. Constitution." *Constitutional Commentary* 31 (2016): 1–53.

Muñoz, Vincent Phillip. "Two Concepts of Religious Liberty: The Natural Rights and Moral Autonomy Approaches to the Free Exercise of Religion." *American Political Science Review* 110, 2 (May 2016): 369–81.

Muñoz, Vincent Phillip. "Block that Metaphor." Review of *Church, State, and Original Intent*, by Donald L. Drakeman. *Claremont Review of Books* 10, 4 (Fall 2010): 49–51.

Muñoz, Vincent Phillip. *God and the Founders: Madison, Washington, and Jefferson*. New York: Cambridge University Press, 2009.

Muñoz, Vincent Phillip. "The Original Meaning of the Establishment Clause and the Impossibility of Its Incorporation." *University of Pennsylvania Journal of Constitutional Law* 8, 4 (August 2006): 585–639.

Murrill, Brandon J. *Modes of Constitutional Interpretation*. Washington, DC: Congressional Research Service, 2018.

Natelson, Robert G. "The Founders' Hermeneutic: The Real Original Understanding of Original Intent." *Ohio State Law Journal* 68, 5 (2007): 1239–306.

National Archives and Records Administration. *The Founders Online: Open Access to the Papers of America's Founding Era; A Report to Congress*. Washington, DC: National Archives and Records Administration, 2008.

Neuberger, David. "The UK Constitutional Settlement and the Role of the UK Supreme Court." Lecture presented at Legal Wales Conference, Bangor, Wales, October 10, 2014, www.supremecourt.uk/docs/speech-141010.pdf.

Neumann, Ulfrid. "Juristische Argumentationstheorie." In *Handbuch Rechtsphilosophie*, eds. Eric Hilgendorf and Jan C. Joerden. Stuttgart: J. B. Metzler, 2017, pp. 234–41.

Nourse, Victoria. *Misreading Law, Misreading Democracy*. Cambridge, MA: Harvard University Press, 2016.

Oliphant, Benjamin and Léonid Sirota. "Has the Supreme Court of Canada Rejected 'Originalism'?" *Queen's Law Journal* 42, 1 (Fall 2016): 107–64.

O'Neill, Johnathan. *Originalism in American Law and Politics: A Constitutional History*. Baltimore, MD: Johns Hopkins University Press, 2005.

Oxford English Dictionary. Oxford: Oxford University Press, 2000.

Oxford English Dictionary Online. New York: Oxford University Press, 2010.

Page, Scott E. *The Difference: How the Power of Diversity Creates Better Groups, Firms, Schools, and Societies*. Princeton, NJ: Princeton University Press, 2007.

Paschal, George W. *The Constitution of the United States Defined and Carefully Annotated*. Washington, DC, 1868.

Paulsen, Michael Stokes. "How to Interpret the Constitution (and How Not To)." *Yale Law Journal* 115, 8 (June 2006): 2037–66.

Pearson, Ellen Holmes. "1775–1815." Chap. 3 in *A Companion to American Legal History*, eds. Sally E. Hadden and Alfred L. Brophy. Malden, MA: Wiley-Blackwell, 2013.

Pendleton, Edmund. "United States against Hilton: Some Remarks on the Argument of Mr. Wickham." *Aurora General Advertiser*, February 11, 1796.

Peterson, Merrill D. "Mr. Jefferson's 'Sovereignty of the Living Generation.'" *Virginia Quarterly Review* 52, 3 (Summer 1976): 437–47.

Phillips, James C., Daniel M. Ortner, and Thomas R. Lee. "Corpus Linguistics and Original Public Meaning: A New Tool to Make Originalism More Empirical." *Yale Law Journal Forum* 126, 101 (May 2016): 21–32.

Phillips, James Cleith and Sara White. "The Meaning of the Three Emoluments Clauses in the U.S. Constitution: A Corpus Linguistic Analysis of American English from 1760–1799." *South Texas Law Review* 59, 2 (Winter 2017): 181–236.

Pocock, J. G. A. *Political Thought and History: Essays on Theory and Method*. Cambridge: Cambridge University Press, 2009.

Pojanowski, Jeffrey A. and Kevin C. Walsh. "Enduring Originalism." *Georgetown Law Journal* 105, 1 (November 2016): 97–158.

Pojanowski, Jeffrey A. "Reading Statutes in the Common Law Tradition." *Virginia Law Review* 101, 5 (September 2015): 1357–424.

Popkin, William D. *Materials on Legislation: Political Language and the Political Process*. 3rd ed. New York: Foundation Press, 2001.

Popkin, William D. *Statutes in Court: The History and Theory of Statutory Interpretation*. Durham, NC: Duke University Press, 1999.
Posner, Richard A. "Law School Professors Need More Practical Experience: Entry 9; The Academy Is out of Its Depth." *The Breakfast Table* (blog), *Slate*, posted June 24, 2016, https://slate.com/news-and-politics/2016/06/law-school-professors-need-more-practical-experience.html.
Posner, Richard A. *How Judges Think*. Cambridge, MA: Harvard University Press, 2010.
Post, Robert and Reva Siegel. "Originalism as a Political Practice: The Right's Living Constitution." *Fordham Law Review* 75, 2 (November 2006): 545–74.
Potter Jr., Parker B. "If Humpty Dumpty Had Sat on the Bench . . . : An Eggheaded Approach to Legal Lexicography." *Whittier Law Review* 30, 3 (2009): 367–532.
Potter Jr., Parker B. "Wondering about Alice: Judicial References to *Alice in Wonderland* and *Through the Looking Glass*." *Whittier Law Review* 28, 1 (2006): 175–318.
Powell, H. Jefferson. "The Original Understanding of Original Intent." *Harvard Law Review* 98, 5 (March 1985): 885–948.
Radin, Max. "Statutory Interpretation." *Harvard Law Review* 43, 6 (April 1930): 863–85.
Rakove, Jack N. "Joe the Ploughman Reads the Constitution: Or, the Poverty of Public Meaning Originalism." *San Diego Law Review* 48, 2 (May–June 2011): 575–600.
Rakove, Jack N. "Confessions of an Ambivalent Originalist." *New York University Law Review* 78, 4 (October 2003): 1346–56.
Ramsey, Michael D. "Beyond the Text: Justice Scalia's Originalism in Practice." *Notre Dame Law Review* 92, 5 (2017): 1945–76.
Rawle, William. *A View of the Constitution of the United States of America*. Philadelphia, 1829.
Raz, Joseph. *Authority of Law: Essays on Law and Morality*. 2nd ed. Oxford: Oxford University Press, 2009.
Raz, Joseph. *Between Authority and Interpretation: On the Theory of Law and Practical Reason*. New York: Oxford University Press, 2009.
Raz, Joseph. "Intention in Interpretation." Chap. 9 in *The Autonomy of Law: Essays on Legal Positivism*, ed. Robert P. George. New York: Oxford University Press, 1996.
Rehnquist, William H. "The Notion of a Living Constitution." *Texas Law Review* 54, 4 (May 1976): 693–706.
Robertson, William. *The History of the Reign of Charles the Fifth, Emperor of Germany and of All the Kingdoms and States in Europe, During His Age: To Which Is Prefixed, a View of the Progress of Society in Europe, from the Subversion of the Roman Empire, to the Beginning of the Sixteenth Century: Confirmed by Historical Proofs and Illustration: In Three Volumes*. Vol. 1. Philadelphia, 1770.
Roosevelt, Franklin D. "Fireside Chat: On the Reorganization of the Judiciary," March 9, 1937. Online by Gerhard Peters and John T. Woolley. *The American Presidency Project*, www.presidency.ucsb.edu/documents/fireside-chat-17.
Rosenberg, Gerald N. *The Hollow Hope: Can Courts Bring about Social Change?* 2nd ed. Chicago: University of Chicago Press, 2008.
Rosenfeld, Michel. "Constitutional Adjudication in Europe and the United States: Paradoxes and Contrasts." *International Journal of Constitutional Law* 2, 4 (October 2004): 633–68.
Rossum, Ralph A. *Understanding Clarence Thomas: The Jurisprudence of Constitutional Restoration*. Lawrence: University Press of Kansas, 2014.

Rubin, Edward L. and Malcolm M. Feeley. "Judicial Policy Making and Litigation against the Government." *University of Pennsylvania Journal of Constitutional Law* 5, 3 (2003): 617–64.
Rubin, Peter J. "Taking Its Proper Place in the Constitutional Canon: *Bolling v. Sharpe, Korematsu*, and the Equal Protection Component of Fifth Amendment Due Process." *Virginia Law Review* 92, 8 (December 2006): 1879–98.
Rutledge, Wiley. To Ernest Kirschten, February 20, 1947. Wiley Rutledge Papers, Box 143.
Sales, Philip. "*Pepper v Hart*: A Footnote to Professor Vogenauer's Reply to Lord Steyn." *Oxford Journal of Legal Studies* 26, 3 (Autumn 2006): 585–92.
Sawyer III, Logan E. "Principle and Politics in the New History of Originalism." *American Journal of Legal History* 57, 2 (June 2017): 198–222.
Scalia, Antonin. *A Matter of Interpretation: Federal Courts and the Law*. Princeton, NJ: Princeton University Press, 1997.
Scalia, Antonin. "Judicial Deference to Administrative Interpretations of Law." *Duke Law Journal*, 3 (June 1989): 511–21.
Scalia, Antonin and Bryan A. Garner. *Reading Law: The Interpretation of Legal Texts*. St. Paul, MN: Thomson/West, 2012.
Schauer, Frederick. *Playing by the Rules: A Philosophical Examination of Rule-Based Decision-Making in Law and in Life*. New York: Oxford University Press, 1991.
Scheppele, Kim Lane. "Jack Balkin Is an American." *Yale Journal of Law and the Humanities* 25, 1 (Winter 2013): 23–42.
Schwartz, Bernard. *The Bill of Rights: A Documentary History*. New York: Chelsea House, 1971.
Schwartzman, Micah. "Judicial Sincerity." *Virginia Law Review* 94, 4 (2008): 987–1027.
Scutt, Jocelynne A. *Women and Magna Carta: A Treaty for Rights or Wrongs?* Basingstoke: Palgrave Macmillan, 2016.
Segall, Eric J. "Originalism as Faith." *Cornell Law Review Online* 102 (2016): 37–52.
Shapiro, David L. "In Defense of Judicial Candor." *Harvard Law Review* 100, 4 (February 1987): 731–50.
Siltala, Raimo. *Law, Truth, and Reason: A Treatise on Legal Argumentation*. New York: Springer, 2011.
Sirico Jr., Louis J. "Original Intent in the First Congress." *Missouri Law Review* 71, 3 (Summer 2006): 687–720.
Sirota, Léonid and Benjamin Oliphant. "Originalist Reasoning in Canadian Constitutional Jurisprudence." *University of British Columbia Law Review* 50, 2 (2017): 505–76.
Sloan, Herbert. "'The Earth Belongs in Usufruct to the Living.'" In *Jeffersonian Legacies*, ed. Peter S. Onuf. Charlottesville: University Press of Virginia, 1993, pp. 281–315.
Slocum, Brian G., ed. *The Nature of Legal Interpretation: What Jurists Can Learn about Legal Interpretation from Linguistics and Philosophy*. Chicago: University of Chicago Press, 2017.
Smith, Adam. *An Inquiry into the Nature and Causes of the Wealth of Nations*, ed. Edwin Cannan. London: Methuen, 1904.
Smith, Stephen D. "That Old-Time Originalism." Chap. 10 in *The Challenge of Originalism: Theories of Constitutional Interpretation*, eds. Grant Huscroft and Bradley W. Miller. Cambridge: Cambridge University Press, 2011.

Smith, Steven D. "The Jurisdictional Establishment Clause: A Reappraisal." *Notre Dame Law Review* 81, 5 (2006): 1843–94.
Smith, Steven D. *Law's Quandary*. Cambridge, MA: Harvard University Press, 2004.
Smith, Steven D. *Foreordained Failure: The Quest for a Constitutional Principle of Religious Freedom*. New York: Oxford University Press, 1995.
Smith II, George P. "*Marbury v. Madison*, Lord Coke and Dr. Bonham: Relics of the Past, Guidelines for the Present; Judicial Review in Transition?" *University of Puget Sound Law Review* 2 (1979): 255–68.
Solan, Lawrence M. "Legal Linguistics in the US: Looking Back, Looking Ahead." Legal Studies Paper, No. 609, Brooklyn Law School, July 2019, https://papers.ssrn.com/sol3/papers.cfm?abstract_id=3428489.
Solan, Lawrence M. "Can Corpus Linguistics Help Make Originalism Scientific?" *Yale Law Journal Forum* 126, 101 (May 2016): 57–64.
Solan, Lawrence M. and Tammy Gales. "Corpus Linguistics as a Tool in Legal Interpretation." *Brigham Young University Law Review*, 6 (2017): 1311–57.
Solum, Lawrence B. "Originalism versus Living Constitutionalism: The Conceptual Structure of the Great Debate." *Northwestern University Law Review* 113, 6 (2019): 1243–96.
Solum, Lawrence B. "Originalist Methodology." *University of Chicago Law Review* 84, 1 (2017): 269–96.
Solum, Lawrence B. "Triangulating Public Meaning: Corpus Linguistics, Immersion, and the Constitutional Record," *Brigham Young University Law Review*, 6 (2017): 1621–82.
Solum, Lawrence B. "We Are All Originalists Now." Chap. 1 in *Constitutional Originalism: A Debate*, eds. Lawrence B. Solum and Robert W. Bennett. Ithaca, NY: Cornell University Press, 2011.
Solum, Lawrence B. "What Is Originalism? The Evolution of Contemporary Originalist Theory." Chap. 1 in *The Challenge of Originalism: Theories of Constitutional Interpretation*, eds. Grant Huscroft and Bradley W. Miller. Cambridge: Cambridge University Press, 2011.
Solum, Lawrence B. "The Interpretation–Construction Distinction." *Constitutional Commentary* 27, 1 (2010): 95–118.
Starr, Kenneth W. "Observations about the Use of Legislative History." *Duke Law Journal* 36, 3 (June 1987): 371–9.
Stead, William T. "My First Visit to America: An Open Letter to My Readers." *Review of Reviews*, March 10, 1894.
Stein, Peter. *Roman Law in European History*. Cambridge: Cambridge University Press, 1999.
Stein, Peter. "Interpretation and Legal Reasoning in Roman Law." *Chicago-Kent Law Review* 70, 4 (1995): 1539–56.
Steinberg, David E. "The Original Understanding of Unreasonable Searches and Seizures." *Florida Law Review* 56, 5 (December 2004): 1051–96.
Stewart, David O. *The Summer of 1787: The Men Who Invented the Constitution*. New York: Simon & Schuster, 2007.
Steyn, Johan. "*Pepper v Hart*; A Re-examination." *Oxford Journal of Legal Studies* 21, 1 (Spring 2001): 59–72.

Storing, Herbert J., ed. *The Complete Anti-Federalist*. Vol. 2, *Objections of Non-Signers of the Constitution and Major Series of Essays at the Outset*. Chicago: University of Chicago Press, 1981.
Story, Joseph. *Commentaries on the Constitution of the United States: With a Preliminary Review of the Constitutional History of the Colonies and States, before the Adoption of the Constitution*. 2nd ed. Boston, 1851.
Story, Joseph. *Commentaries on the Constitution of the United States: With a Preliminary Review of the Constitutional History of the Colonies and States, before the Adoption of the Constitution*. Boston, 1833.
Strang, Lee J. *Originalism's Promise: A Natural Law Account of the American Constitution*. Cambridge: Cambridge University Press, 2019.
Strang, Lee J. "How Big Data Can Increase Originalism's Methodological Rigor: Using Corpus Linguistics to Reveal Original Language Conventions." *UC Davis Law Review* 50, 3 (February 2017): 1181–242.
Strang, Lee J. "The Original Meaning of 'Religion' in the First Amendment: A Test Case of Originalism's Utilization of Corpus Linguistics." *Brigham Young University Law Review*, 6 (2017): 1683–750.
Strauss, David A. "The Supreme Court 2014 Term: Foreword; Does the Constitution Mean What It Says." *Harvard Law Review* 129, 1 (November 2015): 1–61.
Strauss, David A. *The Living Constitution*. New York: Oxford University Press, 2010.
Sunstein, Cass R. "There Is Nothing that Interpretation Just Is." *Constitutional Commentary* 30, 2 (2015): 193–212.
Tamanaha, Brian Z. *Law as a Means to an End: Threat to the Rule of Law*. Cambridge: Cambridge University Press, 2006.
Tankersley, Daniel C. "Beyond the Dictionary: Why *Sua Sponte* Judicial Use of Corpus Linguistics Is Not Appropriate for Statutory Interpretation." SSRN, February 2018, http://dx.doi.org/10.2139/ssrn.3117223.
Taylor, John. *An Argument Respecting the Constitutionality of the Carriage Tax; Which Subject was Discussed at Richmond, in Virginia, in May*, 1759. Richmond: Augustine Davis, 1795.
Teles, Steven M. *The Rise of the Conservative Legal Movement: The Battle for Control of the Law*. Princeton, NJ: Princeton University Press, 2008.
Tetlock, Philip E. *Expert Political Judgment: How Good Is It? How Can We Know?* Princeton, NJ: Princeton University Press, 2005.
Tew, Yvonne. "Originalism at Home and Abroad." *Columbia Journal of Transnational Law* 52, 3 (2014): 780–895.
Thayer, James B. "The Origin and Scope of the American Doctrine of Constitutional Law." *Harvard Law Review* 7, 3 (October 1893): 129–56.
Thorne, Samuel E., ed. *A Discourse upon the Exposicion and Understandinge of Statutes: With Sir Thomas Egerton's Additions*. San Marino, CA: Huntington Library, 1942.
Thumma, Samuel A. and Jeffrey L. Kirchmeier, "The Lexicon Has Become a Fortress: The United States Supreme Court's Use of Dictionaries," *Buffalo Law Review* 47 (1999): 227–302.
Tinling, Marion. "Thomas Lloyd's Reports of the First Federal Congress." *William and Mary Quarterly* 18, 4 (October 1961): 519–45.
Toobin, Jeffrey. "How Scalia Changed the Supreme Court." *New Yorker*, February 13, 2016, www.newyorker.com/news/news-desk/how-scalia-changed-the-supreme-court.

Trumbull, Benjamin. "Act of Assembly Adopting the Saybrook Platform, Oct. 1708." In *A Complete History of Connecticut: Civil and Ecclesiastical, from the Emigration of its first Planters from England, in the Year 1630, to the Year 1764, and to the Close of the Indian Wars, in Two Volumes*. New Haven, CT: Maltby, Goldsmith & Co., 1818.

Tucker, St. George, ed. *Blackstone's Commentaries: With Notes of Reference, to the Constitution and Laws, of the Federal Government of the United States; and of the Commonwealth of Virginia*. Philadelphia, 1803.

Tushnet, Mark. "The Dilemmas of Liberal Constitutionalism." *Ohio State Law Journal* 42, 1 (1981): 411–26.

Tyler, Tom R. *Why People Obey the Law*. Princeton, NJ: Princeton University Press, 2006.

US Department of Justice, Office of Legal Policy. *Original Meaning Jurisprudence: A Sourcebook*. Washington, DC: Government Publishing Office, 1988.

Uzzell, Lynn. *Redeeming Madison's Notes*. Unpublished manuscript.

VanBurkleo, Sandra Frances. "'Honour, Justice, and Interest': John Jay's Republican Politics and Statesmanship on the Federal Bench." In *Seriatim: The Supreme Court before John Marshall*, ed. Scott Douglas Gerber. New York: New York University Press, 1998, pp. 26–69.

Van der Sloot, Bart. "The Practical and Theoretical Problems with 'Balancing': Delfi, Coty and the Redundancy of the Human Rights Framework." *Maastricht Journal of European and Comparative Law* 23, 3 (2016): 439–59.

Varol, Ozan O. "The Origins and Limits of Originalism: A Comparative Study." *Vanderbilt Journal of Transnational Law* 44, 5 (2011): 1239–98.

Vermeule, Adrian. *The Constitution of Risk*. New York: Cambridge University Press, 2014.

Vermeule, Adrian. *Law and the Limits of Reason*. Oxford: Oxford University Press, 2009.

Vogenauer, Stefan. "A Retreat from *Pepper v Hart*? A Reply to Lord Steyn." *Oxford Journal of Legal Studies* 25, 4 (Winter 2005): 629–74.

Waldron, Jeremy. "The Rule of Law." In *Stanford Encyclopedia of Philosophy*. Article published June 22, 2016, last modified July 1, 2016. https://plato.stanford.edu/entries/rule-of-law/.

Waldron, Jeremy. "Judicial Review and Judicial Supremacy." *NYU School of Law, Public Law Research Paper*, No. 14–57 (October 2014). https://ssrn.com/abstract=2510550.

Waldron, Jeremy. *The Dignity of Legislation*. Cambridge: Cambridge University Press, 1999.

Waldron, Jeremy. *Law and Disagreement*. Oxford: Oxford University Press, 1999.

Webster, Noah. *An American Dictionary of the English Language*. 1st ed. New York, 1828.

Webster's New Dictionary of the English Language: Revised and Updated. New York, Popular Pub, 2002.

Weir, David A. *Early New England: A Covenanted Society*. Grand Rapids, MI: Wm. B. Eerdmans, 2005.

Weis, Lael K. "What Comparativism Tells Us about Originalism." *International Journal of Constitutional Law* 11, 4 (October 2013): 842–69.

Whitney, Edward B. "The Income Tax and the Constitution." *Harvard Law Review* 20, 4 (February 1907): 280–96.

Whittington, Keith E. *Repugnant Laws: Judicial Review of Acts of Congress from the Founding to the Present*. Lawrence: University Press of Kansas, 2019.

Whittington, Keith E. "Is Originalism Too Conservative?" *Harvard Journal of Law and Public Policy* 34, 1 (Winter 2011): 29–41.

Whittington, Keith E. *Political Foundations of Judicial Supremacy: The Presidency, the Supreme Court, and Constitutional Leadership in U.S. History*. Princeton, NJ: Princeton University Press, 2007.

Whittington, Keith E. "The New Originalism." *Georgetown Journal of Law and Public Policy* 2, 2 (Summer 2004): 599–614.

Whittington, Keith E. *Constitutional Construction: Divided Powers and Constitutional Meaning*. Cambridge, MA: Harvard University Press, 1999.

Whittington, Keith E. *Constitutional Interpretation: Textual Meaning, Original Intent, and Judicial Review*. Lawrence: University Press of Kansas, 1999.

Williams, Daniel K. *Defenders of the Unborn: The Pro-Life Movement before* Roe v. Wade. New York: Oxford University Press, 2016.

Wilson, James. "Of the Study of the Law in the United States." In *The Works of James Wilson*, ed. Robert Green McCloskey. Cambridge, MA: Harvard University Press, 1967.

Wilson, John F. and Donald L. Drakeman, eds. *Church and State in American History: Key Documents, Decisions, and Commentary from Five Centuries*. 4th ed. New York: Routledge, 2020.

Witte Jr., John. *God's Joust, God's Justice: Law and Religion in the Western Tradition*. Grand Rapids, MI: Wm. B. Eerdmans, 2006.

Witte Jr., John. "'A Most Mild and Equitable Establishment of Religion': John Adams and the Massachusetts Experiment." *Journal of Church and State* 41, 2 (Spring 1999): 213–52.

Worcester, Joseph E. *Dictionary of the English Language*. Boston, 1860.

Wurman, Ilan. *A Debt against the Living: An Introduction to Originalism*. Cambridge: Cambridge University Press, 2017.

Yodelis, Mary Ann. "Who Paid the Piper? Publishing Economics in Boston, 1763–1775." *Journalism Monographs* 38 (February 1975): 6–54.

Yowell, Paul. *Constitutional Rights and Constitutional Design: Moral and Empirical Reasoning in Judicial Review*. Oxford: Hart Publishing, 2018.

Zimmerman, Jonathan. *Whose America? Culture Wars in the Public Schools*. Cambridge, MA: Harvard University Press, 2002.

Zines, Leslie. "Dead Hands or Living Tree? Stability and Change in Constitutional Law." *Adelaide Law Review* 25, 1 (2004): 3–20.

ZoBell, Karl M. "Division of Opinion in the Supreme Court: A History of Judicial Disintegration." *Cornell Law Quarterly* 44 (1958–1959): 186–214.

Index

Ingram Content Group UK Ltd.
Milton Keynes UK
UKHW021317180423
420369UK00021B/461